THE LANGUAGE OF GOD:

METAGETICS AND THE BIBLE

LAURA BARRETT BENNETT

THE LANGUAGE OF GOD:

METAGETICS AND THE BIBLE

metagetics.

METAGETICS PUBLICATIONS

METAGETICS PUBLICATIONS

The Language of God: Metagetics and the Bible
Second Edition

First printing 2018.

Printed in the United States of America

ISBN-13: 978-0999312711
ISBN-10: 0999312715

In Loving Memory of
Dr. Paul C. Barrett
My Father, Mentor, Colleague, and Friend

Foreword

by Michael A. Maday

I was raised Catholic and so I never really learned to read the Bible. At least in my church, it was more important to know the Catechism, and while I did hear some Bible stories and got to know some of the main characters, I didn't really know the Bible. This made things challenging when I entered Unity's ministerial school as most of my fellow students seemed to be well versed. Fortunately, I had wonderful teachers, like Rev. Wayne Manning and Rev. Frank Giudici to give me the historical context. That helped a lot. I was fortunate then to also befriend two of my fellow students, Alden Studebaker and Laura Barrett who really knew the Bible. Both were religion majors in college. Alden tested out of our history classes, and so did Laura. Laura's father was Dr. Paul Barrett, who used to run the ministerial program, and who was one of Unity's great Bible teachers.

It was in my training in metaphysical Bible interpretation, that I was able to perk up and engage the material. I had always excelled in interpreting literature and the skills I had learned in all those English lit classes in high school and college, served me well. And I was fortunate enough to befriend Dr. Barrett and both he and his daughter Laura thought I had a talent for metaphysical interpretation. That of course made my day and gave me a huge boost in my ministerial education. Years later, I was also fortunate to serve as Unity's book editor and so I worked with Studebaker on his excellent book, *Wisdom for a Lifetime*. That was a delightful challenge and we had help from others, especially Frank Giudici. But Alden did a great job of integrating his academic background in religious studies with Unity's treatment of Bible interpretation.

One of the core ideas of that book is that everyone interprets the Bible, that even the so-called "literal" reading of the Bible, the one that fundamentalists insist upon, is still an interpretation. That is quite a stunning claim but it is a sound one. "Facts" are hard to find about the Bible even from traditional historical viewpoints and there are virtually no sources one can go to determine the truth. We do have archeological and historical writings that are reasonably accurate, or so we think. There is a need to keep current too and new discoveries keep coming. One doesn't need to be a post-modern philosopher to know that we all interpret everything using our own self-styled frames of reference.

But what made Studebaker's book so compelling was that rather than seeing all this as a problem, he saw it as a virtue, as something that made Bible interpretation exciting, and worth pursuing. And he gave some fascinating examples of the ways we can interpret the Bible, including the dramatic and the comedic!

Now Laura Barrett Bennett has taken all this to a whole new level, reframing metaphysical Bible interpretation in the context of her own scholarship, her years of Bible teaching, her profound spiritual development, and the work with her father, Dr. Paul Barrett. In many ways, metagetics is emphasizing the most important aspect of metaphysical interpretation, the need to live our insights in our lives. This distinction cannot be underestimated for most of us are content to keep it all in our heads, pull those ideas out to impress or influence our friends or congregants or students, and then to carry on as before. That is being human, and living our spirituality in what integral philosopher Ken

Wilber calls "translative" terms. But to be truly transformed, our insights need to change our lives, and help us to die to our former selves. That is exactly what *The Language of God* promises.

It has been my honor to edit this book, not that it needed much from me, and to provide this Foreword. I honestly have thrilled to be part of this story, to learn all the aspects of it, to read about the history of Bible interpretation, of hermeneutics, and to discover the depths and diversity of it, and to know the many players over all the years. I've been grateful to Laura for offering all this in such a clear and lighthearted way. Anyone who has ever read philosophy or theology knows what a virtue that is!

I can feel Paul Barrett's influence on almost every page. His passion for the Bible and his clarity of thought taught me how to approach the Bible and offer it as a transformative teaching. In fact, I learned to both transcend and include the Unity teachings, and what they have to offer the world that is unique and compelling. And now his daughter is bringing that to us again in an even more powerful way. Dare I say it, that this is what Bible Interpretation has always intended, and all of Unity's great Bible teachers, from Charles Fillmore, to Herbert Hunt, to Ed Rabel, and to Paul Barrett, have paved the way on this path. *Metagetics* walks this path, and goes beyond it for all who are truly motivated to make the interpreting of Scripture a life-changing event.

Rev. Michael A. Maday, M.A. is an ordained Unity minister (1984) who has served churches in Michigan and Missouri as well as Unity Village where he has been book editor for Unity Books and Unity House, adjunct faculty for Unity Institute and Seminary, and prayer associate for Silent Unity.

THE LANGUAGE OF GOD: METAGETICS AND THE BIBLE

ACKNOWLEDGMENTS

My heartfelt thanks to the following people.

Larry Bennett, my beloved husband, for his love, support, and technical assistance, without whom I could not have done this.

Michael Maday, for his professional editing, counsel and great friendship.

April May, for taking a chance on me and giving me the opportunity to bring this book for the first time to my beloved colleagues.

Harriet Chezem, my sister and inspiration on what it means to be a truly good human being.

Carolyn and Frank Keller, Aunt and Uncle, whose generosity and love encouraged me to make this a reality.

Rev. Mildred Park and Mary Storm, in memoriam for my grandmother and mother, two strong women who made a difference in many lives, and who taught me to do the same.

Harriet Bennett, for all of the dinners, laundry, and housecleaning while I was writing.

Rev. Sandra Campbell, and exemplar of ministry and contribution, and my good friend.

The Sunday morning Bible group at Unity Temple on the Plaza in Kansas City for your encouragement and fresh ideas of what Bible study is.

Gary Jones, in memoriam, my friend and boss while I was teaching at Unity Village, who first encouraged me to write a book.

The congregations of Unity Church of Flint, Michigan and Unity Renaissance of Chesapeake, Virginia who inspired me to expand the possibilities for everyone in Bible self-interpretation.

To all of the students, faculty, and staff of Unity School for Religious Studies, now Unity Worldwide Spiritual Institute, past and present, who have been, and still are, a source of great love for what I do.

Finally, to Angel, in memoriam, my friend and fur-person who stayed by my side at her pillowed post on my desktop until this book was complete.

CONTENTS

Unit One: The Language of God

Part I: Introduction

Part II: Word

Part III: Truth

Part IV: Life

Unit Two: Metagetics and the Bible

Part V: The Spirit of the Word

Part VI: The Soul of Truth

Part VII: The Body of Life

UNIT ONE: THE LANGUAGE OF GOD

PART I: INTRODUCTION

.

.

CHAPTER 1: OVERVIEW

"Your word is a lamp to my feet and a light to my path (Psalm 119:105)."

FREETHINKER

There is a language that is timeless, and that renders an immediate sense of the now moment. It clears the mind and illuminates the path of life. It emerges from absolute silence, and yet it has been spoken by countless voices. It has no visible form, and yet it has been written in innumerable languages. When expressed, it has been called Word, Truth and Life, providing guidance, assurance, revelation, and enlightenment. What is this language that expresses the ideas and insights that have for ages been sought through religion, science, and philosophy; and is also beyond all religious, scientific, and philosophical constructs? It is the language of God.

To put it simply, the language of God is communication through which spiritual principle is translated into understandable and practical expression. Even to call it "the language of God" is to use a religious term to which it cannot be confined. Yet, as human beings we must use what is available to us to explain the unexplainable and let the intention of our hearts carry the wisdom and power of this language to others. Because of this, the language of God can be heard in the message of a good speaker or the encouraging words of a friend. It can be read in the pages of a newspaper, a magazine, or a best seller.

Certain "best sellers", or popular writings of ages past, have come to hold a special place in human society and history. They have been, and still are, revered and seen by religious authorities, leaders of nations, spiritual practitioners, and others as connecting links between what is human and what is divine. Along with other scriptures, they include the Quran of Islam; the Vedas, Upanishads, and Bhagavad Gita of Hinduism; the Tripitaka and Lotus Sutras of Buddhism; the Six Classics and Four Books of Confucianism; and the Tao Te Ching of Taoism. Most of these writings, or collections of writings, are closely associated with one of the world's great religions or philosophies, for without them, it is unlikely that these religions and philosophies would be so great, or even exist at all.

One collection of such scriptures from both the Jewish and Christian cultures is the Bible. The Bible's global influence on human society and behavior, even on other religions, is unsurpassed. It is an important foundational work in both the world of humankind, and the spiritual life of the individual. Yet, much of its spiritual relevance seems to have faded in recent decades. While there are many reasons for this, two of them stand out.

One reason is the technology of today's global communications which includes the immediacy of sharing experiences, images, and opinions on Social Media, as well as the information that is received through the Internet. These provide easy access to a variety of religious and philosophical thought as well as to a diversity of spiritual insight, guidance, and practices. Right at the fingertips, and/or voice command, of many people are multiple perspectives in how to pursue Truth and righteous living. The well of options runs deep, and rather than church, temple, mosque and/or scripture, people are turning to their phone, pad, or laptop for their spiritual experience of life.

Such freedom of information is a tricky thing, however. While some world governments block certain websites and communications that they deem as disruptive, many others allow for a free flow of information. Yet, with such freedom comes the risk of making information available that renders false understanding, incites violence, and/or encourages a way of life that takes away basic human rights. One must be discerning in his or her choice of the truths and life practices that speak to him or her.

Another reason for the loss of interest in the Bible is the way people are using their discernment. The academic information regarding the Bible that is available to the individual today puts into question its literal validity, creating skepticism toward its religious value, and in some cases, toward religion in general. Research performed in recent years has shown that the number of people in the United States with no religious affiliation is growing rapidly, while the number of those who are actively involved with America's predominant religion, Christianity, is declining.[1] This kind of tolerance for the freethinking individual that is found in many countries today is a good thing, for authenticity in our spirituality depends upon our ability to choose freely what brings us closest to the Divine in our awareness and experience. Yet, these trends also indicate that many freethinkers are turning away from ancient scripture,

---

[1] "ATHEISM ON THE RISE IN AMERICA," BY LEAH BARKOUKIS, TOWNHALL, ACCESSED SEPTEMBER 8, 2016, HTTP://TOWNHALL.COM/TIPSHEET/LEAHBARKOUKIS/2015/05/12/RISE-OF-ATHEISM-IN-AMERICA-N1997822

dismissing it as archaic and no longer relevant, even though it is extremely relevant.

While the Bible in many cases may no longer be used, or trusted, as a singular source of spiritual and moral guidance, it is still an integral part of life today. Laws, business practices, family and community relationships, societal behaviors, governmental and legal systems, all have their roots in the cultures that influenced biblical writing. Whether or not people believe in God or are even aware of what God means to them, they live in a world formed and shaped by those who did, and who wrote about it so long ago. They also govern themselves according to the ethics and behaviors that found a permanent place in the human psyche through the continued existence and growing availability of such writings. So, what can the freethinker do to best interact with life and the world the way they are today, while at the same time finding within himself or herself the ability to transcend what has been and bring into existence what can be?

What if a new relationship with the Bible could be formed for you, the freethinking individual with an open heart and discerning mind? What if this relationship connected heart and mind to immerse you in the mystical experience and mindful interpretation that leads to masterful living? What if it liberated you from the limitations of the past through the revelation of a fresh outlook on the present, and a new possibility for the future?

The development of such a relationship is why metagetics was created. Wherever you are in life; whatever your politics, nationality, ethnicity, or place in society; whether you practice any form of religion, or have a skeptical attitude toward religion in general, The Language of God: Metagetics and the Bible was created for you. This is more than a writing of inspirational material, or guide on how to interpret Scripture. Metagetics is a revolutionary approach to scriptural interpretation.

In its application to the Bible, metagetics reaches into the writings and stories from ages of human struggle, evolution, and wisdom to draw forth the spiritual teachings that are as powerful and pertinent today as they were several millennia ago. It then shapes these teachings into language and practices that not only work for your life, but also have the potential to uplift all of humankind. In this way, it pierces the veil of time and space, connecting you with the whole of human evolution and bringing you to the next phase of your own spiritual development and personal fulfillment.

The accomplished metagetical interpreter can pick up the Bible, go to any verse, passage, or story on any page, read it, understand its meaning, and draw forth from it definitive direction and inspired motivation for joyful living, loving relationships, and positive contributions in the world - all within a few minutes. In fact, metagetical interpretation can be applied to any of the world's scriptures, or to any literary work, even to the stories, experiences, relationships and things of your life. Yet, this book is focused on the Bible. Why?

BIBLE

RELATIONSHIP

One reason for the biblical focus is my own relationship with the Bible. This relationship has provided me with the awareness, knowledge, and experience necessary for the realization of what the Bible can be as a tool of transformation, a doorway to deeper understanding, and a portal for practical guidance in life. The following passage from my tape set, The Wisdom and Power of Scripture: Truth and the Gospels, Part I, best describes how this relationship began:

"Somewhere in storage in the house where I grew up there is a small black King James Bible with a hard cover that is peeling off, water stained pages, and the penciled in scribble of a young child's hand on the inner cover. It was given to me when I was two years old as I entered the nursery school of the Unity Church in Topeka, Kansas. I treated it like I would a beloved stuffed animal, with lots of hugs and squeezes, and of course I drew in it on its blank pages, because at two years old that's what you did with any book that was given to you. Perhaps at that age I was too young to receive a book I could neither read nor even come close to understanding, let alone treat with great reverence and care. Yet, I believe this was the beginning of what for me has been a lifetime positive relationship with this large and complex work; for all that my toddler's mind knew to do with this special thing was to love and play with it, and this I have been doing ever since."[2]

For more than thirty years, I studied and taught Bible history, literature, and interpretation, including serving more than ten years as the Chairperson of Biblical Studies for the Ministerial and Adult Education Programs of Unity School for Religious Studies, now known as Unity Worldwide Spiritual Institute. At this point in my experience I have come to know the Bible as a resource of mystical communion, mindful awareness, and masterful living. This is because the work I have done with the Bible, both on my own and with others,

---

[2] BENNETT, LAURA BARRETT. THE WISDOM AND POWER OF SCRIPTURE, TRUTH AND THE GOSPELS, PART I: TAPE 1, SIDE A. UNITY VILLAGE, MO: UNITY, 1999.

has deepened and matured my relationship with it, while keeping the joy and playfulness intact.

Through my relationship with the Bible, I have had the privilege of working with great biblical mentors, including my own father; hundreds of wonderful students, many of whom have gone on to inspire me with their own ministries, writings, and biblical work; and incredible colleagues with whom I have had great friendships and from whom I have learned a great deal. It is my intention with this work to honor these people who are so dear to me, as well as you who are reading this book on your spiritual search. In so doing, I am bringing together all the forms of biblical interpretation that I have taught, learned, and applied in life in a singular process that anyone can use. That process is known as metagetics.

The word metagetics came from a discussion with my husband, Larry, about what to call this process. It is a term that has emerged from three interpretive styles that I had used in my personal life, and in my career as a minister and educator. One is the eisegetical approach in which a predetermined meaning is placed onto the chosen scripture, the words of which, for the interpreter, support that predetermination. Another is the exegetical scholastic approach that explores historical context, literary meaning, and the original languages of scripture giving one's biblical understanding a solid foundation in human history and evolution.

The third interpretive style, and the greatest contribution to the transformational process of metagetics, is metaphysical interpretation. To apply metaphysics is to seek the spiritual Truth behind the literal word. This is done through the metaphorical connection between the things, characters, and stories of Scripture and the qualities, states of mind, and ways of thinking and feeling within the consciousness of the individual. Metaphysical interpretation provides invaluable insight into the nature and evolution of consciousness, both for the individual and the whole of humanity.

One evening as I was beginning the preparation of this book I shared with my husband, Larry, that the interpretive process within it evolves out of the work I had been doing with the Bible for many years as a teacher and a student. It contains exegetical elements of enlightening scriptural study and metaphysical elements of evolutionary understanding. In addition, a transformational experience emerges from the process itself. As I was sharing all of this, Larry stopped me and shouted, "Metagetics!" This was the perfect word. When you examine the meaning of its two parts you have the Greek prefix, meta, which means after, beyond, pursuit, or quest; and the Greek suffix gesthai, which is from the word hegeisthai meaning guide and lead.[3] Metagetics, then, is the pursuit of a deeper meaning in Scripture, and in life, that leads beyond enlightening study to spiritual revelation, personal transformation, and empowering leadership that moves spiritual ideas into action. My relationships with the Bible, and with the people who have filled my life and work, have culminated in the awakening of something that can be used in spiritual transformation for years to come.

---

[3] "META" AND "EXEGESIS", ONLINE ETYMOLOGY, ACCESSED SEPTEMBER 5, 2016, HTTPS://WWW.ETYMONLINE.COM/WORD/META AND HTTPS://WWW.ETYMONLINE.COM/WORD/EXEGESIS.

FOUNDATION

The second reason I am focusing on the Bible is because of its influence on our humanity as an integral part of our modern society. Over the years I have come to know the Bible as a solid foundation to knowing ourselves as individuals, as communities, and as a human race. From its modest origins to its role as a cornerstone in the structure of many societies throughout the world, this combination of various scriptures embraces a plethora of culture and religion as well as the whole spectrum of spiritual and human experience.

In the most basic sense, the Bible is a collection of books written between 900 BCE and CE 135, that was compiled and canonized over centuries from the seventh century BCE to the fifth century CE. Over time it has been integrated into the structure of our present-day society, and is, therefore, a basic influence on all who are part of our world today - including you. Whether or not you realize it, or even want it to be this way, the Bible has played a part in forming and shaping who you know yourself to be. In examining the history of the Bible, you can gain insight not only into global issues and events, as well as human relationships and interactions, but also into your own thoughts, acts and reactions to life and to the world.

As you spiritually contemplate and metagetically interpret the Bible's stories, characters, and passages, the language of God reveals to you the mysteries of your own soul as you acquire, or enhance, your ability to love and accept yourself and others. You also gain the skills and motivation for constructively responding and contributing to those with whom you share your life and world. Through the application of metagetics, the Bible can find you wherever you are in life - in whatever condition, state, or circumstance - and show the way to greater peace, deeper healing, higher awareness, and sweeter joy. Unity Minister and Bible Scholar, Dr. Paul C. Barrett, my father, has said the following:

Can you conceive that, whatever the condition of your present life, the Bible can tell you about it? It can tell you how you got where you are. It can tell you what to expect while you are there. It can tell you how to advance from your present state of being, into a higher state of joy, peace, love, and success.[4]

As both a collection of diverse writings and a single volume of spiritual evolution, the Bible can empower the individual in living a miraculous life. It can reach into the realm of your relationships, environment, and personal well-being, supporting and strengthening you in your daily living, and becoming for you an unlimited resource for your own spiritual evolution, if you just know how to approach it.

To my father, Dr. Paul Barrett, the Bible was the most sacred of scriptures. Like the rest of us, he struggled with personal challenges, and the whole gamut of human emotions that went with them. Yet, the Bible for him was not only a healing balm to the soul, but a powerful reminder that our true nature is of God, and can, therefore, never be less than whole. He had a way of relating to the Bible that not only gave him the ability to see the Spirit of God at work in his life, it also gave him the gift to facilitate the emergence of this awareness in others. He could bring out of even the most complex scriptures simple steps that when applied in life rendered a practical approach for moving through challenges and fulfilling one's dreams.

---

[4] BARRETT, DR. PAUL C. INTRODUCTION TO BIBLE INTERPRETATION, TAPE 1, SIDE A. FAIRFAX, VA: DIVINE LIFE MISSION, 1986.

One such teaching I recall from the book of Revelation, "*So, because you are lukewarm, and neither cold nor hot, I am about to spit you out of my mouth. (Revelation 3:16).*" Who wants to be rejected for being lukewarm? Yet, my dad did not read harsh judgment or rejection in this. He saw a practical lesson about the quandary of being stuck in indecision when faced with a life choice - neither hot nor cold. His message was to consciously choose whatever it is you do in life, and move forward with confidence, knowing you will be shown the way.

If your choice is hot and right on, you will prosper and benefit by it. If it is cold and way off the mark, you will soon learn through your decisive action what not to do and how to change course toward the right solution. Yet, if you are afraid to move forward with your choice, and you don't invest yourself fully in what you are doing, the indecision eats away at you and you lose your appetite for what is spiritual and your motivation in doing what is for your highest good. One of my students who had experienced my dad's teachings on the book of Revelation remarked, "Your dad has a way of making Revelation read like a comic book - simple, entertaining and with a good message."

My dad never claimed any special gift. He simply understood the words and language of the Bible from their deeper intention, and not just from their literal meaning. In his tape entitled, Introduction to Bible Interpretation, he made the following three points about the Bible:

1. "It is a Book of Truth. It speaks to what is true in the mind of God, though not necessarily to what is fact in the mind of man."
2. "It is a Book of Life. It is humanity's textbook of self-discovery."
3. "It is the Word of God. The Bible is Esoteric, that is to say it is filled with hidden meanings that are revealed, not so

15

much through the literal word, as through the inspired mind and heart."[5]

The Language of God: Metagetics and the Bible highlights my dad's biblical understanding by first examining the Bible as the "Word of God", then as a "Book of Truth", finally as a "Book of Life", in that order. The three terms of Word, Truth, and Life form the foundational framework of metagetics. They are presented as domains in which nine principles of the interpretive process are found - many of which originated with Dr. Barrett's work, and all of which will be explored and put into practice in this book.

In this exploration, you learn how the Word evolved as a principle of spiritual reality known as the Logos; how Truth was explored through the discipline of interpretation known as hermeneutics, and how the vitality of the Life-force is experienced, not only when the Bible comes alive, but when you become the living language of God through your relationship with the Bible. This includes meeting some of history's greatest religious and philosophical thinkers and connecting with some of humanity's deepest spiritual teachings.

Then you engage with the principles of these three domains as they apply to biblical scripture. Through contemplative communion you experience the Spirit of the Word; through the wisdom of the heart-centered mind, or heartmind, you know the Soul of Truth; and through breath and movement you embrace the Body of Life as you become the living language of God in your world. This takes place when you

---

[5] DR. PAUL C. BARRETT AS QUOTED IN INTRODUCTION TO BIBLE INTERPRETATION, TAPE 1A. PALM SPRINGS, AURETHA BIBLE CENTRE, 1983.

read the text of this book as well as of the recommended biblical passages and participate in its exercises.

TEXT

CONTENT

What you are now reading is the Overview. It is the only Chapter in Part I of Unit One: The Language of God. Part I is simply entitled Introduction. This is because this chapter introduces you to metagetics and the Bible, and to the content of the book. Following the Overview are thirteen chapters of text, divided into six more parts of the book.

Part II: Word begins in Chapter 2 with the evolution of the idea of Logos. This chapter addresses how Logos evolved from a universal philosophical principle to the incarnation of Christ, the proclamation of salvation, and the manifestation of Scripture. Following in Chapter 3, Scripture, you will discover for yourself what sacred scripture is, as well as how it shows up in your world. Included is a brief history of how the biblical scripture came to be considered canon, or the authoritative Word of God.

You may notice how the terms, "Word," and "Scripture," are often capitalized, as well as the other domains of "Truth," and "Life." Capitalization, and italics are used in the following ways:

1. As titles and names for the Being, Presence, and/or active expression of God.
2. As the names of those writings at the center of the world's great religions, or as terms used in place of, or in reference to, those names.

3. As titles of the three key domains and nine principles that outline this course.
4. As titles for chapters or sections.

Part III is called Truth. Chapter 4, Knowing, introduces the three tiers of knowing that measure how we know what Truth is. The first tier is called Perception, which is knowing based on previously formed viewpoints and opinions. The second is Conception, which is fresh insight reasoned out from what we already know combined with new information and experience. The third is Inception, which is the influx of new and creative ideas that come from a connection with the Spirit of God beyond intellectual thought and concept. Chapter 5, Interpretation, addresses the history and practice of biblical interpretation, otherwise known as Hermeneutics, as a search for spiritual Truth. From the Greek word, hermeneutike, hermeneutics literally means interpretation.

With our investigation into hermeneutics through time we see the roots of how we interpret the Bible today through the three approaches of Eisegesis, Exegesis, and Metaphysics. These types of interpretation bring the Bible alive. What they are and how they work are brought forth in Chapter 6: Alive. It is the first of two chapters in Part IV, called Life. Chapter 7 is called Living because of its examination of the living spiritual energy that is awakened through the metagetical process and applied to the living of life. It includes an exploration of Spirit, Soul, Body, and World as aspects of Being that are enlivened in this process.

CURRICULUM

Unit Two, entitled Metagetics and the Bible, takes you through seven chapters that address the "7 principles of interpretation" used in the transformational experience of metagetics. It includes experiential exercises as the principles and method of metagetics are explored. It begins with Part V: The Spirit of the Word. The first principle, and the eighth chapter, is Love. Love attracts to you the inspiration that you seek in Scripture and clears away the inner obstructions to receiving that inspiration. Through communion with God, the next principle and ninth chapter of Prayer aligns you with the "Spirit of the Word" and its creative activity in you. Then you delve into the tenth chapter on Contemplation. This activity shows you how to reach into the core of your being and reveal how God's Word speaks to you, and through you, in new ways that are relevant to your present experience.

In Part VI, The Soul of Truth, you move through three more interpretative principles to engage in exegesis and metaphysics from the wisdom of the soul, or heartmind, an aspect of your being that will be explored later in this book. This puts you into a living conversation with the author and text of Scripture. It begins with the principle of History in Chapter 11, through which you touch upon the collective memory of humanity that is part of your own soul's development. There are three types of Bible history: The history *In* the Bible, the history *About* the Bible, and the history *Of* the Bible. Through the principle of Meaning, in Chapter 12, you discover new meaning for your life in the History, Metaphor, Etymology, and Metaphysics of biblical words, stories and passages.

The principle of Logic, in Chapter 13, assimilates what you have learned into a revelation of Truth that is beyond any pre-

19

conceived notions. It follows a recipe that brings together the "7 Principles of Interpretation" with a "7" Step Method of Metagetics". These steps that result in a practical message for life are Choose, Commune, Contextualize, Combine, Conclude, Constitute and Console. This message leads you to the last chapter and the final principle. From this revelation emerges a message that leads you to the last chapter and the final principle.

Part VII, The Body of Life, contains one chapter. In Chapter 14, the principle, Mastery brings form and function to the metagetical process. It begins with the section, Embodiment, by addressing the hero who has attained mastery, not through domination and control of others, but through becoming the embodiment of that which awakens one's true nature and uplifts all of humankind. The section on Message focuses on what has been revealed to you through your work with Scripture, and how you can become the embodiment of its message in your life and world.

To aid you in the development of your metagetical skills several things have been provided throughout this book. Following the chapter's text, the main points are re-written, paraphrased and/or repeated in the Summary of the chapter's teachings. There is also an Inquiry consisting of questions using ideas from the chapter to deepen your spiritual insight and expand your self-awareness. In chapters 2, 3 and 5, Tables summarizing the historical timelines described within those chapters will follow the Summary at the end of the chapter. Three appendixes can be found at the end of the book as well. One is the Endnotes, listing the chapter by chapter citations. Another is the Bibliography of resources used in writing this book. Finally, there is the Index of Names and Authors, and the Index of Terms and Titles.

PROMISES

While the extent of your participation in the reading and lessons of the metagetical process is up to you, it is your full participation that will fulfill the promises of this book. What are these promises? At the completion of your experience with this text, you will have the following:

1. The basic skills for the transformational spiritual practice of metagetical Bible interpretation.
2. A way of relating to the Bible as a doorway for mastery in life.
3. The ability to hear, read, speak, and be an expression of the living language of God. This will lead to the following experiences:
a. Empowering inspiration through the Spirit of the Word.
b. Personal and spiritual freedom through the Soul of Truth.
c. Increased enthusiasm and vitality through the Body of Life.

The work of metagetics does not promise that you will be able to fix everyone and everything, especially yourself. "Mastery" is not so much about controlling life, as it is about being fully present to it and the blessings it brings. In the adventure that is your life's journey, challenges will continue to arise, and you will be faced with the fears and inner obstacles that come with being human. What your participation in metagetics does promise is access to the Bible as an infinite resource and steadfast support system of love, wisdom, and new and practical insight into who you are and what you are capable of doing and being.

So now I invite you to experience the freedom found in loving and playing with the Bible. Why would you bother to do this when there is so much that has been revealed and written in the way of spiritual and transformational literature since the

21

Bible was completed? Perhaps it is because whatever your relationship with the Bible is, whether you think of it as powerful, pleasant, painful, or virtually irrelevant, you cannot help but experience its effects every day of your life, for it has woven itself into the very fabric of the human psyche, and of our global societies.

In fact, there is no human experience, no news event, no drama, no comedy, no popular form of entertainment, scandal, heroism, or pure ecstatic inspiration that is not reflected, and maybe even rooted in the Bible. Therefore, by metagetically coming to know and understand the Bible from the place of divine love, joy, and wisdom, you come to know and understand yourself, and all of humanity, from that same place. In this state of awareness, God is present in all people, in all things, and as all possibility.

Are you ready and willing to live in a world of possibility in which the language of God speaks directly to you through every person, place, and thing? Are you ready and willing to engage in transformational conversations that transcend space and time? Are you ready and willing to learn how to love and play with the Bible, and to let it teach you how to love and play with your life? All you need to do is work with The Language of God, Metagetics and the Bible, and let it work in and through you. When you do, a brighter light will shine into the world - the light of your own true Self. Let us embark together in this great journey through the realm of spiritual wisdom as we join the Psalmist in proclaiming to God, "Your word is a lamp to my feet and a light to my path (Psalm 119:105)." Welcome to metagetics!

SUMMARY

- The Language of God is communication that translates spiritual principle into understandable and practical expression.
- The Language of God is spoken by countless voices and read in many writings. One such writing is the Bible.
- The Bible's global influence on human society and behavior, even on other religions, is unsurpassed.
- The Bible is an important foundational work in both the world of humankind, and the spiritual life of the individual.
- Metagetics is an approach to the Bible for the freethinking individual with an open heart and discerning mind. It is for anyone from any background.
- Metagetics combines principles from previous interpretive methods, specifically eisegesis, exegesis and metaphysics, from which it got its name.
- Through your engagement with metagetics, you will learn to hear, read, speak, and be an expression of the living language of God.
- This book is divided into seven parts with a total of fourteen chapters that address the three domains, the seven principles, and the six-step method of metagetics.
- To the degree that you participate in this course, its promises will be fulfilled for you.

Inquiry

1. When have you experienced the Language of God speaking to you?

2. Through what writings have you encountered the Language of God?

3. What is the Bible to you and/or for you?

4. What, if any, experience have you had in interacting with the Bible?

5. What would you like to get out of reading this book and doing its exercises?

PART II: WORD

CHAPTER 2: LOGOS

"In the beginning was the Word, and the Word was with God, and the Word was God. (John 1:1)."

ROOTS

Have you ever noticed that your environment is filled with objects, events, and relationships that depend on the reasoning faculty of your mind to know what they are and to translate that knowledge into ways that you can relate to them? Have you also noticed that the way knowledge translates itself in your mind is in the form of words, and that words are the primary vehicles through which your relationships with the people and things of your world are established?

For example, if you wanted a cup of hot tea, you might go to your kitchen, heat up water in a teapot, get a cup from the cupboard, pour the water through a filter or bag of tea leaves, let it brew – and you have tea. How would you have known what to do if you did not understand such words as "kitchen," "water," "teapot," "cup," "cupboard," "tea leaves," and "brew"? How would you have been able to make tea if your reasoning faculty had not put those words together in a way that guided your actions? Even your understanding of a word like "hot" reveals to you the care necessary in your handling and sipping of the tea. You do not even have to speak the words, for in your early learning of their meaning your brain stored them in your memory and is consistently running them through

27

your mind as you reason out your environment and your relationship to the things within it. Thus, words and reason give you a relationship to the world in which you live and shape your experience of that world.

Words and reason come together in the wisdom of ancient Greece as well, not just as the activity of individual consciousness relating to the world around it, but also as the source of being and existence. This source of being and existence is called Logos, translated into English as "Word," with a capital "W." To fully understand the Word, or Logos, we must look to its roots and go to its beginning – not its cosmic beginning, but when it was first conceived as existing on a cosmic scale. Following is an introduction to some of the key figures at the roots of the Logos idea, and an overview of how it grew through their exploration and insights. This is a glance into Greek philosophy and its influence on the evolving religions of Judaism and Christianity.

GROWTH

PHILOSOPHY

Meet Heraclitus (c. 535 – 475 BCE), the first philosopher to introduce the idea of the Logos. I like to picture him standing in a stream contemplating the activity of its changing condition counterbalanced by the constancy of its presence. Perhaps the most well-known statement of this 5th century philosopher was,

"You cannot step into the same river twice," implying that the unstable movement of water creates the stable presence of the river.[6]

For Heraclitus, the Logos was a permeating principle bringing rationality and order into the world, but in a very interesting way. He believed that out of the all-pervading Logos came the world of form and nature. He also conveyed that within form and nature were opposing forces creating change and flux in their opposition to each other. Cosmic equilibrium, or balance, was found in the change and flux as opposition was burned off in the energy of what Heraclitus referred to as "fire," the primal element out of which all things were made. As quoted by university professor Daniel W. Graham, Heraclitus observed that "Cold things warm up, the hot cools off, wet becomes dry, dry becomes wet."[7]

This balancing act was the creative activity of the Logos which functioned as a singular principle in the overarching world-order. Heraclitus is again quoted by Dr. Graham. "This world-order, the same of all, no god nor man did create, but it ever was and is and will be: ever-living fire, kindling in measures and being quenched in measures."[8] Does this seem "logosical," or excuse me, logical to you? If so, great. If not, that's okay. We as a humanity have evolved in our understanding of the universe since the time of Heraclitus, and our understanding of the Logos has evolved along with us. Let us continue the evolution with Plato.

---

[6] "HERACLITUS," BY DANIEL W. GRAHAM, *THE INTERNET ENCYCLOPEDIA OF PHILOSOPHY*, ISSN, ACCESSED SEPTEMBER 8, 2016, HTTP://WWW.IEP.UTM.EDU/.

[7] IBID.

[8] IBID.

If we could go back in time and observe Plato (c. 427-347 BCE), we might find him in a dialogue with a group of students from his Academy, espousing the wisdom of his mentor, Socrates. For Plato, Logos was the principle behind the *Dialectic* of Socrates, the scenario through which so many of Plato's writings are composed. A "dialectic" was an exchange of ideas in which inquiries were made, and two opposing points of view were discussed, regarding the assumed nature of a given topic. Rather than the fiery cosmic activity of creation, Logos for Plato was the perfect argument, or conceptualization and communication of the perfect nature of a thing. Such perfection could only emerge through the pure logic of the dialectic. In the *Dialectic* of Socrates as portrayed by Plato in *The Republic*, it is written:

> *"So here, the summit of the intelligible world is reached in philosophic discussion by one who aspires, through the discourse of reason unaided by any of the senses, to make his way in every case to the essential reality and perseveres until he has grasped by pure intelligence the very nature of Goodness itself."* [9]

Got that? Let me put it another way. In Plato's writing, Socrates is pointing out that the pure logic of the in-depth dialectic leads to the experience of the Logos, or the expression of words that account for perfection beyond words. The search for such pure logic through philosophical debate did not stop with Plato.

Aristotle (c. 384-322 BCE) was a student of Plato, and a graduate of his Academy. We might envision him as a young man engaged in the dialogue Plato is having with his students and asking questions that stretch the very boundaries of Plato's own logic. Aristotle viewed Logos as one of three ways

---

[9] IBID.

to present an argument of persuasion. In his work on *Rhetoric*, he wrote:

"Of the modes of persuasion furnished by the spoken word there are three kinds. The first kind depends on the personal character of the speaker [ethos]; the second on putting the audience into a certain frame of mind [pathos]; the third on the proof, or apparent proof, provided by the words of the speech itself [logos]. Persuasion is achieved by the speaker's personal character when the speech is so spoken as to make us think him credible (Modes of Persuasion. 1356a, 2-3)."[10]

Here, language itself points to Logos as the undeniable proof that someone, or something, is credible. This is known as logic.

The idea of persuasive logic is later expanded, becoming the Logos of universal reason. It is this Logos that Zeno (c. 336-265 BCE), the founder of the Athens Stoic School of Philosophy, conveys as the ultimate good and the highest purpose in life. With logic ruling over passion and emotions, Zeno may very well have been the prototype of the Vulcans and the inspiration of the character Mr. Spock in the Star Trek universe. Diogenes Laertius, a 3rd century biographer of the Greek philosophers, preserved some of Zeno's teachings in his work *Lives and Opinions of Eminent Philosophers* where he quotes Zeno in saying the following:

"But when in the case of animals impulse has been superadded, whereby they are enabled to go in quest of their proper aliment (nourishment), for them, say the stoics, Nature's rule is to follow the direction of impulse. But when reason by way of a more perfect leadership has been bestowed on the beings we call

---

[10] ETHOS, PATHOS, AND LOGOS – MODES OF PERSUASION (ARISTOTLE), ACCESSED JUNE 22, 2017, HTTP://WWW.EUROPEAN-RHETORIC.COM/ETHOS-PATHOS-LOGOS-MODES-PERSUASION-ARISTOTLE/.

rational, for them life according to reason rightly becomes the natural life. For reason supervenes to shape impulse scientifically (Baird, 507)."[11]

In other words, it is natural for animals to live by instinct, but the natural expression of the human is to live by reason. This supersedes instinct by accessing the Logos, or logic, wherein what is right and good in life can be experienced.

THEOLOGY

Influenced by Heraclitus, Plato and Aristotle, as well as the Stoics, Philo Judaeus of Alexandria (c. 20 BCE – 50 CE), a Hellenistic Jewish philosopher and theologian, wrote extensively on the interconnection of philosophy and the Scripture. We might picture Philo standing in the great halls of the Alexandrian Library in Egypt with five scrolls of papyri in his hands. The Greek name for the Torah is Pentateuch, literally meaning "five vessels," or "five scrolls." This is possibly because scrolls of papyrus, from which paper gets its name, could not be sewn together into one large scroll, as with the kosher animal skin of the Hebrew Torah.

Philo's scripture was the Septuagint, a Greek translation of the sacred Hebrew writings. Considered by many to be the father of metaphysical Bible interpretation, Philo interpreted the stories found in the Septuagint as metaphors, and the teaching of its laws as a guide for the journey of the individual soul toward enlightenment. According to his writings, the anthropomorphic and emotional depictions of God in the Bible were limited human concepts of a universal Form beyond

---

[11] ZENO QUOTED BY F.E. BAIRD, PHILOSOPHIC CLASSICS: ANCIENT PHILOSOPHY, VOLUME I (PRENTICE HALL COLLEGE DIV, 2008) AS REFERRED TO BY JOHN J. MARK, ZENO OF CITIUM, ACCESSED JULY 17, 2017, HTTP://WWW.ANCIENT.EU/ZENO_OF_CITIUM/.

motion and emotion in which was found the perfect blueprint for the whole of the universe.

In addition, Philo saw the Logos as an intermediary being. This being was not separate from God, but a thought in the mind of God through which God's power to create, and to govern, could be activated and accomplished. It was, and is, the eternal and first begotten of God. From this transcendent firstborn being in the mind of God, came the birth of all things. It is the Logos that brought, and continues to bring, balance to the opposing forces of nature. It is the Logos that moves invisible and intangible forms, known to both Plato and Philo as Ideas, into visible and tangible existence and experience.

> *"For it is out of that essence that God created everything, without indeed touching it himself, for it was not lawful for the all-wise and all-blessed God to touch materials which were all misshapen and confused, but he created them by the agency of his incorporeal powers, of which the proper name is Ideas, which he so exerted that every genus received its proper form (LA 1.329)."*[12]

The "agency" of God's incorporeal powers bringing "Ideas" into their proper form was the Logos. "And the Logos, which connects together and fastens every thing, is peculiarly full itself of itself, having no need whatever of any thing beyond (*Her.* 188)."[13] For Philo, the Logos was the intermediary that allowed God to know and experience God, "full itself of itself." Thus, from the beginning of existence came a world conceived

---

[12] JUDAEUS PHILO, LEGUM ALLEGORIARUM (ALLEGORICAL LAW), QUOTED BY MARIAN HILLER, PHILO OF ALEXANDRIA, INTERNET ENCYCOPEDIA OF PHILOSOPHY, ACCESSED JULY 17, 2017, HTTP://WWW.IEP.UTM.EDU/PHILO/#H11.

[13] JUDAEUS PHILO, QUIS RERUM DIVINARUM HERES SIT (WHO IS THE HEIR OF DIVINE THINGS?), AS QUOTED BY HILLER.

in the mind of God and created by God through the Logos, the power of the Word.

This is nothing new. The creative power of the Word first appears in the Hebrew Scriptures with the originating words of God, *"Then God said, 'let there be light'; and there was light (Genesis 1:3)."* It is also seen as the wisdom of God in action referred to in the book of Isaiah, *"...so shall my word be that goes out from my mouth; it shall not return to me empty, but it shall accomplish that which I purpose, and succeed in the thing for which I sent it (Isaiah 55:11)."* What is distinct with Philo is that the Logos, the Word, exists as an entity, or being. This being of the Logos becomes the core of Christian theology.

To look at the Logos in Christianity, we begin by going to the seashore of Syria where we encounter Justin Martyr (c. 100 – 165 CE). We can picture him walking along the shore with an elderly Christian who shares with him the wisdom of the Hebrew prophets and the teachings of Jesus Christ. After years of soul searching and philosophical study, with interest in the ideas of Plato, Justin experiences a spiritual awakening and dedicates his life to service of the Divine as it is depicted in Jewish and Christian Scripture. After conversion to Christianity, he teaches in locations around the Empire and debates philosophers in Rome.

Justin was especially focused on the Christian faith as the culmination of Greek philosophy and Judaism. According to theologian Alister McGrath, Justin puts forth the Logos as the ultimate source of all human knowledge. For Justin, the Logos was known temporarily through the manifest appearances of God in the Old Testament. It was the Christ of the New Testament, however, who gave it its fullest revelation.

"Our religion is clearly more sublime than any human teaching in this respect: the Christ who has appeared for us human being represents the Logos principle in all its fulness... Whatever either lawyers or philosophers have said well, was articulated by finding and reflection upon some aspect of the Logos. However, since they did not know the Logos – which is Christ – in its entirety, they often contradicted themselves."[14]

Justin put forth the idea that the incarnation of Christ was the only way to know the Logos fully. While he was martyred for the controversy of his teachings, denounced by the cynic philosopher Crescens, who felt all Christians were atheists, Justin was not alone in his viewpoint.

Those who, like Justin, believed the Logos was found in the being of Jesus Christ included Titus Flavius Clemens, otherwise known as Clement of Alexandria (c.150-215 CE). Like Justin, he was a convert to Christianity who purported the truth of biblical scripture over that of Greek thought and mythology. It would not be surprising to find him teaching about the Logos, not just to men, but to women as well. He was known to advocate for the ability of women to inspire with spiritual insight and for their equality in church leadership. In addition to seeing men and women equally, he believed the Logos was not just equal to the universal and absolute Truth sought by so many, but the same as it. Clement depicted the Logos as "the thought of God," and "the source of creation," which himself was incarnated to become visible. He stated the following:

"...Plato says, who are the true philosophers? Those who wish to see the truth. And in the Phaedrus, he speaks of Truth as an idea.

---

[14] JUSTIN MARTYR SUMMARIZED AND QUOTED BY ALISTER E. MCGRATH, CHRISTIAN THEOLOGY AN INTRODUCTION, (MALDEN, MA: BLACKWELL PUBLISHING, 2001), 357.

But this 'idea' is none other than the thought of God, which the pagans called his logos. Now the logos proceeds from God as the cause of the creation. Then the logos is himself begotten, when he becomes incarnate, in order that he may become visible."[15]

For Clement, Christ as Logos is the logical and incarnated proof of the Truth in Scripture. Truth with a capital "T" will be addressed later in this book.

Perhaps the greatest interpreter of biblical scripture in the later 2nd and early 3rd century was Origen Adamantius of Alexandria (c. 185-254 CE). One of the earliest cut and paste editors, we can envision him carefully piecing together the different translations and versions of the Old Testament to draw forth the actual meaning of its writings and stories. It was Origen who created the six-column translation of the Hebrew Bible known as the *Hexapla*. Along with some of his writings, this work developed at depth what later came to be known as biblical exegesis. This approach to interpretation will be explored in later chapters.

Like Justin and Clement, Origen believed that Christ was the Logos. He also elaborated as to how this was so. He conveyed that the Logos unified with the human soul in the incarnation of Jesus Christ. Through this incarnation, the mediator of the Logos brought divine substance into human form.

"Therefore, with this soul acting as a mediator between God and flesh – for it was not possible for the nature of God to be mingled with flesh without a mediator– there was born the God-man (deus-homo), that substance (substantia) being the connecting link which could assume a body without denying its own nature.

---

[15] TITUS FLAVIUS CLEMENS QUOTED BY MCGRATH, 225.

...The Son of God by whom all things were created is called Jesus Christ, the Son of man."[16]

According to Origen, the mediator of the Logos was the salvation of humankind through the demonstration of his own death and resurrection. Such resurrection was to come for all in the form of the spiritual body that could unite with God in heaven, a salvation to which all souls had access, including the most sinful.

"By the command of God the body which was earthly and animal will be replaced by a spiritual body, such as may be able to dwell in heaven; ...even for those destined for eternal fire or for punishment there will be an incorruptible body through the change of the resurrection."[17]

Teaching salvation and eternal life for all, Origen was excommunicated from the Church. Still, he clung to his faith. Ironically, in his later life he was persecuted and martyred for being a Christian.

Thus, the Logos, which was originally perceived as a universal principle of creation, came to be known as the perfection behind logical words and reason which was the highest purpose in life. Later, it was seen as the Divine blueprint of being and existence, which was personified in Jesus Christ as the mediator of salvation and eternal life for all of humanity.

---

[16] ORIGEN ADAMANTIUS IN *THE CHRISTIAN THEOLOGY READER*, ED. ALISTER MCGRATH, THIRD EDITION, (MALDEN, MA, BLACKWELL PUBLISHING, 2007), 265.

[17] IBID. 649.

WRITING

POWER

In the English translation of the Gospel of John, Logos is transliterated into Word, and is used as a name for Jesus. This is seen in John's early verses, the first verse of which is quoted at the opening of this chapter.

> *"In the beginning was the Word, and the Word was with God, and the Word was God. He was in the beginning with God. All things came into being through him, and without him not one thing came into being. What has come into being in him was life, and the life was the light of all people (John 1:1-2)."*

To many devout Christians, then and now, Jesus was – and is – the Logos. Donald McKim, author of *The Westminster Dictionary of Theological Terms*, points out that in Christology, Jesus is perceived as the "concrete, historical expression" of the Logos.[18] But wait – there's more. The Word of God reaches into other arenas as well.

In his book *Christian Theology an Introduction*, Alister Mcgrath writes, "The term is also used to refer to 'the gospel of Christ' or 'the 'message or proclamation about Jesus.'"[19] He also writes, "The term is used in a general sense to refer to the whole Bible, which can be regarded as setting the scene for the advent of Christ, telling the story of his coming, and exploring the implications of his life, death, and resurrection

---

[18] MCKIM, DONALD K. *WESTMINSTER DICTIONARY OF THEOLOGICAL TERMS.* LOUISVILLE: JOHN KNOX PRESS,

2003, 164.

[19] MCGRATH, CHRISTIAN THEOLOGY, AN INTRODUCTION, 166/167.

for believers." [20] What McGrath is saying is that in Christianity the power of the Word takes on three forms of revelation. Not only is it revealed through a person, but also through a proclamation, as well as through the Sacred Scripture of the Bible.

This approach to Scripture as the Word of God is also connected with Jewish mysticism, which views the letters and syllables of the Torah as carrying the spiritual power of God, and of having a deeper meaning that reveals this power to the sincere seeker. A popular medieval commentary known as *Mikra-ot Gedolot*, or *The Interpreter's Bible*, purports that the Torah is the "Revealed Word of God." In his book, *Essential Judaism: A Complete Guide to Beliefs, Customs, and Rituals,* author George Robinson writes, "Because the commentators believed the Torah to be the Revealed Word of God, every single letter, even the ornamentations on the letters, was believed to have a meaning. One only needed a method with which to plumb the depths of the text."[21] Abraham Joshua Heschel, the renowned Jewish philosopher of the twentieth century, shared these thoughts in his work entitled *God in Search of Man: A Philosophy of Judaism*:

> *"There is a theory in Jewish literature containing a profound parabolical truth which maintains that the Torah, which is eternal in spirit, assumes different forms in various eons. ...Just as man assumed a material form when he was driven out of the Garden of Eden, so has the Torah assumed a material form. If man retained 'the garments of light,' his spiritual form of*

---

[20] IBID., 167.

[21] ROBINSON, GEORGE. ESSENTIAL JUDAISM: A COMPLETE GUIDE TO THE BELIEFS, CUSTOMS, AND RITUALS. NEW YORK: SIMON AND SCHUSTER/ATRIA PAPERBACK, 2000. P. 303.

existence, the Torah, too, would have retained its spiritual form."[22]

We have seen how the Logos evolved into the God-man of Jesus Christ, but how did the reasoning of humanity reach this point of belief where words on a page carried the governing principle, light of wisdom and life, creative power, and even the very spirit of the Divine? A brief look at the evolution of language might help us in answering this question.

LANGUAGE

Most mornings I do not need to set my alarm. Like the crow of the rooster, my cat starts with a *meow* that in her training of me implies it is time for breakfast, and she keeps it up until she sees me get up and out of bed. Just as the animals around us do today, our human ancestors most likely attempted to communicate through sound. Over time their expressive noises formed into specific syllables that became individual words. As the brain of humankind evolved, and the need to connect with other humans for survival and protection became more evident and distinct, so did the words that were used, and whole vocabularies came into being. These vocabularies were used to give direction, make exchanges, cry for help, and eventually to tell stories that bound a community together in shared history and spiritual meaning.

With the advent of stationary settlements and civilizations language evolved, and visual symbols were used to preserve specific types of communication. Numbers were formed and

---

[22] HESCHEL, ABRAHAM JOSHUA. *GOD IN SEARCH OF MAN: A PHILOSOPHY OF JUDAISM.* NEW YORK: FARRAR, STRAUS AND GIROUX, 1983. P. 262/263.

alphabets were taken from images of daily life. For example, did you know that the letter "A" was originally the head of an ox, and "B" the yoke? Turn "A" upside down and "B" sideways and you will see what I mean. Other images came in the forms of wedges, lines, and dots that were used to convey business agreements and divine ordinances that brought law and order to whole societies.

The cuneiform script of the early Acadians was used to communicate the laws given by the gods that Hammurabi brought down from the mountain to give to the people. Wait a minute! Wasn't it Moses on the mountain, and the Hebrew Script that communicated God's Law? In any case, the alphabets that emerged from these ancient scripts became words, which became written phrases and sentences, which led to written languages. Even the word "alphabet" is from the good old "A" and "B" letters – this time in the Greek language as *alpha* and *beta*.

As civilizations prospered and grew, they developed military systems that enhanced their ability to expand their influence as they spread their cultures and languages to the world around them. The interactions with local forms of indigenous culture and spirituality integrated into the societal and religious systems of the great and conquering empires, creating new forms of language and religion. Hence, Hammurabi in one culture, might become Moses in another, each culture having its own revered version of how Divine Law came into the world of humankind. Sacred Scripture became sacred when it bound a society or civilization together in a common story, set of laws, and language. Thus, the written word became the vehicle for the governing principle and creative power of the Divine, and language made that word coherent. Therein lies the answer to our earlier question.

Which language, however, is the language of God? Is it the language of an ancient earth religion that first connected humankind to nature and the cosmos? Is it oriental in origin, such as the Sanskrit of the Hindu *Vedas*, or the ancient Chinese of the *Tao Te Ching*, or the Japanese of the *Lotus Sutra*? Perhaps God's true language grew and developed in the Middle East, Europe, and the West. Is it Hebrew, the writings of which gave the world a singular God, Creator, and Law Giver? Is it Aramaic, the spoken language of Jesus? Is it Greek, the language of ancient philosophy that gave birth to the concept of the Logos, and to much of the New Testament? It could be Latin, the language of the *Holy Bible* of Rome, and many of the later translations of ancient Greek philosophy. Maybe it is the German Renaissance language used by Martin Luther to inspire a Reformation of Christianity. Perhaps it is King James English, which brought the Christian scriptures to North America. Or – it just might be the Arabic of the *Quran* of Islam as it was given to Mohammed by the archangel Gabriel.

Each of these languages, at one point or another, has been put forth as the language whose very syllables are infused with the power of God. Yet, the creative and authoritative power of God's Word cannot be bound to a single written language, nor can it be limited to the words and descriptions given by all these languages put together. The Language of God is, therefore, none of these. Yet, because it is none of these, it could very well be all of them.

PRINCIPLE

The language of God is the universal and intermediary principle that moves the invisible into the visible, the unspeakable into the spoken, and the unformed into dynamic and organic existence. It gives us the experience of that which is Infinite and Eternal through that which is finite and temporal. It is the Logos, incarnated and expressed through you, through your words and proclamations, and through the writings and things of life that are sacred to you.

As we have learned, the Word of God in Christian theology refers to the person of Jesus, the message about Jesus, and the whole text of the Bible. In the same way, the Logos is the Divine Principle of your being, expressing as you, as the message you have for life, and as the Truth that is revealed to you through your interaction with the Bible. As you discover the Logos, or the Word of God, in the text of Sacred Scripture, you awaken it in yourself.

To enable you in doing this, our next chapter is focused on Scripture. You will come to know what Sacred Scripture is for you, and how the Bible became the canon of Sacred Scripture for the Judeo-Christian world. As with this chapter, you will delve into the past and meet some of the more interesting characters in the development of human understanding regarding God's Word as Scripture. You will also get to know how the Bible was, and still is, evolving in its meaning for humankind and for you as a living, dynamic expression of the Logos.

SUMMARY

- Words and reason come together as the creative activity of individual consciousness relating to the world around it.
- The creative power of word and reason is taken to a cosmic scale in Greek philosophy as the source of being and existence called Logos, translated into English as "Word," with a capital "W."
- The Logos also came to be known in philosophy as the perfection behind logical words and reason, the expression of which was the highest purpose in life.
- In Theology, the Logos was seen as the Divine blueprint of being and existence, which was personified in Jesus Christ as the mediator of salvation and eternal life.
- In Christianity the power of the Word is revealed through a person (Jesus Christ), a proclamation (the Gospel message), and through the Christian Bible (sacred scripture).
- In Jewish mysticism, the Torah was believed to be eternal in spirit and the revealed Word of God.
- Writings that bound a society together in a common story, set of laws, and language became sacred scripture.
- The languages of sacred scripture have for a long time been believed to be infused with the power of God.
- While it is not limited to language - God's Word can be found in every language.
- The language of God is the universal and intermediary principle of the Logos, incarnated and expressed through you, through your message and proclamations, and through your interaction with the writings and things of life that are sacred to you, including the Bible.

TABLES

GROWTH OF THE LOGOS IDEA IN PHILOSOPHY		
SOURCE	DATES ©	LOGOS IDEA
Heraclitus	535-475 BCE	An overarching principle bringing rationality, order, and balance to all of existence, out of which comes the world of form and nature.
Plato	427-347 BCE	The perfect dialectical argument. The expression of words that accounts for perfection beyond words.
Aristotle	384-322 BCE	Persuasive Logic. The undeniable proof that someone, or something, is credible.
Zeno	336-265 BCE	Universal reason. The ultimate good and highest purpose in life, with logic ruling over passion and emotions.

GROWTH OF THE LOGOS IDEA IN THEOLOGY		
SOURCE	DATES ©	LOGOS IDEA
Philo Judaeus	20 BCE-50 CE	The universal Form in the mind of God. The perfect blueprint for all of existence. The eternal and transcendent being that gives birth to all things.
Justin Martyr	100-165 CE	The ultimate source of all human knowledge, revealed through Christ of the New Testament.
Clement of Alexandria	150-215 CE	The "thought of God," and the "source of creation," incarnated to become visible. Universal and absolute Truth, found in the being of Jesus Christ.
Origen of Alexandria	185-254 BCE	Divine substance that unified with the human soul through Jesus Christ and became a mediator through which the salvation of spiritual unity with God in heaven could be experienced by all.

45

INQUIRY

1. How would you describe the Logos?

2. Is the Bible the Word of God? Why or why not?

3. Is Jesus the Word of God? Why or why not?

4. Are you the Word of God? If so, in what way? If not, why not?

5. Can you speak the language of God? If so, how? If not, why not?

Chapter 3: Scripture

"...and the ears of all the people were attentive to the book of the law (Nehemiah 8:3b)."

Sacred

What is sacred scripture? That depends upon whom you ask. To many it is the hallowed writings at the center of their practiced religion. To others, it can be a popular book that left them inspired and uplifted. We have already seen how the Bible came to be considered the Word of God, which is what makes it sacred for a lot of people, but what does being sacred mean? Marcus Borg, theologian and best-selling author of *Reading the Bible Again for the First Time*, tells us that being sacred includes being a sacrament. He states,

"...a sacrament is commonly defined as a mediator of the sacred, a vehicle by which God becomes present, a means through which the Spirit is experienced. He also tells us, "Virtually anything can become sacramental: nature, music, prayer, birth, death, sexuality, poetry, persons, pilgrimage, even participation in sports, and so forth. Things are sacramental when they become occasions for the experience of God, moments when the Spirit becomes present, times when the sacred becomes an experiential reality."[23]

---

[23] Marcus J. Borg, Reading the Bible Again for the First Time (San Francisco: Harper, 2002), 31.

47

What Borg is saying is that whatever makes God real and experiential for you is sacred to you. This brings us to the understanding that there are two kinds of Sacred Scripture.

First, there is that which speaks to us as a collective humanity, binding people together in common history, ethical values, and religious practices. These would be the scriptures of the world's great religions, some of which were mentioned earlier in this book, including the Bible. The very fact that human beings have gone to great lengths to preserve these scriptures through the ages speaks to their timeless value as spiritual resources. It also adds confusion to modern day living as ancient ethical practices and strategies are strongly held to as fully appropriate in their execution for all time. The writing that reveals Truth and promotes human evolution, in its preservation, can also conceal Truth and impede that evolution when taken strictly at face value. That is why it is so important to understand its deeper meaning and intention, and to apply that to today's world and experience. In this way, enlightenment from that which is timeless promotes the evolution of consciousness in our time.

The second kind of sacred scripture is that which speaks to each one of us individually. This could be one or more of these great scriptures. It could also be anything from the journaling of a meditative experience to a good book, article, poem, or story that provides comfort, inspiration, or motivation. This scripture does not even have to use religious words or language, but can, for the individual, still be infused with spiritual power. For example, the poetry from the *Song of Solomon,* or *Song of Songs*, is more erotic than religious in nature. It never even mentions God. After all, what is so religious about such utterances as *"Let him kiss me with the kisses of his mouth! (Song of Solomon 1:2)"* Yet, whether it is factual or not, the belief that it was wise King Solomon who composed these words transforms the lover's encounter to the ecstatic union between God and his people in the eyes of the later interpreter. Thus, the secular literature of erotic love poetry can be considered as part of the Hebrew and Christian Scriptures. No less, a secular writing of a non-biblical source could be considered by you as sacred to your life experience.

Spiritual insight from the written word could have touched our lives any number of times. Who knows? If we were to select a best-selling book that has been a spiritual inspiration for us, and if we were able to gather together a global council of religious authorities with the common purpose to declare that this work is the authoritative Word of God, there may be a new, New Testament, or even a new religion altogether. We would need to ask ourselves in the effort, however, is there such a thing as the authoritative Word of God, and how is this determined? Looking back on the history of our present biblical canon can give us insight as to why the Bible is considered a book of religious authority. It can also help us in determining its spiritual value for us, as well as reveal how we can discern the spiritual value of any language or literature we encounter.

CANON

CRITERIA

"Canon" is a term that refers to Sacred Scripture as the authoritative Word of God. The term comes from the Greek word, *kanon*, which means, "measuring line;" "fixed reference point;" and "rule." It refers to that which has measured up to the criteria of having divine power and authority, and has therefore become the rule or reference point by which the things of life are measured. While sacred scripture for you can

49

be any writing that inspires you, many of the central writings of the world's great religions achieved this status over long periods of time, and with much discernment, discussion, and declaration. So how was the criterion for the biblical canon determined?

No known checklist of criterion existed as such for the determination of scriptural canon. No religious council or leadership sat down with a universally agreed upon list to create the exact biblical contents that are available to us today. To emerge as the Sacred Scripture of a people, or religion, from the vast collections of writing over time, however, the books of the Bible had to contain qualities that helped them in becoming what they are. In reflecting on the process of biblical formation, and on previous criterions set forth by the teachers and writers who have contributed to my knowledge and understanding, I have discerned certain qualities based upon what the books of canon have in common. I have also given them terms that are relevant to our present day understanding of what makes something valuable to us. These can be summed up in four primary criteria:

1. Popularity: The canonical writings were widely circulated, read, and studied by those within the given religious movement, and therefore, already had great influence in the societies and communities that were part of that movement. To put it into today's terms, they were "best sellers" and part of the pop culture of their time.

2. Credibility: The author of any one of these writings was believed to be a divinely chosen prophet, leader, or apostle, writing on behalf of God. Remember the "Song of Solomon?" Were it not for Solomon's name associated with this poetry, it may not have made the Hebrew canon.

3. Intentionality: The writing revealed stories and teachings that were in alignment with the religious

and/or political intentions of those who declared their authority.

4. Practicality: The teachings of scripture could be universally applied to a diverse and widespread collection of communities, as well as put into practice by the individuals within those communities.

Is this not, also, how you determine the writings that are inspirational and life changing for you? First, it may help catch your attention if a piece of literature is a "best seller." More importantly, best seller or not, what you read must resonate well enough with you to have its own sense of popularity within your personal choice of life resources.

Secondly, you must have some respect for the author of this writing. Whether or not you have heard of those who put together a particular work, he, she, or they must have some credibility. Either the credibility is evident in the author's reputation, or in the author's experience, education and/or spiritual wisdom as you read the material. Perhaps the author is simply someone you trust through their skill of communicating directly to the heart of who you are. Whatever types of credentials an author may have, communication that is relevant to your life is essential, and this brings us to the third criteria.

What becomes spiritual guidance and authority for you must inspire, or align with, your personal intentions. Perhaps you are looking for greater skills development and organizational acumen; or more peace, healing, and prosperity for your life; or maybe you wish to expand your global awareness and ability to contribute to society. Whatever your intention, if you find writing that brings a spiritual essence to its fulfillment, it is one vehicle through which you can hear the language of God speaking to you. Fourth, and finally, what you read must call forth in you the practical motivation, ideas,

51

and confidence to put into action the inspiration you have received.

This is what the Bible has done for countless individuals through time. It has also been viewed as the source of disappointment, disillusionment, and downright discouragement. Because of its diverse perspectives on God, and its broad spectrum of the human experience, the Bible can be used to condemn or justify any type of human behavior and action. Yet, even with its misinterpretations and misuses, it has still managed to maintain a viable place in inspirational literature for the individual.

It was not only its individual appeal and practicality, however, that gave it a lasting presence in human development. The writings of the Bible were born out of the shared experience of a great people who gave the world a singular God and/or a small and growing religious community of those who sought to follow the ways of a radical healer and teacher. Because of this, these writings became popular, credible, intentional, and practical, and were determined by those with influence and authority as the vehicles through which God spoke to the whole of humanity. In other words, they became canonical, or biblical canon.

How did the canon of the Bible emerge? Who decided what it would be, and how did these decisions get made? Was it, as Alister McGrath inquires, from *imposition* or was it from *recognition*? [24] *Imposition* means that the process of determination by religious leaders primarily involved imposing their authority on scripture in declaring its value and validity. In other words, the Bible was, and is, the Word

---

[24] ALISTER E. MCGRATH, *CHRISTIAN THEOLOGY AN INTRODUCTION*, (MALDEN, MA: BLACKWELL PUBLISHING, 2001), 160.

of God because they said so. Therefore, it was, and is, a means through which their authority and beliefs about eternal Truth as it applies to life could be conveyed and preserved. *Recognition*, on the other hand, implies that the determination process was one of recognizing and selecting the scripture that already had intrinsic spiritual authority. Most likely through discernment and discussion, certain writings emerged as those already having universal spiritual value. Alister McGrath has written:

> *"In practice there has been increased recognition of late that the community of faith and Scripture, the people and the book, coexist with one another, and that attempts to draw sharp lines of distinction between them are somewhat arbitrary. The canon of Scripture may be regarded as emerging organically from a community of faith already committed to using and respecting it."[25]*

Nowhere is this more evident than in the biblical record of Ezra's reading of the Torah to the people in Jerusalem after the re-building of the wall. According to the book bearing his name, Nehemiah, who was governor in Jerusalem, realized it was time to bring the people together under one faith and one God, and he calls on Ezra to do so. While it seems that the Torah was first read at the dictate of Nehemiah, an imposition if you will, this dictate actually came from the recognition of these writings as already holding great value for the people. In fact, in the biblical account it was the people who told Ezra to bring "the book of the law of Moses" to them. While the accuracy of the specifics of this account have been questioned, this event is key to the authority given to the Torah. Thus, recognition of what was canon may well have begun with this presentation, or some similar event,

---

[25] Ibid.

estimated to have taken place in the fifth century BCE. It then continued with the work of a number of religious Councils from the 1st to the 5th centuries CE.

This early beginning is clearly implied in the following verses from the Hebrew Scriptures.

"All of the people gathered together into the square before the Water Gate. They told the scribe Ezra to bring the book of the law of Moses, which the Lord had given to Israel. Accordingly, the priest Ezra brought the law before the assembly, both men and women and all who could hear with understanding. This was on the first day of the seventh month. He read from it facing the square before the Water Gate from early morning until midday, in the presence of the men and the women and those who could understand; and the ears of all the people were attentive to the book of the law (Nehemiah 8: 1-3)."

Imagine yourself to be in the crowd at the square next to the Water Gate just outside the newly restored Temple of Jerusalem, listening to the first complete reading of the Torah. After years of exile in Babylon, and the resulting struggle with your identity as a human being, now come the words that tell your story, that give you guidance on how to live your life, and that reveal your relationship with the God of all Creation. What a powerful moment! What a great awakening to your spiritual identity! What a deep connection you share with all of those around you! You now know who you are and where you belong.

This is the power of sacred scripture, first depicted within the Judeo-Christian tradition by the priest and prophet, Ezra. It was shared in celebration of the new Temple, the re-building of the wall of Jerusalem, and the restoration of the people to their homeland. It became the foundation of a renewed religion with an emphasis on the monotheistic singularity of God, and God's special relationship with the people of Judah.

54

With the advent of a sacred and commonly shared scripture, the religion of the Hebrews became "Juda-ism".

TANAKH

The Torah was just the beginning of the Hebrew canon. By the time of Jesus, it was clear that the oracles of the great prophets and the historical adventures of the kings and leaders of Israel, known as the lesser prophets, were very much part of the scriptural canon in Judaic practice and tradition. In Matthew, Jesus refers to them in his own teachings:

> *"Do not think that I have come to abolish the law and the prophets; I have come not to abolish but to fulfill. For truly I tell you, until heaven and earth pass away, not one letter, not one stroke of a letter, will pass from the law until all is accomplished (Matthew 5: 17-18)."*

What of the rest of the Hebrew Bible? How did it become canon? Not long after the lifetime of Jesus, the people lost their Temple and Jerusalem was left in ruins for the second time. This time, it was not the Babylonians, but the Romans, and the year was approximately 70 CE. With their Temple gone and their priests vanished, or put to death, the people of Judah scattered to the winds over the next twenty years. Rather than let this be the end of their religion, however, they made it a new beginning. They started with the writings that tied them all together as God's chosen people. In his book, *Understanding the Old Testament*, Bible historian Bernhard W. Anderson wrote the following:

> *"The new crisis that came upon Judaism in the centuries just before and after the dawn of the Common Era provided great impetus for the 'stabilization' and 'fixation' of the whole tradition. The loss of Judaism's vital center – the Temple in the Holy Land – posed the threat that the tradition would be*

55

distorted or weakened by various cultural influences and that the scattered Jews would lose their sense of identity and vocation. The result was an increasing concern for 'scripture' (what is written) and 'canon' (the writings that are normative for faith and practice)." [26]

In this great crisis of approximately 90 CE, the Hebrew canon took on its final form under the influence of the late first century discussions held at a small academy of rabbis, or teachers, on the Palestinian coast. The academy at Jabneh, or Jamnia, as it was known in Christianity, became a center of cultural shift for the Jewish people. Judaism evolved into a religion, not based on Temple worship and sacrifices performed by priests, but instead based on scriptural wisdom and rabbinical understanding shared in the synagogue, the place of gathering. At the center of the synagogue was not the Holy of Holies, as with the Jerusalem Temple, rather it was the Torah, the foundational scripture of Judaism.

Along with the Torah, the books of the Prophets were acknowledged as works of spiritual authority, and finally, through the Jamnia deliberations, selected Writings of wisdom and poetry joined the Law and the Prophets. Thus, by 100 CE, the content of the Hebrew Bible became Torah (Law/Teachings); Nebi'im (Prophets); and Kethubi'im

(Writings), known today by the acronym TNK. The TNK, or Tanakh, became the contents for the Old Testament of Protestant Christianity. Here is a brief outline.

---

[26] ANDERSON, BERNHARD W. *UNDERSTANDING THE OLD TESTAMENT*, ABRIDGED FOURTH EDITION. PRENTICE-HALL, 1998. P. 578.

HEBREW CANON

I. TNK, or Tanakh
   a. **Torah** = Law/Teachings. It consists of five books of the Law.
   b. **Neviim** = Prophets. It consists of eight books of the Former and Latter, or Lesser and Great, Prophets.
   c. **Kethubim** = Writings. It consists of eleven books which include wisdom, poetry, and apocalyptic literature, as well as historical chronicles and editorial stories.

II. Hebrew Bible
   a. **Description.** The 24 books of the Tanakh with the same basic content, yet different divisions and order as that of the Protestant Old Testament.
   b. **Contents.**
      • Law/Teachings. Genesis, Exodus, Leviticus, Numbers, Deuteronomy
      • Prophets. Joshua, Judges, Samuel, Kings, Isaiah, Jeremiah, Ezekiel, The Book of Twelve
      • Writings. Psalms, Proverbs, Job, The Song of Solomon (Song of Songs), Ruth, Lamentations, Ecclesiastes, Esther, Daniel, Ezra/Nehemiah, Chronicles

As you can see from the above outline, the Tanakh is a complete Bible. To acknowledge this, many scholars and students of the Bible refer to the "Old Testament" as "Hebrew Scriptures," or the "Hebrew Bible." I will do the same in this book, except in a context of Christian theology where it has been referred to as the "Old Testament".

What term, then, should be applied to the writings of the Christian Bible that follow the Old Testament? Many people today refer to them as the Christian Scriptures because they came out of the early Christian culture. This is a good and valid reference that is also in alignment with the term "Hebrew Scriptures." In this book, I choose to refer to them as the New Testament. Just as with the Hebrew Bible, "New Testament" is the given title from the culture within which its canon was selected. Christian Scriptures include the Hebrew Scriptures plus the New Testament or both the Old and New Testaments.

In addition, I grew up in the Christian culture and have a particularly close relationship with the figure of Jesus Christ as presented in the New Testament. I do not think of the New Testament as superior, or inferior, to other Scripture. It is simply my most familiar touchstone and spiritual resource. It is also incomplete as a resource without the depth of understanding given by the Hebrew culture and the Tanakh. As for what you call these scriptures, consider which titles mean the most to you in your relationship with them. This will tell you what to call them. In the meantime, let us consider how twenty-seven books of the New Testament emerged from the evolution of the Christian culture.

NEW TESTAMENT

Early into the second century CE the "Patristic Period" began, so named for the contributions of the patriarchs of church and state to the theological and scriptural canon of Christianity. It started with the completion of the writings that were to become the New Testament around 135 CE, and ended with the declaration of the dual nature, both divine and human, found in the figure of Jesus Christ at the Council of Chalcedon in CE 451. It was within this period that Christian Scripture took the form that carried it into the Protestant Reformation of the 16th century CE. Because the forming of canon was an organic process that grew out of the acknowledged practicality and popularity of Scripture, it is good to recognize some of the contributions toward this canon that are milestones in its evolution.

We begin with Marcion (85-160 CE), son of the Bishop of Sinope, a shipping port on the Black Sea. Marcion was a wealthy ship owner who gave large contributions to the Christian church in Rome. Nevertheless, he was brought before a hearing of church leadership in Rome for his questionable teachings. We can picture him before the Roman council, charismatically making a case for what he believed and taught.

Marcion believed that the message of the Gospel had nothing to do with the Old Covenant, or Law, of the Hebrew Scriptures. He indicated that the Father of Christ was the only true God, and that Christ was not connected to Judaism, but was rather a whole new non-incarnate being in God.[27] He conveyed that the only true New Testament was to be found in portions of the Gospel of Luke, and of ten letters from Paul. Putting forth his own radical version of the Gospels and New Testament got him declared a heretic by the Christian congregations of Rome in 144 CE. He was ex-communicated and his money was returned to him. Yet, he continued to teach and gain a following, known as the Marcionites, that

---

[27] SOULEN, RICHARD N. AND KENDAL R. HANDBOOK OF BIBLICAL CRITICISM. LOUISVILLE, WESTMINSTER JOHN KNOX PRESS., P. 109

lasted into the 10th century CE. Marcion's so-called heretical approach to Scripture was a major impetus for seeking clarity around the canon of the New Testament. Among those who wrote against Marcion, and in so doing moved the New Testament canon forward toward its final form, were Irenaeus, Clement, and Tertullian.

According to his own accounts, Irenaeus, the Bishop of Lyons (c. 130-200) could be found as a young boy listening to the sermons of Polycarp of Smyrna, who claimed a connection with some of Christianity's original apostles. Influenced by Polycarp and his caution against heretical teachings, Irenaeus was concerned with defending orthodox Christianity against Marcion and the philosophy of early Christian groups like the Gnostics. For Irenaeus, the Scripture must represent the Apostolic Tradition, or the tradition of Gospel teaching and insight passed down from the early Apostles.

In his writings, Irenaeus quotes from every book in the current New Testament, except Philemon, 2 Peter, 3 John, and Jude. Yet, his most critical focus was on the Gospels. They must have apostolic authority and there must be four of them. In his work *Adversus Haereses*, or *Against the Heresies*, he states:

> *"The Gospels could not possibly be either more or less in number than they are. Since there are four zones of the world in which we live, and four principal winds, while the Church is spread over all the earth, and the pillar and foundation of the Church is the gospel, and the Spirit of life, it fittingly has four pillars, everywhere breathing out incorruption and revivifying men. From this, it is clear that the Word, the artificer of all things,*

being manifested to men gave us the gospel, fourfold in form but held together by one Spirit." [28]

For Irenaeus, these four gospels had already risen to the top in usefulness and popularity. They were, and are, Matthew, Mark, Luke, and John. Thus, the foundation of the New Testament was widely accepted, but there was more to come.

We have already met Clement of Alexandria (c. 150 – 215), and have become acquainted with some of his thoughts on the Logos, which for him is the absolute and universal Truth incarnated as the Christ. In his approach to the Logos and other developing ideas of early Christianity, he quotes from many non-canonical sources. He also makes references to books that became the canon of the New Testament with the exceptions of Philemon, James, 2 Peter, and 2 and 3 John. To him, the Acts of the Apostles, the letters of Paul, and the Revelation to John all held the qualities of spiritual authority and practical application.

Wait a minute! The Revelation to John – how is that practical? I have read that Thomas Jefferson referred to it as "…the ravings of a maniac, no more worthy nor capable of explanation than the incoherencies of our own nightly dreams." [29] In actuality, this work is filled with common metaphor that could be easily understood in its application to Christian life in a time of Roman imperial oppression, and

---

[28] GLENN DAVIS QUOTING FROM IRENAEUS, AGAINST THE HERESIES (3.11.8). IRENAEUS OF LYONS. THE DEVELOPMENT OF THE CANON OF THE NEW TESTAMENT. (ACCESSED APRIL 6, 2017). HTTP://WWW.NTCANON.ORG/IRENAEUS.SHTML#4_GOSPELS.

[29] JEFFERSON, THOMAS. FROM HIS LETTER TO GENERAL ALEXANDER SMYTH, MONTICELLO, JANUARY 17, 1825. HTTP://FOUNDERS.ARCHIVES.GOV/DOCUMENTS/JEFFERSON/98-01-02-4882, FEBRUARY 22, 2016.

applied to the ability to overcome all obstacles through faith. This was important enough to Clement to be included. It was also a view that met with broad consensus by the end of the second century.

Next, we look at Quintus Septimus Florens Tertullianus, or Tertullian of Carthage (c. 160 – 225). Tertullian was eloquent and prolific in his speech and writing. Well educated, he could engage a crowd of listeners with his intelligent insight and sharp wit. When he felt drawn to Christianity in Rome, and later converted after returning home to Carthage in Africa, he astounded the Christian world with a lively propagandist style that presented Latin as a viable language for the whole of Christianity. His literary perspective included the doctrinal sufficiency of Scripture. In one of his books, Mcgrath shares Tertullian's most famous quote, "What is there in common between Athens and Jerusalem?"[30] This is a clear indication of Tertullian's indignation regarding Greek philosophy as a means of interpreting scripture, not unlike that of Irenaeus. He took a stand against what he considered to be the heresy of all who were influenced by Greek thought such as Marcion (c. 85 – 160) and his followers, as well as the Gnostics.

While Tertullian re-affirmed the value of the four Gospels and the Acts of the Apostles, he also expanded on the New Testament in his own writings by referring to a few evangelical and apostolic letters that included teachings against "false prophets." These included the Pastoral Epistles of 1 and 2 Timothy and Titus; and the General Epistles of Hebrews and Jude. The Pastoral Epistles and Hebrews are considered by scholars to be deutero-Pauline because of being

---

[30] MCGRATH, ALISTER E. HISTORICAL THEOLOGY: AN INTRODUCTION TO THE HISTORY OF CHRISTIAN THOUGHT. OXFORD: BLACKWELL PUBLISHING, 1998, 91.

written in Paul's name and attributed to him, even though it is likely they were not Paul's writings. Tertullian also pointed to the Shepherd of Hermes and the Acts of Paul as Christian scripture, but these did not make the final canon. Still, his contribution to the New Testament is clear through some of its later Epistles.

We have now seen some of the early development of what became the New Testament, as we know it, taking us well into the third century. In the early fourth century, a major shift took place in the world of Christianity. In 311, the Roman emperor Galerius called for the end to Christian persecution. In 312, after being victorious in a series of civil conflicts, Constantine conquered Rome and became the soul emperor of both the eastern and western parts of the Roman Empire. Soon after, he declared himself to be Christian and through the Edict at Milan in 313 CE, Christianity, not Christian persecution, came to be supported by the Empire. And why not? It was already widespread, and Constantine could use it as the perfect vehicle through which to exert his own power and political agenda.

At the Capitoline Museum in Rome there are remnants of a colossal marble likeness of Constantine. You can stand within a few feet of his upward pointing hand that is taller than you are. You can also go face to face with his giant head. The strong facial features with eyes looking toward the heavens give you a sense of awe in experiencing the presence of one who was literally humanity's largest figure, yet whose gaze was toward things of a divine nature. Although Christianity removed the possibility that the Emperor was also the Son of God, this was good for Constantine because it also removed the possibility that anyone could compete with him for that claim. The Son of God was found in the person of Jesus, who was no longer on earth. Yet, His representative on earth was

Constantine. Thus, Constantine demonstrated his divine connections and authority within a Christian context to rule supremely in the world of humanity.

As he asserted his Christian based authority, Constantine drew together the church fathers from around the Empire. Beginning in 325 CE, the Council of Nicaea in Asia Minor, or present-day Turkey, set upon the task of discerning the meaning and creed of true Christianity. This was in large part due to a debate that was going on in the church at that time. Arius of Alexandria (c. 250 – 336), and his followers, taught that Jesus was the supreme creation of God, but human, and not God, Himself. The Latin term for this was *homoiousios*, meaning *of like substance*. Athanasius of Alexandria (c. 296 – 373) opposed Arius. For him and his followers, Jesus was God incarnate, or *homoousios*, meaning *of the same substance*. I like to picture the two men on a major news network being interviewed and verbally battling it out with each other. After all, that is what the Arian Controversy certainly resembled.

Faced with differing perspectives on God and Jesus, the Nicaean Council set upon the task of defining both of these subjects and bringing clarity to the Arian Controversy. In so doing, they created a statement of faith based on a baptismal creed from the Church in Jerusalem that was also a response against the Arians. The statement from Nicaea was later expanded at the Council of Constantinople in 381 CE, and is most accurately referred to as the Niceno-Constantinopolitan Creed. Wow - that's a mouthful! Perhaps that is why we still commonly refer to it as the Nicene Creed.

"We believe in one God, the Father, the almighty (pantocrator), the maker of all things seen and unseen. And in one Lord Jesus Christ, the Son of God; begotten from the Father; only-begotten – that is, from the substance of the Father; God from God; light from light; true God from true God; begotten not made; of one

substance with the Father (homoousion tu patri); through whom all things in heaven and on earth came into being; who on account of us human beings and our salvation came down and took flesh, becoming a human being; he suffered and rose again on the third day, ascended into the heavens; and will come again to judge the living and the dead. And in the Holy Spirit."

As for those who say that 'there was when he was not,' and 'before being born he was not,' and 'he came into existence out of nothing,' or who declare that the Son of God is of a different substance or nature, or is subject to alteration or change – the catholic and apostolic church condemns these." [31]

Even before 381 in Constantinople, the Nicene Creed influenced the standards of orthodoxy, or right belief, regarding Christian scripture and teachings. Holding these standards high, Athanasius shared what he believed the Christian canon to be in a series of annual letters that were written to affirm the dates of Lent and Easter, known as the *Festal Letters*. In his thirty-ninth Festal Letter of 367 CE, he put forth a list of twenty-seven books. Further consideration and debate followed.

Another group adding to the controversial conversations of early Christianity, and mentioned previously in this text, was the Gnostics. Gnosticism is an umbrella term that encompasses smaller religious sects that existed from the 2nd to the 4th centuries CE. They taught neither that Jesus was God in human form, nor that Jesus was God's supreme human creation. To the Gnostics, Jesus was not human at all. He was a spiritual being who only appeared to be human. Gnosticism also taught that within each person was God's Divine Spark, and that God's own Being was in every

---

[31] THE NICENE CREED AS QUOTED BY MCGRATH IN CHRISTIAN THEOLOGY, AN INTRODUCTION, P. 21.

creature. Salvation, therefore, was found in turning away from the evil of the material world and seeking inner communion with God. Such teachings were deemed heretical and many Gospels that have been attributed to the Gnostic sects, were never seriously considered as part of the Christian canon.

While the followers of Arius, like those of Marcion and the Gnostics, were declared as heretics, and their writings and teachings as heretical, their ideas remained influential throughout the history of Christian thought. For example, in 451 CE at the Council of Chalcedon, near what is now Istanbul, Turkey, Jesus was declared to be both fully human and fully divine. This expanded beyond the *homoousios* idea of Athanasius to include the *homoiousios* nature of Jesus. Nevertheless, the perspective of Athanasius on God and Jesus won out in Nicaea, and his book list became what we now know as the New Testament.

In 397 at the Synod, or Council, of Carthage in Africa, a document was written espousing the scriptural canon of the universal Catholic Church. It included the twenty-seven books that were put forth earlier by Athanasius. This New Testament was confirmed by Pope Innocent I in 405 in a letter directing all bishops to make use of this authoritative resource. Admittedly, all of this seems a bit like an *imposition* of the standards of the Nicene Creed on the selection of the scriptures of Christianity, and not simply the *recognition* of the innate spiritual value of this literature. Perhaps this is the case. Yet, *recognition* of its value was key to this literature even being considered.

Through discussion and discernment, the qualities of popularity, credibility, and practicality were seen in each of the New Testament books. When these writings could also be considered as having alignment with the core creed of Christianity, intentionality was also discernable. Thus, the process of canonization included both the organic evolution of intrinsic scriptural value and the imposition of previously fixed religious standards. The New Testament then took shape as seen in the following outline.

NEW TESTAMENT CANON

I.   New Testament
    a.   **Description.** As recommended by Athanasius, the New Testament was, is, and always will be twenty-seven books.
    b.   **Contents.** Four sections outline the books of the New Testament as follows:
- Gospels. Matthew, Mark, Luke, John
- Acts. The Acts of the Apostles
- Epistles. Romans, 1 Corinthians, 2 Corinthians, Galatians, Ephesians, Philippians, Colossians, 1 Thessalonians, 2 Thessalonians, 1 Timothy, 2 Timothy, Titus, Philemon, Hebrews, James, 1 Peter, 2 Peter, 1 John, 2 John, 3 John, Jude
- Revelation. The Revelation (or Apocalypse) of John

The New Testament became part of the Christian Bible along with the Old Testament. "Old Testament" is a term specific to the Christian Bible. It compares the writings of Judaism with the New Testament, finding a theological basis for this comparison in the oracles of Jeremiah.

"The days are surely coming says the Lord, when I will make a new covenant with the house of Israel and the house of Judah. It will not be like the covenant that I made with their ancestors

when I took them by the hand to bring them out of the land of Egypt – a covenant that they broke, though I was their husband, says the Lord. But this is the covenant that I will make with the house of Israel after those days, says the Lord: I will put my law within them, and I will write it on their hearts; and I will be their God, and they shall be my people. No longer shall they teach one another, or say to each other, 'Know the Lord,' for they shall all know me, from the least of them to the greatest, says the Lord; for I will forgive their iniquity, and remember their sins no more (Jeremiah 31:31-34)."

Jeremiah's passage on the new covenant is an example of prophetic oracles that became signposts for the New Testament writers. For these writers, the prophets of the Hebrew Scriptures pointed to the coming of the Messiah, a time when the old covenant of obedience to the Law was superseded by the forgiving grace of Jesus Christ as portrayed in the new covenant. The Apostle, Paul, compared what he saw as the bondage of sin and death in the old covenant to the veil of Moses that hid the full glory of God from the people. "Indeed, to this very day, when they hear the reading of the old covenant, that same veil is still there, since only in Christ is it set aside (2 Corinthians 3:14b)."

According to Christianity, the Old Testament heralded the coming of the Christ by leading the people through history to the time of Jesus. Yet, the creators of the early Christian Bibles noticed a gap in history and teaching between where the Hebrew Bible left off, and the life of Jesus began. To make the Old Testament complete in its purpose, an expanse of Hebrew literature, now known as the Apocrypha, was used to bridge the gap.

EXPANSION

APOCRYPHA

For centuries the only available versions of the Christian Bible included a New Testament of twenty-seven books and an Old Testament with an expansion that included works that were not in the Hebrew Bible. Versions of the Old Testament with added literature can be found in the Greek Orthodox and Roman Catholic Bibles of today. These versions are based respectively on the Old Testaments of the Septuagint and Latin Vulgate translations with some differences that evolved over time.

"Septuagint," is the Latin word for "seventy." The original Greek reference to this work was *kata tous ebdomekonta* which means, "according to the seventy." Septuagint is so named for the seventy plus scholars who were commissioned by Ptolemy II of Egypt to translate writings of Hebrew Scripture into Greek under the rule of the Greek Empire, c. 300 BCE. Thus, the language of Greek began to play a key role in the development of Scripture. For example, the Greek terms Genesis, meaning "origin," and "Exodus," meaning "a going out," became the names of books found in the Pentateuch. As mentioned before, Pentateuch means "five vessels" which is the Greek word for the first five books, or the Torah.

While Greek had a strong foothold that would always influence biblical understanding, over time Latin was declared the official language of the Bible by the Roman Catholic Church. This Latin Bible was known as the "Vulgate." "Vulgate" was the term used for the translated manuscript of the fifth century CE that was commissioned to provide a Bible for the common, or "vulgar," Latin speaking population of the Roman church. Jerome was the translator.

Eusibius Sophronius Hieronymous, otherwise known as Jerome (c. 347-420), lived a youth of both wanton behavior and great education. Born along the northern coast of the Agean Sea in the village of Stridon, near Dalmatia, he went to school in Rome, learning Latin, and familiarizing himself with the Greek classics. Later, to cleanse the guilt of his youth, he became a Christian ascetic, learned Hebrew, and became ordained as a priest. He then lived in Constantinople for two years, engaging in intense scriptural study before becoming the secretary of Pope Damasus I in Rome in 382 CE. It was this Pope who commissioned him to revise the Latin Bible which he completed in 405 CE, the same year Pope Innocent I confirmed the New Testament canon. He spent his later life writing commentaries on Scripture in Alexandria, Egypt, following which time he went to Bethlehem and lived in a cave that he believed was the birthplace of Jesus. It is in Bethlehem that he died in the year 420 CE.

Taking his appointed task of translation seriously, Jerome compared the Septuagint with the Hebrew Bible and noticed extra literature. We can imagine him hunched over these great texts and comparing them with each other to create an authentic translation of the Old Testament. He noticed that some writings added whole books to the contents of the Hebrew Bible, while others added portions to already existing books. He referred to these writings as *apocrypha*, a Greek word which means "hidden writings." They were writings hidden within the Old Testament of the Septuagint, but not part of the Hebrew Canon.

It was in the time of the Reformation that these books were taken out of the Old Testament of the Christian Bible altogether. Martin Luther in his German Bible of 1534 was the first to create a distinct section between the Old and New Testaments called the Apocrypha. In response to this, the Council of Trent put forth Jerome's "Vulgate" as the only true Bible of the Church. While the Council of Trent determined that it was necessary to include apocryphal books in the canon, the growing population of Protestant Christians did not. They believed that recognition, and not imposition from the church, was the way to determine Sacred Scripture. Noticing that none of these "hidden writings" were directly quoted in the New Testament scriptures, they asserted that what had already naturally evolved as part of the Hebrew canon held authoritative value, and what had not could not be Old Testament canon, even if it supported Christianity's central creed.

There was, however, some awareness of value in these works of what became known as the secondary canon, or deutero-canonical literature. They did, after all, provide history and teachings of faith that filled in the gaps between the Hebrew Bible and the New Testament. Deutero-canonical literature is that which can be, to put it in terms of the Anglican Church, "...read for example of life and instruction of manners; but not to establish any doctrine."[32] In other words, it makes good reading, but is not equal to the power and authority of the rest of the canon. Therefore, in translating the Bible from its original languages into their local vernacular, the Protestant reformers separated the Apocrypha from the rest of the Scripture, and the Protestant Christian Bible took shape.

---

[32] ARTICLE VI OF THE ARTICLES FOR RELIGION IN THE BOOK OF COMMON PRAYER AS QUOTED IN THE CANONS OF SCRIPTURE FOUND IN THE NEW INTERPRETER'S STUDY BIBLE, NEW REVISED STANDARD VERSION WITH THE APOCRYPHA. NASHVILLE: ABINGDON PRESS, 2003, P. XXXI.

Some editions of this Bible include a section of the Apocrypha, some do not. Some apocryphal sections are shorter than others, as with the early Anglican Church whose version only has twelve books, rather than the eighteen books of the standard Protestant Apocrypha. Eventually, the literature of the Apocrypha was dropped out completely, being viewed by later Protestants as having no divine authority whatsoever. Such a difference can be seen in the Bible of King James I of England. The original version of 1611 contains the apocryphal writings, but none can be found in the King James Bible after 1666. Even some Catholic Bibles of the twentieth century have omitted the Apocrypha. Growing interest in biblical scholarship has created a demand, however, and the Apocrypha has been once again included as its own section in some biblical translations and versions since the 1960's. For most Protestants, however, the Bible consists of thirty-nine books based on the contents of the Hebrew Bible, and twenty-seven books of the New Testament – the same books that Athanasius declared as sacred.

The following table contains an outline of the Old Testament as it appears in most protestant Bibles today, along with the Apocrypha which has been included in some scholastic versions. Should you want to expand your work with the Bible beyond the Protestant canon, I do highly recommend exploring the Apocrypha, particularly for its value in the development of biblical history and literature. It can even be of some inspiration to the biblical interpreter.

PROTESTANT SCRIPTURE

I.   Old Testament
  - a. **Description.** Used by most Christians, and others, today, consisting of thirty-nine books in four main sections: Five books of Law; twelve books of History; five books of Wisdom and Poetry literature; and seventeen books of the Prophets.
  - b. **Contents.** As distinct from the Hebrew Bible, Samuel, Kings, and Chronicles were divided into two books each, and the "Book of the Twelve" was divided into twelve books of the prophets, resulting in the following:
  - c. **Law.** Genesis, Exodus, Leviticus, Numbers, Deuteronomy
  - d. **History.** Joshua, Judges, Ruth, 1 Samuel, 2 Samuel, 1 Kings, 2 Kings, 1 Chronicles, 2 Chronicles, Ezra, Nehemiah, Esther, Job
  - e. **Wisdom and Poetry.** Psalms, Proverbs, Ecclesiastes, Song of Solomon
  - f. **Prophets.** Isaiah, Jeremiah, Lamentations, Ezekiel, Daniel, Hosea, Joel, Amos, Obadiah, Jonah, Micah, Nahum, Habakkuk, Zephaniah, Haggai, Zachariah, Malachi

II.   Apocrypha
  - a. Description. Writings and books found in the Old Testament of the Greek Orthodox and Roman Catholic Churches based on the Greek Septuagint and Latin Vulgate Bibles. They are not part of the Hebrew Bible and were separated out of the Old Testament by the Protestant Reformers.
  - b. **Contents.** The following books can still be found in some scholastic versions of the Protestant Bible today as their own section of deuterocanonical literature, or secondary canon.
  - c. The Apocryphal/Deuterocanonical Books. Tobit, Judith, Esther (The Greek Version Containing Additional Chapters), The Wisdom of Solomon, Sirach, Baruch, The Letter of Jeremiah, The Additions to Daniel (The Prayer of Azariah and the

73

Song of the Three Jews, Susanna, Bel and the Dragon), 1 Maccabees, 2 Maccabees, 1 Esdras, The Prayer of Manesseh, Psalm 151, 3 Maccabees, 2 Esdras, 4 Maccabees

The Protestant Bible of sixty-six books is the Bible that has been used by a religious movement that started in the 19th century, matured in the 20th, and continues to evolve through today, known as Unity. This is the movement in which I grew up, and this is the Bible that is being used as the scriptural resource for this book. The primary canon of thirty-nine books based on the Hebrew Bible, and twenty-seven books of the New Testament, are more than enough for the purposes of this work. In fact, they are more than enough for a lifetime of humanistic insight and spiritual wisdom. Still, the Apocrypha is a valuable part of the evolution of the biblical canon.

EVOLUTION

Biblical canon, though seemingly fixed for all time within each religious tradition, is not the end of evolution in the Judeo-Christian culture. The dogma of creeds and canon cannot stop what my good friend and colleague, Robert Brumet, calls "the evolutionary impulse." This is the innate human drive to be, know, experience and express more than what has been given by the past.

Even the Nicene Creed did not escape revision over time. As of the eighth century CE, a new form of the central creed of Christianity took shape. The Apostle's Creed has been divided into twelve statements as a representation of the twelve Apostles and has carried the standard of what it means to be Christian into Protestant practice and present-day declaration. The eastern version varies slightly in that it does not include what is seen below in the square brackets, but the creed overall reflects much of the Christian belief system of today.

1. I believe in God, the Father almighty, creator of the heavens and earth;
2. And in Jesus Christ, his only (unicus) Son, our Lord;
3. Who was conceived by the Holy Spirit and born of the Virgin Mary;
4. He suffered under Pontius Pilate, was crucified, dead and buried; [he descended to hell;]
5. On the third day he was raised from the dead;
6. He ascended into the heavens, and sits at the right hand of God the Father almighty;
7. From where he will come to judge the living and the dead.
8. I believe in the Holy Spirit;
9. In the holy catholic church; [the communion of saints;]
10. The forgiveness of sins;
11. The resurrection of the flesh (resurrectio carnis);
12. And eternal life.[33]

I remember repeating this creed when I was a young girl visiting the Lutheran Church with my friend. That which is centuries old certainly contributes to modern life, but modern life continues to evolve and expand beyond it. Today, religion is experienced as a living system of dynamic change and organic growth. While canon and creed have laid the foundations of the Judeo-Christian tradition, new interpretations on how to approach them are being seen and demonstrated in Catholicism, Protestantism, and in the rules and regulations of our present society.

---

[33]THE APOSTLE'S CREED AS QUOTED BY MCGRATH IN CHRISTIAN THEOLOGY, AN INTRODUCTION, P. 20.

New traditions and practices are being created every day, and in this time of escalating technological communication, the widespread value of these new ideas is accelerating our connection in the universal spirituality of multiple creeds, and the common ethics of the human experience. Because of this I can write a book about the Bible that measures its validity, not by historical creed, but by my own evolving beliefs and experiences. Why then bother with the history of scripture and belief at all?

The value of this book is found in your ability to use the Bible as a means through which to experience the language of God speaking to you, not just in Scripture, but in all of life. To do so, you must discover yourself in the Bible, and this calls for looking beyond the surface of the words on its pages. To separate the Bible from its history and evolution through time is like looking at the Grand Canyon without looking down. The Bible is deeply carved into the landscape of human society, and in being so, is part of who you are today. Coming to know its history and evolution, even to a small degree, is to better understand your own humanity in your search for spiritual Truth.

To fully embrace the language of God is to honor what has already been set forth in Scripture, while at the same time drawing from it new revelation and spiritual insight. The key to doing this is metagetics. Metagetics is the latest revolution in scriptural interpretation. It will take you farther in your spiritual journey, and deeper in your self-discovery, than the previous interpretive methods put together. To continue our preparation for the transformational process of metagetics, we will next explore the domain of Truth by climbing the three tiers of knowing and becoming acquainted with some of the interpretive methods of Scripture out of which the transformational work of metagetics evolved.

SUMMARY

- Whatever makes God real and experiential for you is sacred to you.
- This includes sacred writings, otherwise known as scripture, of which there are two kinds:
  - The first kind is commonly shared by whole societies and cultures, and refers to the scriptures of the world's great religions.
  - The second kind appeals to the individual and does not have to use religious words or language to render the experience of spiritual power and inspiration.
- The history of our present biblical canon can give us insight as to why the Bible is collectively considered sacred scripture, as well as reveal how we discern the spiritual value that any writing may have for us.
- "Canon" refers to that which has become the rule, or reference point, by which the things of life are measured.
- To emerge as canon, the books of the Bible had to contain qualities that helped them in becoming what they were, and are as the sacred scriptures of a people, or religion. These are summed up in present day terms as follows:
  - Popularity: The writings that became biblical canon were widely circulated, read, and studied. Today, they would be called the "best sellers".
  - Credibility: The author of any one of these writings was believed to be a divinely chosen prophet, leader, or apostle, writing on behalf of God.
  - Intentionality: The writing revealed stories and teachings that were in alignment with the religious and/or political intentions of those who declared their authority.
  - Practicality: The teachings could be universally applied to diverse communities, as well as put into practice by the individuals within those communities.

- For the writings that are sacred to you, they must have some amount of "Popularity", or resonate with you. Your respect for the authors gives them "Credibility". What they convey can align with your "Intentionality" in life and can have some "Practicality" in how it applies to your personal experience.
- Alister McGrath distinguished the process of discerning canon as either *imposition* or *recognition*?
  o Imposition refers to religious leaders imposing their authority on scripture in declaring its value and validity.
  o Recognition implies that the determination process was one of recognizing and selecting the scripture that already had intrinsic spiritual authority.
- In meeting the four criteria of Popularity, Credibility, Intentionality, and Practicality, the process of developing the Christian canon included both the *recognition* of intrinsic scriptural value and the *imposition* of previously fixed religious standards.
- To make the Old Testament complete in its purpose, and fill in the gap of history between Testaments, Hebrew literature, now known as the Apocrypha, was included in the Catholic, but not the later Protestant Bibles.
- To fully embrace the language of God is to honor what has already been set forth in Scripture, while at the same time drawing from it new revelation and spiritual insight. The key to doing this is metagetics.

TABLES

DEVELOPMENT OF THE HEBREW CANON			
HISTORICAL PERIOD	DATES ©	SCRIPTURE	NAMES AND OCCURENCES
The Persian Empire (550 – 330 BCE)	450-400 BCE	Torah, or Pentateuch	Ezra reads the Torah after the re-building of the Temple and wall in Jerusalem.
The Greek Empire (331 – 163 BCE)	300 BCE	Septuagint	Ptolemy II commissions the "Septuagint" which becomes the basis of the Greek Old Testament.
Roman Empire prior to Christianity (63 BCE – 313 CE)	1-30 CE	Torah and Neviim	The Torah (Law) and Neviim (Prophets) were considered Sacred Scripture by the time of Jesus.
	90 CE	TNK/Tanakh, or Hebrew Bible	The Council of Jabneh, or Jamnia, gives the Hebrew Bible its final form: Torah; Neviim; and Kethubim (Writings).

DEVELOPMENT OF THE APROCYPHA AND PROTESTANT CHRISTIAN CANON			
HISTORICAL PERIOD	DATES ©	SCRIPTURE	NAMES AND OCCURENCES
The Reformation	1534 CE	The Protestant Bible	Martin Luther completes the German Bible, giving the Apocrypha its own section between Testaments.
	1611 CE		The King James Bible in English is completed with some apocryphal writings included.
	1666 CE		A new version of the King James Bible is produced with no writings from the Apocrypha.
	1960's onward		As interest in biblical scholarship increased the Apocrypha was included as its own section and considered to be a secondary canon, or deutero-canonical.

DEVELOPMENT OF THE NEW TESTAMENT AND CATHOLIC CHRISTIAN CANON			
HISTORICAL PERIOD	DATES ©	SCRIPTURE	NAMES AND OCCURENCES
The Patristic Period **(135 – 451 CE)**	85-160 CE	Portions of Luke; Letters from Paul	Marcion implies that the only true scripture is found in portions of Luke and ten of Paul's letters.
	130-200 CE	Four Gospels	Irenaeus suggests a foundation for the New Testament in the four Gospels of Matthew, Mark, Luke and John.
	150-215 CE	Acts; Paul's Letters; Revelation	Clement of Alexandria adds to Scripture the Acts of the Apostles, the letters of Paul, and the Revelation to John.
	160-225 CE	1 and 2 Timothy; Titus; Hebrews; Jude	Tertullian includes the Pastoral Epistles of 1 and 2 Timothy and Titus, and the General Epistles of Hebrews and Jude.
	311 CE	The Catholic Bible	Roman Emperor Galerius calls for an end to Christian persecution.
	312-313 CE		Constantine becomes Emperor and Christianity is supported by Rome.
	325 CE		The Council in Nicaea formulates the Nicene Creed to address the Arian Controversy.
	367 CE		The Thirty-Ninth Festal Letter for Easter written by Athanasius, lists twenty-seven New Testament books.
	381 CE		At the Council of Constantinople, the Nicene Creed is amended, becoming the standard of belief for Christian Doctrine and Scripture.
	397 CE		The Synod of Carthage produces a document espousing the twenty-seven books put forth by Athanasius as canon.
	405 CE		Pope Innocent I confirms the Christian canon. Jerome completes the Latin Vulgate Bible, calling Old Testament writings that are not in the Hebrew Bible "hidden writings," or *apocrypha*.
	451 CE		The Council of Chalcedon amends Christian Doctrine stating that Jesus is both fully human and fully divine.

80

INQUIRY

1. Name some things in your life and world that are sacred to you?

2. Is the Bible sacred to you? Why or why not?

3. What other literature is sacred to you?

4. Why is the Apocrypha important to biblical development?

5. What does a greater understanding of the biblical canon do for you in relating to the Bible? What does it do for you in your own personal development?

PART III: TRUTH

CHAPTER 4: KNOWING

"If you continue in my word, you are truly my disciples; and you will know the truth and the truth will make you free (John 8:32)."

QUEST

In my classes on religion and Scripture, one of the most frequently asked questions from my students has been "How do you know when something is the truth?" I often answered from a statement I learned from some anonymous source a long time ago. I would get a little smile on my face and with an heir of unfailing confidence I would tell them, "The Truth is known by three criteria. You know - that you know - that you know." I have spoken this somewhat humorously over the years, and when I started writing this book I really contemplated what that statement meant, and why the question was so frequently asked.

Since the dawn of rational thought humankind has been on a quest to know the truth. We want to know the truth behind what we see on the news or hear in shared gossip. We want the organizations that serve us to be transparent and truthful in the information they share so that we can interact with them from a place of knowledge and understanding. We want to know that the people in our lives are truthful with us. Beyond this, we want to know the truth of our existence. What is the truth of who we are and how we came to be? What is our true connection to the people and things around us, to the universe – and beyond?

We believe that if we know the truth of something – it reveals itself to us, whether it is the energy of the sun, a close relationship, or the health of our own bodies. Then, through this revelation we can choose how to relate to it in a way that promotes our sense of purpose and well-being. For example, in our enhanced awareness of the sun's power, we might harness its energy and contribute to the greater ecology of our planet. When we know a person better in a relationship, we might see how that individual is trying to reach out to us in ways we may have previously missed. If we know the root cause of physical discomfort or pain, we might put in practices that optimize the life of our bodies and enhance the quality of our lives. Knowing the truth about someone, something, ourselves, and the cosmos gives us a way of relating to each one of these things that brings peace in our ability to be with what is so, power in our ability to create and accomplish, and freedom in the self-expression of how we choose to live our lives and interact with our world. What does it mean to know the truth? Let us begin our exploration of this inquiry with another look at Scripture.

TIERS

PERCEPTION

At the opening of this chapter is the famous quote from the Gospel of John, "If you continue in my word, you are truly my disciples; and you will know the truth and the truth will make you free (John 8:32)." The Greek word for "to know" is ginosko. The following words have been used to describe what it means: learn, come to know, get a knowledge of, perceive, understand, and feel."[34] Nothing surprising here. In fact, you may already know what the word know means. Yet, if you really look at these words, you can see the different tiers of knowing, especially with the words perceive, understand, and feel.

To know is the first tier. It is to perceive something from a place of already knowing about it - like what you already know about the word – know. You may have said to someone at some point, "I know that," relating what was said to what you already know. This is a knowledge based on experience and learning of the past that has given you a lens of perception through which to view your world. It's the old American catch phrase, "Been there, done that, got the T-shirt."

Like the tourist picking up the T-shirt with a depiction of a locale to prove where he or she has been, we pick up a perception regarding the truth about something based upon where we have been in life. This has been helpful to our becoming who we are in the present, but there is a catch. Our perception about things usually has more sway over us than any new knowledge we may receive regarding those same things. Even when something entirely new is presented to us, we tend to see it in the light of what we already believe. The Christopher Columbus legend of the indigenous people being blind to his ships in the harbor because they had not previously seen anything like them speaks to this. Another example from everyday life is not seeing the keys where we put them down because we do not believe they would be there.

---

[34] JAMES STRONG, STRONG'S CONCORDANCE WITH HEBREW GREEK LEXICON, ACCESSED AUGUST 2, 2017, HTTPS://WWW.BLUELETTERBIBLE.ORG/LANG/LEXICON/LEXICON.CFM?STRONGS=G2 25&T=KJV.

We have a whole drawer full of T-shirt perceptions called our belief system. For example, what do you already believe about the statement quoted from the Gospel of John? Do you believe Jesus said that? Do you believe knowing the truth is what it takes to be a disciple of Christ? What does that mean? On the other hand, are you familiar with the scholarly theory that John was written based on a list of miracles and that this may or may not be an accurate statement and should be taken with a grain of salt?

My belief includes both a grounding in scholarship and the insight of spiritual experience. My own scholarship tells me that the author put these words into the mouth of Jesus. Yet, for me this makes them no less inspired than if someone had a smart phone to video Jesus saying them. This is because my own faith has rendered an experience of the Jesus Christ figure beyond the historical person, and I know that I can have a spiritual vision of this figure speaking those words directly to me from the Source of the Spirit of God within me.

Right now, if you think that I am somehow duped by religion, or off in my thinking – that's okay. It could be that my experience is bumping up against your belief system. Perhaps for you, truth is only known through empirical evidence and intellectual thought. Or perhaps you believe you are so at one with everything that there is no need to encounter a Jesus Christ figure at all. While I am familiar with my own beliefs, I do not know what beliefs work best for you. What's in your T-shirt drawer? Only you can discern that.

CONCEPTION

This brings us to the second tier. *To know that you know* is to open the T-shirt drawer and sort through it. It is to examine each belief, contemplate its reality amid present life experience, and discern if you want to keep it, or not. You may even look at some new T-shirts based on more recently acquired information and experience and decide whether you want to hold on to them, or not. You can take things into a process of rational consideration and make some decisions – "Yes, this is true," and, "No, this is not true." This is conceptual understanding, or *conception*. Conception is an understanding that comes from reflection on what you already know, combined with your consideration of it in the light of new learning and knowledge. You know that what you know is true. At least that is your concept in this moment.

To sum it up – the first tier of knowing is perception based on already established beliefs. The second tier of knowing is conception gained from rational consideration. Both tiers are an integral part of who we are and what we do. For example, it is my already established beliefs that gave me the perception that I could write this book – first tier. I would not have much to write, however, were it not for the conceptual understanding that comes from the rational consideration of my beliefs combined with new ideas gained through research – second tier. Even as I am writing to you in this very moment I am discerning the truth about Truth. So now comes the big question – "What is Truth?"

GOLD

In its Greek form found in John 8:32, the word for truth is *aletheia*.[35] This word carries a double meaning. Objectively it refers to "what is true in any matter under consideration."[36] Subjectively it implies "personal excellence," based upon "that

---

[35] IBID.

[36] IBID.

candor of mind which is free from affection, pretense, simulation, falsehood, and deceit."[37] Charles Fillmore, author and co-founder of the Unity movement, wrote the following definition: "Truth – the Absolute; that which accords with God as divine principle; that which is, has been, and ever will be; that which eternally is."[38] This is like the objective meaning of "what is true in any matter under consideration" found in the word, *aletheia*. Yet, what of the subjective meaning?

In Unity ministry and teaching, I have often found that the objective Truth is spelled with a capital "T" while the subjective truth is spelled with a small "t." Inspired by Fillmore's definition, Truth with a capital "T" refers to principles of eternal reality by which the universe exists and functions. Adding to Fillmore's insight, truth with a small "t" refers to the individual's perception, beliefs, and concepts regarding the capital "T" Truth. The small "t" subjective truths are formed when an experience of the capital "T" Truth has led to personal freedom, peace, and excellence in life.

In the quest for Truth with a capital "T", human beings have created fields of subjective thought and objective research that have resulted in the religious, philosophical and scientific disciplines of Theology, Ontology, Psychology, Cosmology, Anthropology, and the list continues. Why? What is it we really want to find, and how do we find it? What will give us lasting peace and make us truly free? Is it the Source, or the Force? Is it the Bliss of the Divine, the Life of the Eternal, the Wisdom of the Infinite, the Love of the Lord, the Knowledge of the Principle, the Power of the Presence? Is it

---

[37] IBID.

[38] CHARLES FILLMORE, THE REVEALING WORD - A DICTIONARY OF METAPHYSICAL TERMS, 2ND EDITION (UNITY VILLAGE: UNITY BOOKS, 2006), 200.

90

the fulfillment of all of these, or the emptiness of none of these?

Any human discipline that pursues Truth with a capital "T" develops the definitions, models and concepts that we know as truth with a small "t." These small "t" truths help point the way to the capital "T", truth, but are not that Truth in themselves. That Truth can only be known through a present and authentic experience of it. For the introduction to my tapes *The Wisdom and Power of Scripture, Truth and the Gospels: Part I,* I wrote the following:

"...any definition, model, or lesson of Truth is not really the Truth any more than a description of gold is really gold. Like gold, Truth can only be known through the direct experience of it. It is in our experience of the One that we know the One. It is in our practice of Principle that we know Principle. It is in our sense of being Eternal that we know the Eternal. So what are all of these wonderful definitions, lessons, and models for? They are for that aspect of sentient awareness that we call the mind.

It is the mind's nature to think, and to always be searching for something to think about. Like an infant exploring its new environment, the mind reaches out to touch, examine and comprehend the world around it. This is a good thing. Because of this, you have acquired enough knowledge to accomplish some things in life and to enjoy some things, whether it is a good career, quality time with the family, a peaceful moment with nature, or reading a great book. Yet, also because of this what you already know through your mind's previous explorations can get in the way of your present and spontaneous experience of the Truth. The mind's longing to truly understand has brought you a long way, yet it is also what has gotten in the way.

So, you throw the mind a bone. You say to the mind, 'This is what Truth is.' Then the mind can respond, 'Aha, now I know. Now I can stop thinking, thinking, thinking and searching, searching, searching – and take hold of this concept, focus on it, contemplate it, and in that contemplative focus find quiet and rest.' It is then that the definition or model or lesson of Truth becomes the signpost, pointing the way to the Truth by giving the mind a focus through which it can be stilled so that the Truth, the Eternal, the Principle, the One, can be experienced."39

Following through with the metaphor mentioned in this passage, let's see how this works with a description of gold. Gold is a precious metal with the warm yellow color of sunrise that shines like the dawn. It is malleable enough to mold into works of art that you can wear. It has been pressed so thin as to be used for an outer layer of great architecture and sculpting, as well as a thin pigmentation that highlights some of the world's greatest paintings. It has been used to create the reflective material that protects satellites and space vehicles from solar radiation. If you have ever looked up at night to see one bright spot moving across a starry sky, you may have been looking at sunlight shimmering off a sheet of gold.

Gold can even be formed into financial currency and is not nearly as destructible as paper money. The extraction of it from the earth, and the processing of it for human use takes great care and many working hours. One ton of rock mined from four kilometers under the Earth's surface might yield a small lump of gold that can be held in the palm of your hand. Because of this, it is frequently given a high market value. Not surprising, since the molecular structure of gold was formed in a long ago super nova and is older than the planet. Indeed, when you look at gold on your person, or see it in the museum, or touch its soft metal with your hand, you are encountering the very atoms that formed the Earth.

---

[39] LAURA BARRETT BENNETT. THE WISDOM AND POWER OF SCRIPTURE, TRUTH AND THE GOSPELS, PART I. UNITY, 1995, TAPE 1, SIDE A.

Can you feel it yet? Can you sense yourself touching the soft metal of gold, or seeing its radiant beauty? Can you feel the uplift in your state of mind as you focus on this description of gold? If so, this is because the small "t" truths of gold have pointed the way to the capital "T" Truth. Your mind has focused on descriptive words that not only invite you to think about gold, but to feel the experience of it in your heart – in this case as the awe and wonder that quiets the mind so that the timeless beauty of gold and the power of creation that formed it can be known and experienced. This brings us to the third tier of knowing.

INCEPTION

HEARTMIND

Do you remember the word *feel* in describing the meaning of the word, *know*? To *feel* the Truth in the core of your being is *to know that you know that you know*. While it can inspire great passion, this feeling is more than emotion. Emotion comes under the umbrella of feeling, but not all feeling is emotion. Rather, this feeling calms the emotions and clears the mind, allowing us to see what could not be seen by the mind cluttered with old thinking and reactive emotion. It gives us a new insight and a new creative way to be in life. This is the highest form of reason implied by the ancient philosophers. It is not the intellectual conceptualization of tier two, but an inception of spiritual logic that comes from beyond the intellect. It is the intuitive wisdom of the *heartmind*.

The singular form of the connected heart and mind is what I call the *heartmind*. To anchor the mind in the heart is to feel a presence and power that stills the thoughts and renders a fresh experience of the Truth. This is because there is an intelligence of the heart that is greater than the thinking intellect. Doc Childre and Howard Martin address the intelligence of the heart in their book, *The Heartmath Solution*. They state, "The heart isn't mushy or sentimental. It's intelligent and powerful, and we believe that it holds the promise for the next level of human development and for the survival of our world."[40] They also point out, "The role of the heart as an intelligence within the human system is one of the most prevalent themes in ancient traditions and in inspirational writing." [41] These traditions and writings include the Bible.

When in the Hebrew Bible Solomon asked for wisdom, what exactly was he asking? In the New Revised Standard Version of the Bible we read, *"Give your servant therefore an understanding mind to govern your people, able to discern between good and evil; for who can govern this your great people (1 Kings 3:9)?"* The same verse in the New King James Version reads, *"Therefore give Your servant an understanding heart to judge Your people, that I may discern between good and evil. For who is able to judge this great people of Yours?"* In one translation, Solomon asks for an understanding mind, while in the other, he asks for an understanding heart. This is because in the ancient Hebrew language there is no separation between mind and heart. The original Hebrew word from this scripture is *lev*, or *leb*. It means *heart of a man;*

---

[40] DOC CHILDRE AND HOWARD MARTIN WITH DONNA BEECH, THE HEARTMATH SOLUTION (NEW YORK: HARPERCOLLINS, 1999), 5.

[41] IBID., 7.

seat of passion; *mind of thought and knowledge*; *soul*; and *conscience*.[42] It refers to the heartmind, or the soul.

In approaching the Bible, or anything in our world, from the place the heartmind, we can see the beauty of Spirit, and hear the language of God in the sights and sounds of life, as well as the silence of quiet meditation. When the mental exploits and rational discernment of the intellect are anchored in the intuitive wisdom and passionate commitment of the heart, the soul is fully engaged in an exploration of new discoveries and transformational experiences of the Truth. From this place comes the inception of new inspiration, and we know that we know that we know.

EMPTINESS

When we have made it to the third tier, what about the T-shirt drawer? What do we do with all those T-shirts? When we look at the T-shirt drawer from the place of the heartmind, the drawer is empty and ready for new insights. When the drawer is empty, we have reached the third tier of knowing. From here, we leap off into the realm of the Absolute – beyond soul into Spirit. This is the emptiness, or void of creation, where nothingness exists as all potential and possibility. "In the beginning when God created the heavens and the earth, the earth was a formless void, and darkness covered the face of the deep, (Genesis 1:1-2a). In his book, *A Brief History of Everything*, transpersonal psychologist and philosopher, Ken Wilbur, uses the metaphor of climbing the rungs of a ladder when describing the evolution of consciousness. As with the top tier of knowing, the ladder of consciousness has a top rung – but what is beyond that? Here is what Wilbur says:

---

[42] STRONG, H3820.

95

"When you step off the ladder altogether, you are in free fall in Emptiness. Inside and outside, subject and object, lose all ultimate meaning. You are no longer 'in here' looking at the world 'out there.' You are not looking at the Kosmos, you are the Kosmos. The universe of One Taste announces itself, bright and obvious, radiant and clear, with nothing outside, nothing inside, an unending gesture of great perfection, spontaneously accomplished. The very Divine sparkles in every sight and sound, and you are simply that. The sun shines not on you but within you, and galaxies are born and die, all within your heart. Time and space dance as shimmering images on the face of radiant Emptiness, and the entire universe loses its weight. You can swallow the Milky Way in a single gulp and put Gaia in the palm of your hand and bless it, and it is all the most ordinary thing in the world, and so you think nothing of it." [43]

While I have had such experiences more than once, I can recall one time that has stayed with me throughout my adult life as an example of leaping off the ladder and going to the third tier of knowing – and beyond.

My undergraduate work in Religion Studies and Music was done at Wilson College in Chambersburg, Pennsylvania. Wilson was at that time a small private women's college. It is now coed. The size of its classes allowed the students to bond with their classmates and interact with the faculty at depth for the exploration of the subjects that were being studied. In February of 1979, during my junior year, the Board of Trustees called an all-school meeting of faculty, staff, and students. At this meeting, the President announced the closing of our school at the end of the year. I was deeply upset by this news. My first response was from the first tier of knowing.

---

[43] KEN WILBUR, *A BRIEF HISTORY OF EVERYTHING* (BOSTON: SHAMBHALA, 1996), 156.

Along with many of my classmates, I reacted from anger and fear. I was angry at the Board of Trustees, knowing that they did not do their job right because I perceived that if we do what is right, we cannot fail. I have since come to know that failure is part of how we learn and grow. Back then, however, I was fearful because I did not know what was next for me. This prompted me to do what I now refer to as a move to the second tier of knowing.

I connected with some of my classmates and we conceived a plan that started with a phoning campaign. Day and night, we called the Wilson alumnae to see if we could all work together to raise money for legal action. I even participated in an interview with a prospective law firm. In addition, I applied to another school, just in case. My rational mind had taken hold of my judgmental emotions, but only to push them down for a while. They had not gone away. Between the unacknowledged emotions and responsibilities that went far beyond the classroom, I was totally stressed, along with classmates and faculty members.

The concepts of what to do next helped keep me going amid the stress, but I needed more. In our studies of Bible and World Religions, we had been practicing contemplative prayer and mindful meditation. These practices were like what I had grown up with in Unity, and I enjoyed participating in them. One day – I went for a long walk. It was a cloud covered and cold Saturday morning when I walked the grounds of Wilson College. I took the foot path to the bridge, and crossing the Conococheague Creek, I strolled up to the hills that overlooked the main campus. Snow had fallen in the past few days. It covered the landscape with a soft greyish-white color that matched the thin cloud cover over head. There was no detectable sound in the rolling farmland behind the school's main campus except the squeaky crunch of old snow under my feet and the whisper of a cold breeze. I stood at the top of a hill, overlooking the college.

My mind had been quieted by the silent and bleak landscape. I could feel the nervous energy in the pit of my stomach of the past few days since the time of the announcement. I took a deep breath and moved my focus from the stomach to the heart. There, I could sense how much I loved this place and the people I had come to know here. I even felt compassion for the leaders who concluded that they had no choice but to make this most unpopular decision and announcement. I had gone into the space of the heartmind, the center of the soul.

From this place I saw my beloved school and all who had ever been part of it – like a momentary video through time. I could then see the campus before it was a campus, when it was a farm, then a wilderness of woods and fields. I could sense the struggle of soldiers and citizens in the Civil War, and the skirmishes of early settlers with the native peoples. I felt a connection to the land as did its early inhabitants. Then, I felt a connection to the whole Earth and to all of humanity. Not stopping there, my vision took me to the Cosmos that lay beyond the clouds and I was one with all of space and time. Then ... nothing. No space, no time, no me.

If someone had been looking at me in that moment, I could very well have disappeared. Then a thought went through my mind, "Wow – this is cool!" – and I was back. I was wearing the same clothes, looking at the same scene, but I was not the same. The stress was gone. In its place a new peace and confidence. My precious college, and all that it represented, could never die. This was because the reality of it was not in the buildings, or the organization, or the activities – but in the idea of it. Wilson was the idea that women, and later men as well, could have a liberal arts education that would make a positive difference in their lives and world. It was an education received in an environment of community connection and natural beauty that inspired the soul to do great things in life. This was a fresh idea that was in my heart, and its inception lead to a deeper knowing. I knew it to be the Truth – and not only that – I knew that I knew that I knew!

When I returned, the words I spoke conveyed a new message, "Wilson lives!" I continued my activities of academics and social action to save the school. After weeks of peaceful protests, news headlines, and court engagements, just before the end of the school year in the spring, a judge reversed the decision of the Board of Trustees – and Wilson was saved. Even if this had not happened, it would always be saved in my heart. This is what it is to know with your heart that you know with your mind that you know the Truth. It is like the new discovery of that gold nugget in the silt of the pan. With the fervor of the 19th century forty-niner, you hold to it with all your enthusiasm. Only this Gold Rush never runs dry. Whenever heart and mind are connected as one, Truth is experienced in a novel way that is more valuable than pure gold. The value of this connection will be applied to our interpretive work as we move through this book. In the meantime, let's check-in with where we are right now.

CHECK-IN

In Part One we learned about the Logos, how it evolved, and how it became what has been considered as the Word of God in the canon of the Bible. In this chapter of Part Two, we have sought the Truth by climbing the three tiers of knowing: *perception, conception,* and *inception.* We have discovered that beyond emotion and intellect is the intuitive wisdom of the heartmind. In this discovery, we have touched the great Emptiness, the realm of absolute potential out of which comes the creative power of the Word – whether it is in the form of "Wilson lives," or "Let there be light." In the next chapter, we will become acquainted with how the Truth has been sought through the Word of Scripture over time. We will see how the three tiers of knowing apply to three different interpretive methods, and how those methods lead up to the experience of metagetics.

SUMMARY

- Since the dawn of rational thought humankind has been on a quest to know the truth.

- Knowing the truth gives us a way of relating to the things of life that brings peace in our ability to be with what is so, power in our ability to create and accomplish, and freedom in the self-expression of how we choose to live our lives and interact with our world.

- There are three tiers of knowing:
  o To know is the first tier. It is the perception of something based upon what we already know about it.
  o To know that you know is the second tier. It is conception, or the concept that comes from a rational consideration of what you already know, combined with new learning and knowledge.
  o To know that you know that you know is the third tier. It is the insight, or inception, of Truth with a capital "T" that comes from the mind that is anchored in the heart, or the heartmind.

- There are two kinds of truth:
  o Truth with a capital "T" refers to principles of eternal reality by which the universe exists and functions.
  o Truth with a small "t" refers to perceptions and concepts regarding the capital "T" Truth, as well as any beliefs, definitions, or models that develop from these.

- Small "t" truths help to point the way to the capital "T", truth, but are not that Truth. That Truth can only be known through a present and authentic experience of it from the heartmind.

- To anchor the mind in the heart is to feel a presence and power that stills the thoughts, awakening an intelligence of the heart that is greater than the thinking intellect.

- From the tier of knowing where we dwell in the heartmind, we leap off into the realm of the Absolute – beyond soul into Spirit. This is the emptiness, or void of creation, where nothingness exists as all potential and possibility.

INQUIRY

1. What perceptions do you have stored in your "been there, done that" T-shirt drawer that get in the way of your experience of the Truth regarding...
   - Life?
   - Relationships?
   - Health?
   - Relationships?
   - Politics?
   - Religion?
   - The Bible?
   - Other?

2. What resources are available to you that provide new learning and concepts of any, or all, of these things?

3. What can you do to anchor the mind in the heart and rise to the third tier where you know that you know that you know the Truth?

CHAPTER 5: INTERPRETATION

"He had a dream in which he saw a stairway resting on the earth, with its top reaching to heaven, and the angels of God were ascending and descending on it (Genesis 28:12)."

REVELATION

Capital "T" Truth is transformational. It transcends the form of your perceptions and conceptions, providing the inception of new ideas and fresh insights. Another name for the inception of Truth is inspiration. Inspiration is the awakening of God's Spirit within you. It is the infusion of energy and awareness from beyond what you know your personal resources to be. It leads to revelation.

In the last book of the Bible, the title, *Revelation*, is used as a transliteration of the Greek word *apocalypsis*, which means *disclosure*.[44] Disclosure from apocalyptic literature, like the book of Revelation, relies on its symbolism, archetypal images, and metaphorical messages. These things must be interpreted to be understood. In the experience of being human, revelation also applies to the interpretation of the whole Bible. Humanities professor, W. Randolph Tate writes, "In the context of biblical hermeneutics, revelation is

---

[44] RICHARD N. AND R. KENDALL SOULEN, *HANDBOOK OF BIBLICAL CRITICISM, THIRD EDITION, REVISED AND EXPANDED* (LOUISVILLE, KY: JOHN KNOX PRESS, 2001), 8.

understood as the process of God's self-disclosure to humans."[45]

Because revelation comes from beyond what you can presently perceive or conceive, it seems like a gift from God coming to you from outside of you, or "God's self-disclosure." Biblical scripture of all types has been one of the primary vehicles through which revelation has occurred through time. In actuality, revelation occurs when you go deeper into yourself through the interpretive process to encounter the language of God speaking through the authors and texts of Scripture. It is a new experience for the individual each time it occurs, but it is nothing new in the human experience.

For centuries, great theologians and philosophers have had revelations of what they understood Truth to be, or not to be. Following are highlights from a history of humanity in search of revelatory truths and how they are found through biblical interpretation. These highlights emerge from the growing influence and diversity of Judeo-Christianity as it evolved and spread along with European culture. In fact, it is the evolution of biblical interpretation that is most likely responsible for the long-term popularity and use of the Bible even to today. My intention in sharing them is to render valuable insight into our collective and individual relationships with the Bible. This will support you in sorting through the T-shirt drawer of your concepts and beliefs about God, about life, and about Scripture. Therefore, let us explore this history of traditional, reformed, modern, and post-modern hermeneutics.

---

[45] W. RANDOLPH TATE, BIBLICAL INTERPRETATION, AN INTEGRATED APPROACH (GRAND RAPIDS, MI: BAKER PUBLISHING, 2008), 223.

HERMENEUTICS

TRADITIONAL

Hermeneutics is another word for "interpretation". It is from the Greek, *hermeneuien,* meaning *to express, to explain, to translate,* and *to interpret.* [46] One of its earliest forms as applied to the Bible was the metaphorical approach of Philo Judaeus (20 BCE – 50 CE) that saw the overview of the Hebrew Scriptures as an allegory for the spiritual development of the soul as mentioned earlier in this book. In Christian theology, hermeneutics has been called, "the art of interpretation." As such, it has been viewed as the skillful application of rules for correct interpretation of Scripture according to the dominant theology of a given time.

For example, hermeneutics directed by the Christian tradition according to *Rule of Faith* was applied to defend the Old Testament against Marcion's rejection of it as part of the Christian Bible. The *Rule of Faith,* known in Latin as *Regula Fidei,* is an abridged version of the body of early Christian belief that served as a guide for interpreting biblical writings in the second century. Before the Nicene Creed, it was used by Irenaeus and Tertullian to advocate the unity of the Bible as one evolving story that lead to the salvation of Christ. Through this traditional form of interpretation, the Old Testament stories and prophecies were part of the larger story of the fall, sin, and redemption of humanity, an expansion of the ideas of Philo into the Christian narrative. This was the mainstream approach to scriptural interpretation for centuries, with some enhancements along

---

[46] SOULEN AND SOULEN, 73.

the way. Examples of these are found in *The Fourfold Sense of Scripture*, and the *Lectio Divina*.

The Fourfold Sense of Scripture is an approach to interpretation that became popular in the Middle Ages and was first proposed by John Cassian (c. 360-435 CE). Born in Scythia to wealthy parents, Cassian spent much of his life studying scripture and immersing himself in the ascetic lifestyle of the desert monks of Palestine and Egypt. It was in Egypt that a controversy broke out over whether God had a form like a man, or was more of an incorporeal spirit. This may not seem significant to us, but it hit the heart of how these monks related to God. Believing God to be incorporeal, Cassian found himself, and others of like belief, outnumbered and had to flee for his own safety. He escaped to Constantinople, then to Rome to appeal for protection from Pope Innocent I.

Cassian was offered the opportunity to develop a monastery in Marseilles. He came to be known for his writings on the monastic life and the interpretation of Scripture. Cassian's writings were the main influence on the work of Benedict of Nursia (c. 480-547 CE) in Italy. Heavily influenced by Cassian, *Regula Benedicti*, or *The Rule of St. Benedict*, became the foundational means through which monasteries were created throughout Italy and beyond, influencing the lives of Benedictine, Cistercian, and Trappist monks to this day.

We can envision the older Cassian in quiet contemplation of scriptural Truth in his monastery in southern Gaul, or France. He knew Scripture could be interpreted both literally and spiritually, with its spiritual form being discovered through three distinct approaches. Along with the *literal* approach, there was the *allegorical* approach of implied

106

symbology, the *topological* approach of moral understanding, and the *anagogical* approach of where we are headed in the end. Here is a rhyme describing these four approaches.

"The letter shows us what God and our fathers did;

The allegory shows us where our faith is hid;

The moral meaning gives us rules of daily life;

The anagogy shows us where we end our strife." [47]

Finding meaning behind the literal word of Scripture was also addressed centuries later by the Carthusian monk, Guigo II (c. 1114-1193 CE). Like the tiers of knowing and the ladder of consciousness, ascension in spiritual awareness and experience was the motif of Guigo's *Scala Claustraliaum,* or *Ladder of Monks.* His inspiration was from the story of Jacob. *"He had a dream in which he saw a stairway resting on the earth, with its top reaching to heaven, and the angels of God were ascending and descending on it (Genesis 12:28)."* Guigo's ladder with its four rungs became one of the earliest descriptions of methodical prayer and was named *Lectio Divina,* or *Sacred Reading.* Lectio Divina became the term used for the prayerful contemplation of Scripture. It's four rungs are reading (*lectio*), reflection (*meditatio*), prayer (*oratio*), and contemplation (*contemplation*). We can imagine Guigo's vision of the spiritual journey of monks with Guigo himself ascending a ladder and looking upward toward a light-filled heavenly realm. We could even say that the whole intention of hermeneutics is to journey into the light of greater spiritual awareness and experience.

---

[47] ROBERT M. GRAND AND DAVID TRACY, *A SHORT HISTORY OF THE INTERPRETATION OF THE BIBLE* (MINNEAPOLIS, MN: FORTRESS PRESS, 1984), 85.

REFORMED

As varied as they were, early methods of hermeneutics and biblical scholarship did not go outside the traditional boundaries of the pre-conceived unity of God's Word in the Bible, proclaiming the salvation of Christ. Even the Reformers emphasized these things, but in a way that was distinct from the Catholic Church. The Reformers gave greater authority to Scripture than to human beings, particularly those of the church hierarchy. This allowed for a direct connection between the Bible and the individual reader, or interpreter. According to Richard N. and R. Kendall Soulen, their ideas included, "the priority of scripture's plain sense, the supremacy of the Word over human authority," and "renewed emphasis on philology."[48]

Philology is the study of languages used in classical and scriptural writings in the context of their historical and literary meanings. It was a necessity to the work of the biblical translators of the Reformation. Perhaps the most well-known, although not the first, of these translators was Martin Luther (c. 1483-1546 CE). He completed his German translation of the New Testament in 1522. Twelve years later, in 1534, he completed the Old Testament with a separate deutero-canonical section called the Apocrypha. To create these translations, he used ancient Hebrew, and Greek manuscripts in understanding the texts.

The most famous image of Luther is as an Augustinian monk and University professor, nailing his *Ninety-Five Theses* to the door of All Saints-Church in Wittenburg, Germany. His scholarly theses debated the indulgences that were paid by the poor to the church. This eventually lead to his ex-

---

[48] SOULEN AND SOULEN, 74.

communication, after which he pursued how best to convey the freely given grace of God through faith in Jesus Christ. His highly significant biblical translation not only set standards for the written form of the German language, but also lead to the ability of the common people to read and interpret the Bible.

John Calvin (c. 1509-1564) used scriptural commentary to develop an early form of systematic theology in his work *Institutes of the Christian Religion*, contributing to the Reformation in France. Both Luther and Calvin emphasized the point of *scriptura ipsius interpres* (scripture interprets itself). This gave them a direct connection to God that was not dependent upon human intervention and indulgences.

William Tyndale (c. 1494-1536 CE) was a contemporary of Luther and Calvin. He was an English scholar and linguist who had a passion for theology and the understanding of Scripture free from the dogma of the church. He was influenced by Luther and the works of the classical scholar Desidarius Erasmus of Rotterdam (c. 1466-1536). Erasmus used ancient manuscripts combined with philology, making the already canonized Greek and Latin Bibles more user friendly for his time. Tyndale used ancient manuscripts and philology to translate the Bible into English. He printed the complete New Testament in 1526, but only finished half of the Old Testament, much of which he did in prison. Under Henry the VIII of England, using English to read and understand the Bible was illegal, and Tyndale had to flee England. He was arrested in Antwerp in 1535 and held in Vilvoorde Castle near Brussels until his execution in 1536.

The irony of Tyndale's life and the courage to continue his translations until his death can be seen in several things. Pocket-sized versions of his New Testament flooded the market in England to be used in public book burnings. At his execution, he was strangled before his body was burned as a sign of respect and mercy. It is said that his last words were, "May the Lord open the King of England's eyes." Two years later, after divorcing his first wife, Catherine of Aragon, and marrying Anne Boleyn, Henry created the Church of England. Shortly after that he commissioned the Great Bible, using Tyndale's work as a primary resource.

MODERN

The application of philology and the approach that "scripture interprets itself" on the part of the Reformers began a rationalism that grew over the next two hundred years. This eventually lead to some more humanistic hermeneutics that outgrew previous theological boundaries and started to take on secular forms of verification regarding biblical Truth in the time of the Enlightenment of the late 18th and early 19th centuries. About this growth, the Soulen's wrote the following in their book:

> "...It was inevitable that scholars should begin to read the Bible like any other ancient work and subject it to the same standards of evidence and verifiability. In the new environment, the inherited techniques of Theological Interpretation such as typology (allegorical interpretation) proved largely unworkable, while new techniques such as Historical Criticism produced results that were often religiously inert or seemingly antithetical to faith."[49]

The Soulens go on to say that this tension was brought to some resolution by the German theologian and philosopher, Frederic Daniel Ernst Schleiermacher (c. 1768-1834).

---

[49] IBID.

It was said of Schleiermacher that he was the "Father of Modern Liberal Christianity."[50] In his youth, he developed a strong philosophical skepticism. Not taking the stories and teachings of the Bible, or anything else, at face value, he questioned his teachers and doubted his own Christian faith. As a Chaplain in Berlin, he found little satisfaction in preaching. Rather, he found it in the love of family, as well as the beauty of art and literature. He engaged in philosophical and theological discussions that lead him to continue his career in theology as a University professor, a writer, and a re-constructionist of Protestant Christianity in Germany.

Schleiermacher believed that the ego functioned at the level of the senses and the intellect, and that there was a higher state of non-ego that was not a separate entity. Rather, identity in this state was found in conscious union with the tangible things of life, nature, and the universe. From this place, he approached biblical hermeneutics from what he called "the art of understanding." This understanding came from the interaction between interpreter and text. Within its own context, the text would reveal its meaning through interaction with the feelings and intuitive insights of the interpreter. This interaction with the text then moved the interpreter beyond the sense-based intellect into a deeper spiritual awareness that came from what I have called the heartmind.

The reciprocal interplay of text to context to reader and back to the meaning of the text was one form of what later became known as the "hermeneutical circle". The hermeneutical circle is a descriptive term for the dialogic interplay between the reader, or interpreter, and the text. It is like scientific theory,

---

[50] IBID., 167.

which is the result of both the empirical evidence of what happens, and the observation and interpretation of it through the consciousness of the individual.

This dialogic approach to hermeneutics influenced many theologians and philosophers throughout the 19th and 20th centuries, while others responded with diverse approaches. Following are the names of some of these historical figures, along with the hermeneutics that were most influential on how we interpret the Bible today. I can see them as a group, sitting in a circle and discussing exactly how hermeneutics contributes to the discovery of Truth. Perhaps you will recognize some of their thinking as your own, or perhaps your disagreement with them will lead to more insights for your spiritual journey.

Wilhelm Dilthey (c. 1833-1911) was born in the village of Biebrich, a borough in what is now the city of Wiesbaden, Hesse, Germany. Receiving his doctorate from the University of Berlin, he was greatly inspired by the work of Schleiermacher, whose writings were the subject of his thesis. As a German philosopher and historian, Dilthey expanded the dialogic and the hermeneutical circle into the realm of historical objectivity. He understood humans as historical beings, and history as a reflection of evolving world views rather than simply an account of past events. Instead of reflection and introspection being the key to self-awareness, Dilthey believed that human beings understand themselves within the context of their history. In application to the Bible, it is only in understanding the historical world view of its texts that the individual can more deeply delve into its meaning within the context of his, or her, life.

Rudolph Bultmann (c. 1884-1976) took another approach. Born the son of a Lutheran minister in the German

Confederation in Weisfelstede, Oldenburg, he received his doctorate in theology from the University of Marburg. As a well-respected career theologian, he was a member of the Confessing Church, a church that stood against the state's attempt to unify Protestant churches under a pro-Nazi ideology. Bultmann believed the meaning of the New Testament in modern faith came from understanding the scriptural author's social and cultural intent by using something called Form Criticism. Form Criticism will be addressed in the next chapter.

Bultmann's use of Form Criticism and demythologization of the New Testament pointed out that its stories and teachings were more theology than history. He referred to the stories of Jesus as myth, but this form of myth had meaning through the faith that it inspired. For Bultmann, the proclamation and experience of Jesus as Savior was more important than the determination of what he historically said or did. This emphasis on a form of hermeneutics that depended upon the individual's theological perspective and experience, be it author or interpreter, was most likely influenced both by Schleiermacher and the existentialism of Bultmann's colleague, Martin Heidegger.

The famous existentialist philosopher, Martin Heidegger (c. 1889-1976) shifted the focus of dialogic hermeneutics from an interpretive way of knowing about the text to the experience of a fundamental relationship with the text. His work on *Being and Time* (1927) although incomplete, was one of the most well-known and influential philosophical writings of the 20th century. *Being and Time* addressed what it means to be in relationship with time. In his approach to ontology, or the study of Being, he emphasized authenticity in one's relationship with the world. Authenticity refers to being aware of your already collected perceptions and reactions to life (remember the T-shirt drawer) and choosing freely who you want to be in the moment.

With insights gained from the works of Dilthey, Heidegger believed that in understanding a text within its own context, the interpreter could go beyond what was already known into a new and more authentic understanding. The interpreter could then discern the way in which the parts of the text revealed something about the whole, and the whole text revealed something about its parts – back to the hermeneutical circle. The paradox of Heidegger was his direct support of Nazism and his refusal to denounce it later in life after the Second World War, even though his active involvement with the party only lasted about one year. For this he was banned from teaching. Ironically, his ideas have lived on in both theological hermeneutics and ontological understanding.

Another contemporary of Bultmann and Heidegger was the Swiss theologian, Karl Barth (1886-1968). He was born the son of Fritz Barth, a professor of theology who loved philosophy. Having been exposed to liberal and conservative theology, Karl Barth rejected them both and formed what for him was dialectic theology. His dialectical theology presented both a God of grace and judgment. For Barth, knowing the historical context of biblical content was a support to knowing the Spirit of the Word, which he equated to the salvation of Jesus Christ. He believed that the Word of God was of primary importance in leading to salvation, and salvation was paramount to redeeming humanity from its sins. This was important to him as a member of the Confessing Church, for he perceived humanity's sins in the Nazi regime that he opposed, as well as in those Christians who supported it.

114

While Barth emphasized the Word in the form of the biblical text, Gadamer and Ricœur, like Schleiermacher, emphasized the importance of the individual interpreter. German philosopher, Hans Georg Gadamer (1900-2002) pointed out that context not only applied to the text being interpreted, but also to the experience of the interpreter. The context of the interpreter's traditions and experiences pre-determined how the interpreter understood the text, while the text helped expand the interpreter's understanding of his/her traditions and experiences. It is yet another take on the hermeneutical circle.

Jean Paul Gustave Ricœur of France (1913-2005) emphasized the relationship between self and phenomenon outside of self. In the case of biblical hermeneutics this referred to a relationship between the interpreter and the text which helped the interpreter better understand his, or her, self. Winning the 2000 Kyoto Prize in Arts and Philosophy for revolutionizing hermeneutics with this phenomenological approach, Ricœur stated, "Every hermeneutics is thus, explicitly or implicitly, self-understanding by means of understanding others."[51] Through modern hermeneutics the search for Truth, and the "self-disclosure of God" has led to a greater understanding, not just of God, but of one's self. The opportunity for such understanding on an individual basis expanded with the openness and diversity of post-modern hermeneutics.

---

[51] PAUL RICŒUR, CHARLES E. REAGAN, AND DAVID STEWART, THE PHILOSOPHY OF PAUL RICŒUR: AN ANTHOLOGY OF HIS WORK. BOSTON, MA: BEACON PRESS, 1978, 106.

POST-MODERN

BEYOND

Post-modern hermeneutics began in the 20th century. Yet, it is not based so much on a timeline as it is on a way of interpreting the Bible that leaves the door open beyond the boundaries of theological and rational thought thus far developed in history. For example, Roland Gérard Barthes (1915-1980) questioned the conclusions of traditional, reformed, and rational hermeneutics as favoring the bourgeoise lifestyle of the wealthy and well-educated.

Born into a provincial setting in Cherbourg, France, Barthes lost his father during World War I at an early age. His mother cared for him, moved to Paris, and made sure that he received a good education in classics and literature. Tuberculosis kept him out of World War II and made it difficult for him to complete an advanced degree. Later he admitted that this was not a major focus for him. Still, he became well known for his writings and lectures. Rather than a tool for manipulating the masses into a particular way of thinking, Barthes saw the Bible as part of a body of myth that revealed the cultural character of those who wrote it. He also taught that in breaking down the structure of linguistics within a given writing, one could discern the meaning of its narrative through the characters, functions, and actions within that narrative. This structural analysis became useful to biblical interpreters.

Another post-modern interpreter of literature was Jaque Derrida (1930-2004). He was born in Algeria to an Arabic and French speaking family that was later granted French citizenship. Derrida challenged structuralism like that of Barthes with his approach to what he called Deconstruction.

For him, there was no real linguistic unity, presence of metaphysics, or underlying principle of a given word. Instead there was an unresolvable difference. A word's specific meaning in history, known as its *diachrony*, did not necessarily coincide with the word's meaning in the present moment, known as its *synchrony*. Nor does the present meaning dictate any future meaning. For Derrida, meaning was not found in linguistics, as put forth in traditional and modern hermeneutics, but rather in *semiotics*, or the comprehension of signs.

To clarify semiotics, think of our need to use the bathroom or toilet in a country where you do not know the language. What do you search out in finding it? Perhaps a two-dimensional stick figure with a skirt for Women and two straight legs for Men. This is a form of communication. It is a language beyond linguistics. In semiotics, the signs of the Bible are not logocentric, or found in the meaning of its words. Rather they are noticed in the context of its literature. An example would be the slaughter of the innocents in both the Moses and Jesus stories, validating Jesus' authority in interpreting Jewish law. Another example is apocalyptic imagery that held specific meaning to its original readers, such as the number 666 being a symbol for the Emperor Nero. Yet, what do these things mean to us today? For Derrida there was no once and for all answer to this. Such meaning keeps evolving through time, and only the moment reveals what the meaning is – for the moment.

Jean-Francois Lyotard (1924-1998) was a French philosopher and sociologist. He taught that there is no overarching language that captured all Truth. What could be found, were multiple ways of communicating, or "language games" that came from innumerable systems of thought. The freedom of such independent thought and language, however, is a larger idea, or meta-narrative, of human emancipation. Therefore, any idea worth having must have within it an intention for the greater good and freedom of humankind. The findings of science, for example, must be justified by their contributions to the health and education. In history, biblical or otherwise, the justification for interpreted ideas is found in learning from events how to overcome our faults in favor of our qualities. For Lyotard, the ideological character of what emerged from hermeneutics, needed to be examined carefully in that what is true for one cannot be true for all unless it is good for all.

Another humanitarian approach to Post-Modern hermeneutics comes from Elisabeth Schüssler Fiorenza. Born in Cenad, Romania in 1938, she is an advocate of Feminist Theology, and hermeneutics that include the insight of marginalized population groups. Serving for some time as a professor at Harvard Divinity School, Schüssler Fiorenza studied closely the works of Paul in the Bible. She believed that, not only is it important for women and minorities to interpret Scripture and teach spiritual understanding from their own perspectives, but that Paul taught this as well. In teaching this, she used his quote, *"There is no longer Jew or Greek, there is no longer slave or free, there is no longer male and female; for all of you are one in Christ Jesus (Galatians 3:28)."*

In recent decades, other viewpoints on hermeneutics have evolved. Some believe a return to traditional hermeneutics bound by the theology of the Salvation of Christ is what is necessary in these confusing times. Others feel that the Bible, itself, is not a finished product, but that interpretation and expansion on what it says should continue indefinitely into the future. Still others put forth that any approach to the biblical text needs to be bound to the intended theology of the text as best as can be determined by exegesis, free of imposed theology or individual philosophy and experience.

INTERACTION

Did you see your own way of interacting with the Bible in this account of hermeneutical history? Do you have an approach to the Bible that is distinct from anything that was shared? Do you believe the Bible to be the Word of God, or do you question as to whether or not the Word of God can even be found in this all-too-human text? What is the Truth of the Bible for you? What form of hermeneutics can best reveal that?

In your quest for Truth in the Bible, there is only one interpreter who can provide the answer to all your questions – you! Whatever your relationship is with the Bible, a critical interaction with its text is helpful to your own revelation of Truth and your own understanding of the Word. Of course, I am presuming that the Word and the Truth exist as universal principles as indicated earlier in this book. You may have a post-modern perspective that questions this, as do many other people today. If that is so, perhaps you are open to the possibility that there is That which is greater than you know yourself to be, and That can be found in working with the Bible, whatever "That" is for you.

In Part 3, entitled *Life*, you become acquainted with the Bible as a Book of Life. Working with the Bible as a Book of Life begins with those things that make it come alive. As the Bible comes alive for you, so your life becomes a dynamic expression of being That which is beyond the limitation of your own self assessments. Whatever That is for you, I call it God.

SUMMARY

- Inspiration is the awakening of God's Spirit within you. It leads to revelation.
- Biblical scripture has been one of the primary vehicles through which revelation has occurred through time.
- Revelation occurs when you go deeper into yourself through interpretation to encounter the language of God speaking through the authors and texts of Scripture.
- Hermeneutics is another word for "interpretation".
- As varied as they were, early methods of hermeneutics and biblical scholarship did not go outside the traditional boundaries of unity in God's Word, or the Bible as one story leading up to the salvation of Christ.
- The Reformers gave greater authority to Scripture than to human beings, allowing for a direct connection between the Bible and the individual reader, or interpreter.
- Philology is the study of languages used in classical and scriptural writings in the context of their historical and literary meanings.
- The application of philology over time lead to growing rationalism and humanistic hermeneutics that outgrew previous theological boundaries and started to take on secular forms of verification regarding biblical Truth.
- A reciprocal interplay of text to context to reader and back to the meaning of the text became a widely used approach to interpretation known as the hermeneutical circle. The hermeneutical circle is a descriptive term for the dialogic interplay between the reader, or interpreter, and the text.
- Through modern hermeneutics the search for Truth, and the "self-disclosure of God" has led to a greater understanding, not just of God, but of one's self.
- The opportunity for understanding on an individual basis expanded with the openness and diversity of post-modern hermeneutics.

- Whatever your relationship is with the Bible, a critical interaction with its text is helpful to your own revelation of Truth and your own understanding of the Word.
- See the "Tables" for a summary of the Highlights of Hermeneutics.

TABLES

HIGHLIGHTS OF TRADITIONAL HERMENEUTICS OF THE BIBLE				
Overall Theme: Unity of God's Word in the Bible Proclaiming the Salvation of Christ				
Influential Document	Interpretive Approach	How Used	Practitioners and Authors	When Applied
Rule of Faith	Unity of the Bible as one evolving story leading to the salvation of Christ	Validated the Old Testament as part of the story of Christ	Irenaeus (130-200); Tertullian (160-225)	2nd and 3rd Centuries the Nicene Creed
Fourfold Sense of Scripture	Literal, Allegorical, Topological, and Anagogical	For historical awareness, spiritual reflection, moral instruction, and understanding death	John Cassian (360-435)	4th and 5th Centuries forward
Rule of St. Benedict	Literal study and spiritual reflection.	Provided a guide for the spiritual life of monks	Benedict of Nursia (480-547)	5th and 6th Centuries forward
Ladder of Monks	Reading, Reflection, Prayer, Contemplation.	For *Lectio Divina* or Sacred Reading; Prayerful Contemplation of Scripture.	Guigo II (1114-1193)	12th Century forward

HIGHLIGHTS OF REFORMED HERMENEUTICS OF THE BIBLE				
Overall Theme: Philology – the Study of Scriptural Languages in Their Historical/Literary Context				
Influential Document	Interpretive Approach	How Used	Translators and Authors	When Applied
Latin New Testament with Greek Text of 1516	Humanistic – updating ancient languages from original cultural contexts.	Provided Greek and Latin scriptures more useful for local biblical translations.	Desidarius Erasmus (1466-1536)	16th Century forward
German New Testament of 1522 and Old Testament of 1534	Direct relationship of the individual with Scripture without the need of an intermediary.	Translated Old and New Testaments, plus Apocrypha, in the people's language.	Martin Luther (1483-1546)	16th Century forward
English New Testament of 1526 and half of Old Testament of 1536	Understanding based on the original biblical languages and free from Church Dogma.	Provided access to the Bible for the general English speaking population; A basis for later English Bibles.	William Tyndale (1494-1536)	16th Century forward
Institutes of the Christian Religion	*Scriptura ipsius interpres –* "scripture interprets itself".	Early development of systematic theology used for scriptural commentary.	John Calvin (1509-1564)	16th Century forward

HIGHLIGHTS OF MODERN HERMENEUTICS OF THE BIBLE				
Overall Theme: Humanistic Rationalism with Regard for Secular Verification of Biblical Truth.				
Influential Idea	Interpretive Approach	How Used	Practitioners	When Applied
Hermeneutical Circle	Dialogic interaction - text, to context, to the reader's deeper spiritual insight, and back to text.	Re-constructed Protestant Christianity's approach to biblical interpretation.	Frederic Schleiermacher (1768-1834)	Late 18th Century forward

Humanistic History	Self-awareness and evolving world views drawn from the context of objective biblical history.	Expanded the hermeneutical circle into the realm of historical objectivity.	Wilhelm Dilthey (1833-1911)	19th Century forward
Form Criticism	Faith drawn from understanding scriptural author's social and cultural intent.	De-mythologized the New Testament as containing more theology than history.	Rudolph Bultmann (1884-1976)	Early to mid-20th Century forward
Existential Hermeneutics	Understanding the whole of the text through its parts, and the parts of the text through the context of the whole.	Used the hermeneutical circle to understand the text within its own context by setting aside the interpreter's pre-conceived notions.	Martin Heidegger (1889-1976)	Early to mid-20th Century forward
Dialectic Theology	Understanding historical context as a support in knowing the Spirit of the Word.	Presented Scripture as the Word of God leading to salvation.	Karl Barth (1886-1968)	Early to mid-20th Century forward
Context of Experience	Interpreter's experience influences textual understanding, while the text expands the interpreter's experience.	Included both the text and the experience of the interpreter when applying context.	Hans Georg Gadamer (1900-2002)	20th Century forward
Phenomenological Interpretation	Self-awareness through relationship with the text outside of the self.	Enhanced the understanding of the self by understanding the other.	Paul Ricœur (1913-2005)	20th Century forward

124

HIGHLIGHTS OF POST-MODERN HERMENEUTICS OF THE BIBLE				
Overall Theme: Moving beyond theological and rational thought thus far developed in history				
Influential Idea	Interpretive Approach	How Used	Practitioners	When Applied
Structural Analysis	The Bible is myth that is better understood through the structure of its linguistics.	Questioned the conclusions of traditional, reformed, and rational. hermeneutics.	Roland Barthes (1915-1980)	20th Century forward
Linguistic Deconstruction	Since the meaning of words changes with time, biblical understanding relies on signs, not words.	Challenged the structure of language as significant to biblical understanding.	Jaque Derrida (1930-2004)	20th Century forward
Human Emancipation	Interpretation must advocate freedom and the greater good of humankind.	Advocated learning from history to overcome our faults in favor of our qualities.	Jean-Francois Lyotard (1924-1998)	20th Century forward
Feminist Theology	Interpretation must include the insights of women and marginalized population groups.	Advocated inclusive hermeneutics.	Elisabeth Schüssler Fiorenza (Born 1938)	20th and 21st. Centuries

125

INQUIRY

1. Who interprets the Bible?

2. What is the value of biblical hermeneutics?

3. How does the hermeneutical circle describe your relationship with the Bible? With other literature? With life?

4. Should the Bible be understood free of religious belief? Why or why not?

5. Can God be found in the Bible? Why or why not?

PART IV: LIFE

Chapter 6: Alive

"Return, O my soul, to your rest, for the Lord has dealt bountifully with you (Psalm 116:7)."

Pursuit

In journeying through the historical highlights of hermeneutics in Chapter 4, we saw a variety of ways that the Bible has been interpreted through time in our pursuit of God, of Truth, or of That which is greater than we know ourselves to be. Beginning with traditional forms of interpretation we saw how the Bible was viewed through the lens of being a singular work that led us on the path to Salvation. Even the more allegorical and mystical approaches of the Middle Ages, as well as the humanistic translations of the Reformation, worked within the boundaries of this understanding. In their work with the Bible's original languages, however, the Reformers planted seeds of objective observation and rational thought, and those seeds grew over time into modern hermeneutics.

In modern hermeneutics the Bible came to be critically examined, like other ancient works, for the historical and literary contexts of its contents. This brought interpreters from outside the boundaries of traditional theology into the hermeneutical circle. The hermeneutical circle involved the interpreter in a dynamic reciprocal interaction with what the text was saying about itself. It is still an integral part of much interpretive work that is done today. Not all interpretation, however, relies on this reciprocal interchange. The post-modern interpreters have looked beyond the hermeneutical circle to the point of considering that meaning and truth evolve through time as historical perspectives change. These changes can imply to the interpreter that there is no unchanging Truth, and that any approach to the Bible needs to include the insight of social equality and the greater good of humanity.

And so – here you are at this place in history, seeking a relationship with Scripture, the latest piece of which was written almost two thousand years ago. Why? You would not even be reading this far into the book if you were not pursuing some form of inspiration or transformation through your relationship with the Bible. Are you seeking to demonstrate that the Bible is a unified story of evolution toward wholeness and salvation? Are you looking to work with the hermeneutical circle and discover new meanings in the text? Are you anticipating going beyond all of this to a new revelation of what the Bible can mean for you today? Whatever you seek, you bring it with you, and your work with metagetics brings it forth from you.

The work of metagetics has evolved from multiple approaches to hermeneutics that can be summed up in three words: *eisegesis*, *exegesis*, and *metaphysics*. Metagetics emerged from personal theological insights that have been placed on the Bible through the practice of eisegesis; through interpretive foundations that have been laid through the hermeneutical circle known as exegesis; and through the metaphysical approach of discovering the philosophical principles of Logos and Truth by means of an allegorical interpretation that relates the subjects of Scripture to the activity of individual consciousness. How is that for a statement!? If you want to sound scholarly, simply memorize that last sentence and repeat it to your friends at parties. Aside from doing that, here is how it boils down. Through personal insight, historical and literary understanding, and symbolic connection to personal experience, the Bible comes alive. To understand this more fully, let us look at the three approaches to biblical interpretation that sum up the body of hermeneutics and from which metagetics emerged.

APPROACHES

EISEGESIS

Eisegesis, spoken with a long "i" sound in the first syllable – is the isolation of a verse or passage of scripture from its natural context. I define it as follows:

Eisegesis. (From the Greek, *eis,* meaning *in,* and *into,* and *gesthai,* meaning *to guide,* and *lead.*) It is the interpretation of Scripture done from the perspective of personal belief and concept. It means to put meaning into Scripture. It refers to the practice of finding meaning in Scripture by isolating it from its historical/literary/metaphorical context and using the literal words on the page to support what the interpreter is already thinking.

Eisegesis is for countless individuals an approach to drawing inspiration from the Bible. I use it every day when I look at the *Daily Word Magazine* from Unity. In the *Daily Word,* the oldest daily prayer magazine in the world, a Bible verse or passage is shared to match the theme of the day. The literal wording of the Scripture was chosen from the lens of a pre-conceived spiritual idea for that day. For example, when *Relaxation* was the word for a day, the Word of Scripture said, *"Return, O my soul, to your rest, for the Lord has dealt bountifully with you (Psalm 116:7)."*[52] This teaches nothing about the Psalms, but it does present soothing words for the soul.

While eiesgesis has its drawbacks because it takes the Bible verse out of its context, it does bring inspiration, and even sometimes revelation, when its literal language speaks directly to the reader's experience. Because of this, we witness eisegesis being used in sermons, prayers, weddings and funerals. It, therefore, serves a good purpose. Yet when something is isolated from its context in such a way, its words can also be used to support prejudice, hatred, and even violence. For example, from the book of Joshua we read, *"And the sun stood still and the moon stopped, until the nation took vengeance on their enemies (Joshua 10:13)."*

What's this? It seems that there is divine intervention on behalf of vengeance. Sounds a little terroristic. No wonder people point to the "Old Testament" God as the God of vengeance and the New Testament God as the God of love. Let us remember, however, that this way of looking at God in the Bible comes through the lens of Christian bias seen in how the Bible evolves from the old to the new. In fact, the New Testament has questionable passages of its own. What about this one on slavery? *"Let all who are under the yoke of slavery regard their masters as worthy of all honor, so that the name of God and the teaching may not be blasphemed (1 Timothy 6:1)."* This tells us that to honor God and avoid blasphemy, the slave needs to honor the master. Wow! With these God concepts in both the Hebrew and Christian Scriptures, who wouldn't want to just give up on the Bible altogether? Rather than do that, however, let's look at exegesis.

---

[52] *RELAX, DAILY WORD*, AUGUST 5 2017 (UNITY VILLAGE, MO: UNITY), 51.

EXEGESIS

Exegesis, the first syllable of which is ex, is the interpretation of the text within its own context. It brings you into the hermeneutical circle of a dynamic relationship with the content of Scripture. It has been described as "examining a passage as carefully as possible from as many angles as possible."[53] I have defined it as follows:

> **Exegesis.** *(From the Greek, ex, meaning out of; gesthai, meaning to guide, and lead; and exegeisthai, meaning to draw out, or to explain.) It is the science of textual interpretation. It means to draw the meaning of Scripture out of Scripture, itself, by using the context and content of Scripture as a guide for the factual, ethical, and spiritual insights of the interpreter. When used in application to the Bible it includes an understanding of Bible history, culture, literature, and etymology. The specific techniques employed in the exegesis of Scripture fall under the umbrella of hermeneutics and are known as biblical criticism.*

Biblical Criticism is a key to bringing the Bible alive through the voices of the author and the text of Scripture. These living voices of the Bible are things that speak authentically to its creation and intention, helping to make its stories and teachings relevant for us today. Here is how I define biblical criticism:

> **Biblical Criticism.** *(From Greek, kritikos, meaning able to make judgments, discern, and decide. From Latin, criticus, meaning judge, critic.) A critical look at biblical writing. That is to say, an examination of biblical text that involves theological neutrality, scientific logic, and investigative study.*

---

[53] DOUGLAS STUART AS QUOTED BY RICHARD N. SOULEN AND R. KENDALL SOULEN, *HANDBOOK OF BIBLICAL CRITICISM, THIRD EDITION, REVISED AND EXPANDED* (LOUISVILLE, KY: JOHN KNOX PRESS, 2001), 57.

From the efforts of the great theological and philosophical minds that contributed to hermeneutics, many critical approaches have evolved. For the sake of our work in this book I have selected four of them that stand out as the foundational core of understanding the Bible in its historical, cultural and literary context. Here are some terms with their descriptions.

Historical Criticism: This examines the political, cultural, social, and religious conditions of the time in which the scripture was written and/or read.

Textual Criticism: This examines the phrasing and etymology (root meaning of words), and compares texts with other texts to draw out the original meaning of the Scripture.

Form Criticism: This examines the style and structure of Scripture to more accurately determine the time and environment in which it was written.

Source Criticism: This uses Historical, Textual, and Form Criticisms to determine the authorship, or source, of Scripture.

These criticisms are not about putting the Bible down or making it wrong in any way. Rather, they are part of exegesis, the most relied upon interpretive process in hermeneutics. Now, let's apply a little bit of exegesis to our challenging quotes.

Here, again, is the first of those quotes: *"And the sun stood still and the moon stopped, until the nation took vengeance on their enemies (Joshua 10:13)."* Etymology, or word derivation, of textual criticism tells us that "Joshua", the namesake of the book from which this quote came, is the Hebrew version of the name "Jesus," which means *"God is Salvation."* Historical criticism reveals this verse to be part of an idealistic account of the conquering of the Promised Land, implying that God

134

assures a place for His people. Form criticism conveys that this account is based on an old folk song that survived for generations through oral tradition, probably because of the miraculous victory it conveyed. From this you can see a message that assures God's protection and the overcoming of difficulties, but you may be left with a sense of uneasiness at the violent way in which this assurance was gained.

This is where the wisdom of the heartmind comes into play. With the work of exegesis and biblical criticism, you clean the old concepts that no longer fit out of your T-shirt drawer to try on a fresh understanding. In so doing, you move from the first to the second tier of knowing where you acquire new concepts. This is where the heartmind can do its work and take you to the third tier where your God-centered intuitive voice leads the way.

If you were to take a deep breath with your mental focus on the heart at the center of your being, and inquire in yourself, "How can I overcome obstacles to find my right place in the world?" - what would be the answer? For me, an answer comes from the realm beyond thought. Intuitively I know that the way to find my right place is to serve God through what I do in life. As I live a life seeking ways to uplift and inspire myself and others, I do not have to be concerned about those who would try to stop me, or the time I have in which to do these things. Time will be on my side and obstacles will fall away, just as the sun and the moon stopped for Joshua. My Promised Land of wholeness and salvation will be found in the joy I have for the life I live.

With this interpretation, the story of Joshua and the old song of the sun standing still become metaphors for living a fulfilling life. This approach of using knowledge gained from exegesis, and taking it to the heart, anchors the mind in the heart, and awakens the insight of the heartmind. This takes us beyond the literal meaning of the scriptural words where we are ready to work with metaphysics.

METAPHYSICS

The metaphysical approach expands on the metaphors of exegesis. It renders insight into the psyche, or consciousness, of the individual to discern the universal truths of life and existence. This brings us to two more definitions:

> **Metaphysics.** *(From the Greek, meta, meaning after, beyond, pursuit of deeper meaning, and development; physica, meaning physical matter; and metaphysica, meaning after physics; beyond the physical; underlying the physical.) It is an ancient philosophy that refers to the underlying reality of the physical world. It is the study of the Truth of Being, or the living reality and spiritual essence of all that exists.*

> *"Metaphysics is the science of discerning spiritual ideas and their legitimate expression." (Paul Barrett)54*

> **Metaphysical Interpretation.** *The application of metaphysics to the process of scriptural interpretation with the intention of knowing the Truth or discovering the spiritual reality that lies beyond the literal word. It includes understanding the things, characters, and stories of biblical scripture as metaphors for the qualities, states of mind, thoughts, and feelings within one's own consciousness.*

> *"The Bible is humanity's textbook of self-discovery. Metaphysical Interpretation is the means by which the discovery is made." (Paul Barrett)55*

---

54 PAUL C. BARRETT, *INTRODUCTION TO BIBLE INTERPRETATION*, READ BY DR. PAUL C. BARRETT, FAIRFAX, VA: DIVINE LIFE MISSION, 1986, TAPE 1, SIDE A.

55 IBID.

Metaphysical interpretation conveys that Joshua is part of my inner being. He is the idea of salvation. Salvation for me is the experience of peace and fulfillment that comes from knowing I am whole and complete. In other words, I have all that I need right here and right now, and no obstacle can stand in my way. From this awareness, I move forward to do what is mine to do with the assurance that I will have the time to do it. I can move through, or even beyond, the fight and the struggle to settle into the Promised Land of peace and fulfillment, knowing that my life is a contribution to those in my world.

As for the verse from 1 Timothy advising slaves to honor their masters – let's revisit the Scripture. *"Let all who are under the yoke of slavery regard their masters as worthy of all honor, so that the name of God and the teaching may not be blasphemed (1 Timothy 6:1)."* Talk about obstacles! Talk about struggle! I must admit that when I selected this verse, I was challenging myself to "practice what I preach" in that any passage or verse in the Bible can be interpreted, or understood, in a way that inspires us and calls us to be a positive contribution in our world. How is that possible, when I know that slavery is an abomination? How can Truth be found in such a teaching as was given to Timothy, or in any passages of the Bible in which slavery seems acceptable? Again, I let exegesis lead me into a deeper metaphysical understanding.

Historical criticism tells me that Timothy was the leader of a congregation who was being instructed on how to guide those who were in his community through this letter. Etymology reveals that his name means "honored of God," or "honoring God". Source criticism tells me that the style of the Greek language, and the social conditions in the church at the time, indicated a letter that was likely written later than Paul, the author to whom it is attributed. Writing in tones that were more conservative than Paul's, the author emphasized the importance of holding to a conservative social ethic that put Christianity into a more respectable light in a Roman society of which slavery was an integral part.

In the process of interpretation, I can interact with what the text is saying about itself. Then, compare and contrast my own ideas and values with those of the author. In so doing, I see that being honorable is a good thing, but slavery is not. The wisdom of the heartmind tells me that I can find honor, not in the suppression of freedom and equality, but in the advancement of it. Metaphysics takes this a little further.

Metaphysically speaking, Timothy, the slaves, the masters, and even God, all reside within me as part of my consciousness. Timothy represents my desire to act in honorable ways. Masters are the dominant beliefs through which I interact with the world. Slaves are the ways of thinking and feeling that support those beliefs. When my thoughts and feelings (slaves) support the beliefs (masters) that value freedom and equality, I do not rail against, or blaspheme, the Spirit of God in me. Rather, I find honor (Timothy) in my relationship with God as I commit to freedom and equality for all people.

These interpretations may, or may not, reflect insights with which you have been familiar. Either way is okay. You must explore your own values and develop your own insights in the process of interpretation to have the kind of freedom to which I was referring. If it takes some practice, that is good. I am still practicing. While I have been doing eisegesis for my entire reading life, and exegesis and metaphysics most of my reading life, I still get a thrill out of the revelation of discovering new meaning from Scripture and how it fits into the context of my life today.

RESOURCES

STUDY

This book gives you a general overview of the development of spiritual ideas and literature, such as the Logos and the biblical canon, and the growth of hermeneutics, but if you want to go deeply into biblical study and understanding, and you have not done so already, I recommend finding a ministerial, philosophical, or theological path of education through which you can do this. If you simply want to play with eisegesis, exegesis and metaphysics, that is also good. You can isolate Scripture to your heart's content, or you can become a hermeneutical exegete, or an exegetical hermeneut – whichever you prefer. Or – you could just be a reader, interpreter, and practitioner of the truths you find in Scripture. If you have not worked with biblical interpretation, however, where do you begin?

To aid you in your interpretation there are resources available, both in book form and online. In his book entitled, *Wisdom for a Lifetime, How to Get the Bible Off the Shelf and Into Your Hands*, my colleague and friend, Unity minister Alden Studebaker dedicates two chapters to collecting resources for your interpretive work with the Bible. He calls it the "Bible Study Tool Kit."[56] He expounds on several types of biblical resources that include each of the following: Study Bible, Bible Concordance, Bible Dictionary, Bible

---

[56] ALDEN STUDEBAKER, *WISDOM FOR A LIFETIME, HOW TO GET THE BIBLE OFF THE SHELF AND INTO YOUR HANDS* (UNITY VILLAGE, MO: UNITY, 1998), 101.

Commentary, and Bible Atlas. He also mentions Bible Handbooks of which his book, and this book, are two examples. For now, here is information for the first five types of resources:

Study Bible – A Study Bible is a Bible with information that puts the biblical text into a scholastic context for the greater understanding and knowledge of the reader/interpreter. My recommendation is to select a study Bible with scholastic annotations, commentaries, maps, chronologies, glossaries and/or other things that you find helpful. Be sure it is translated into your own language from the original Hebrew, Greek and Aramaic texts. My current Bible of choice is The New Interpreter's Study Bible, New Revised Standard Version with the Apocrypha (Abingdon). Another good one that I have used is The New Oxford Annotated Bible, New Revised Standard Version with the Apocrypha: an Ecumenical Bible (Oxford University). I have both of these Bibles on my shelf.

I also have two other study Bibles that are helpful to my exegetical work. The Jewish Study Bible, Second Edition, Tanakh Translation (Oxford University). It is a scholastic annotation and study of the Hebrew Bible, or Tanakh. The other is The Jewish Annotated New Testament, New Revised Standard Version (Oxford University). While a lot of the same information is found in all of these resources, The Jewish Study Bible is most useful in presenting the Bible from the understanding and wisdom of Judaism.

Bible Concordance - In his book Alden wrote, "...a Bible concordance is a biblical word book. It is a book of words from the Bible organized with specific scriptural references."[57] My

---

[57] STUDEBAKER, P. 102.

personal and longtime favorite is the James Strong, Strong's Exhaustive Concordance of the Bible (Hendrickson). It has a Hebrew/Greek lexicon, or Dictionary, that is very useful in finding Hebrew and Greek root meanings to biblical words. It is also online. The online version gives you options of English translations when looking up words. This comes in handy since James Strong long ago did this work from an old King James translation of the Bible. I use both the book and the online version in defining my Hebrew and Greek terms.

Bible Dictionary - Bible dictionaries help you understand words, names, places, and their detailed meanings. Two good one volume dictionaries are HarperCollins Bible Dictionary, Revised and Updated (HarperOne); and Eerdman's Dictionary of the Bible (Eerdman). If you are really serious, a good five-volume dictionary is The New Interpreter's Dictionary of the Bible (Abingdon). The only Bible Dictionary ever done for metaphysical work is the Metaphysical Bible Dictionary (Unity), but you would need to update the definitions with your own interpretive work. This is encouraged in the Preface of this dictionary.

Bible Commentary – Studebaker says, "Where study notes end, commentaries begin. These books provide in-depth, scholastically sound information about what's really going on in each verse, chapter, and book of the Bible." He also cautions that they are, "...subject to the interpretive bent of their authors." In other words, a Bible Commentary is a collection of notes that provides historical, cultural, or theological meaning for scriptural passages. My current commentary of choice is The New Interpreter's Bible One Volume Commentary. It also comes in ten and twelve volume sets.

Bible Atlas – A Bible Atlas is a set of maps illustrating the geology of biblical lands and times. This is useful for locating cities, regions, and geological features. Most Bible Atlases are done in the chronological order of the history that is in the Bible. I don't know about you, but I always like to know where I am whether I am home, travelling, or mentally locating myself in a Bible story or passage, and I can't seem to find the ancient Bible lands on my smart phone's GPS. Two good atlases are Adrian Curtis', Oxford Bible Atlas, Fourth Edition (Oxford University); and Berry Beitzel's, The New Moody Bible Atlas (Moody).

Bibles and Bible Resources also come in electronic versions for Kindle and/or Nook. Some are even online, like the *Strong's Concordance*. There is also Bible Software and online resources such as *Olive Tree*, or *Logos* (hmm – that word seems familiar). You can check online for any of the resources mentioned, or types of resources that are listed. Look around, use your wisdom and intuitive insight, and choose what is best for you.

Of course, collecting these resources would take a significant budget if you did it all at once. For our work a good ecumenical Study Bible with detailed annotations, like the ones previously mentioned, will do. You can also use the Greek and Hebrew Dictionary from the *Strong's Concordance* online. These are the two types of resources I use most of the time, even though I make use of the other resources as well when my work seems to call for it. An example of this can be seen in taking another look at the Psalms verse from the *Daily Word* magazine that I referred to earlier in this chapter, *"Return, O my soul, to your rest, for the Lord has dealt bountifully with you (Psalm 116:7)."*

Rest

In revisiting this verse which was used to support the idea of relaxation in the *Daily Word*, I turned to *The New Interpreter's Bible One Volume Commentary*. It had a simple insight into this Psalm in which this verse is found. It said, "This is a song of thankful praise sung following a divine deliverance from a personal crisis."[58] According to *The New Interpreter's Study Bible*, having "first-hand experience" of God's deliverance is enough reason to rest in God. This likely came from surviving a serious illness.

In further research, the verse includes the following words: *rest, soul,* and *dealt bountifully.* I have looked these up online in *Strong's Concordance with Hebrew and Greek Lexicon.* The Hebrew word, *monowach,* can refer to a *place of rest,* as well as to *rest,* itself. The word for *soul, nefesh,* which we also see in the creation of Adam in Genesis 2:7, refers to that which was brought to life through the breath of God. That God *dealt bountifully,* is a singular verb in Hebrew, *gamal.* It means that God did good for the one whose prayer of thanksgiving implies his confidence in God's presence in his life. Now let's look once again at the verse itself, *"Return, O my soul, to your rest, for the Lord has dealt bountifully with you (Psalm 116:7)."*

Exegetically, the Psalmist is telling me that I can rest in the remembrance of the good God has done for me – a simple, sweet, message that works well with eisegesis also. It reminds me that I don't have to be anxious in any pursuit of good or truth in my life. Rather, I can find peace in remembering who

---

[58] *The New Interpreter's Bible One Volume Commentary,* Beverly Roberts Gaventa and David Petersen, Editors (Nashville, TN: Abingdon Press), 342.

God is for me. Metaphysically, I can also find peace in remembering who I am in God. The place of rest is the center of my being where I experience the breath of the living God within me and know myself as an expression of God. As I breathe into life from this place of awareness, I can rest assured that all things are working together for my greatest good.

Working with hermeneutics through eisegesis, exegesis, and metaphysics can make the language of God in the Bible come alive for you as it does for me. Working with metagetics transforms you into becoming the living language of God in your world. How that happens is the subject of the next chapter.

SUMMARY

- Through personal insight, historical and literary understanding, and symbolic connection to personal experience, the Bible comes alive.
- The work of metagetics has evolved from multiple approaches to hermeneutics that can be summed up in three words: *eisegesis, exegesis,* and *metaphysics.*
- Eisegesis is the interpretation of Scripture done from the perspective of personal belief and concept. It means to put meaning into Scripture.
- Exegesis is known as the science of textual interpretation. It draws the meaning of the text from the text through biblical criticism.
- Biblical Criticism is an examination of the biblical text that involves theological neutrality, scientific logic, and investigative study. It has many forms, four of which are as follows:
  o Historical Criticism examines the political, cultural, social, and religious conditions of the time in which the scripture was written and/or read.
  o Textual Criticism examines the phrasing and etymology (root meaning of words) and compares texts with other texts to draw out the original meaning of the Scripture.
  o Form Criticism examines the style and structure of Scripture to more accurately determine the time and environment in which it was written.
  o Source Criticism uses Historical, Textual, and Form Criticisms to determine the authorship, or source, of Scripture.
- The metaphysical approach expands on the metaphors of exegesis. It renders insight into the psyche, or consciousness, of the individual to discern the universal truths of life and existence.
- You have the freedom to explore your own values and develop your own insights in the process of interpretation.

- To aid you in your interpretation there are resources available, both in book form and online. They are as follows:
- A Study Bible is a Bible with information that puts the biblical text into a scholastic context.
- A Bible Concordance is a list of words from the Bible organized according to their scriptural context.
- A Bible Dictionary is a dictionary of words, names, places, and their detailed meanings.
- A Bible Atlas is a set of maps illustrating the geology of biblical lands and times.

INQUIRY

1. What form of biblical interpretation most appeals to you? Why?

2. Why is it important to understand the text of the Bible within its own context?

3. Why is the heartmind an important part of discovering what the Bible is revealing to you?

4. What does metaphysical insight into Scripture provide?

5. How is it that any passage, verse, or teaching from the Bible can be used for inspiration and positive contribution?

CHAPTER 7: LIVING

"...then the Lord, God, formed man from the dust of the ground, and breathed into his nostrils the breath of life; and man became a living being (Genesis 2:7)."

MOUNTAINTOP

For years I had a recurring dream. I was hiking a trail up a mountain, but never making it to the top. Either the air got too thin beyond the tree line and I would become too exhausted to move any farther; or weather would move in and I would have to turn around; or I would get distracted by a comfortable place along the way and never continue my journey. Finally, one night in my dream I made it all the way. I was thrilled! I knew I would find something at the top of the mountain that would give me wisdom to last the rest of my life. I did!

Every mountaintop, hilltop, clifftop, or airplane view that I have experienced, in a dream or in real life, has opened my heart and expanded my mind. This dream was no different. Looking out across the mountains to the valleys and plains below left me with a sense of awe at the vastness of Creation, and a realization that my big life with its significant challenges isn't so big and significant after all. Rather it is an integral part of a whole web of life from which I can draw energy and insight, and to which I can contribute my special gifts. Yet, this was not the culmination of the wisdom received at the top of the mountain in my dream. That came when I found the very thing that makes the mountaintop experience real in my life. It was the beginning of a trail that went down the other side of the mountain.

To become the living language of God in the world, we must climb the three tiers of knowing. We must move through the eisegesis of perceiving things from what we already know, embrace the new ideas and insights conceived through exegesis and metaphysics, and lift ourselves above the tree line of thoughts into the clearing of pure being where the inception of Truth can be received. Then, we must find the trail back down the mountain to where we can make the Truth come alive through the things around us. Even more than this, we can return from the mountaintop to be the living Truth, the living language of God, in our world.

BEING

ELEMENTS

In this book, we have addressed what Truth is, and what the language of God is, but what is living? If someone asked you, "What do you do for a living?" What would be your answer? Would you tell them about your career, vocation, or job? Would you say you are a student, or retired? Perhaps you don't even need to make a living, and that would be your answer. Most likely you would equate the question with, "How do you create enough financial income that supports you in sustaining your way of life?"

While finances are a big part of everyday life, and it is important to be a good steward of these resources, they are not living itself. You are either living, or not. Here is a test. Take a breath. If you can do this – you are living. You do not need to make it happen. In fact, you cannot keep it from happening. If you should stop breathing for any length of

150

time, you are no longer living, at least not in the physical sense of the word.

For our purposes, I am going to ask a different kind of question. Rather than, "What do you do for a living," you can reflect on the question, "What does living do for you?" To respond to this, let's look further on what *living* is through an examination of the elements of *being*. These elements are Spirit, soul, body, and world, and they show up in the two creation stories of Genesis. What do these stories tell us about living? I will give you a hint. It has to do with breathing.

SPIRIT

The first element of being, or existence, is *Spirit*. *Spirit* with a capital "S" refers to God in expression. As Spirit, God is moving into existence, or creating life. This is seen in the two creation stories in Genesis. These two stories are allegories that reveal how God's creative activity works in the world, and in us. In other words, the Truth they reveal is found, not so much in literal understanding, as it is found in the historical, metaphorical, and metaphysical meaning of their main elements. For this chapter, we will examine initial verses in these stories through which the divine act of creation is taking place.

The first creation story in Genesis 1 was written four hundred years later than the second story in chapter 2. Source criticism tells us that it is the work of the "P", or *Priestly* writers. *Priestly* is a large umbrella term for writers who edited and added to the Torah during the 6th century BCE. Their contributions came after the Exile in which the people of the kingdom of Judah were taken into captivity in Babylon. Having been in Exile, they were influenced by the myths of the Ancient Near East. Being priests, the writers and

151

redactors were concerned with ritualistic order and details in their writings. They transformed the pattern of the Babylonian story of *Enuma Elish*, in which creation occurred through six generations of gods, to make the story about one God who did all of the creating in six days and rested on the seventh. That one God was *Elohim*.

Elohim is a descriptive term that translates from Hebrew as "gods." Yet, the Elohim God of the Hebrews was seen by ancient Hebrews as one God that encompassed all gods. In *The Concise Oxford Dictionary of World Religions*, the plural form of Elohim as a singular God is described. It says, "Its plural form may once have been literal – 'mighty ones' – but it became subsumed in the accumulating Jewish sense that if God is indeed *God*, then there can only be what God is: One, and not a plurality of gods."[59]

Elohim is the supreme Creator who is both responsible for, and transcendent over, Creation. In this transcendence Elohim encompasses all of existence and its activity. Creation began with the ex-pression, or pressing out, of the breath, or wind from Elohim God. Before that, there was nothing. After that, Creation came into being through the power of the word. *"In the beginning when God created the heavens and the earth, the earth was a formless void and darkness covered the face of the deep, while a wind from God swept over the face of the waters. Then God said, 'Let there be light,': and there was light (Genesis 1:1-3)."*

In the King James translation of the Bible the wind from God is called Spirit." This is because the Hebrew term for both "wind" and "Spirit" is *ruwach*, which means "wind," "breath,"

---

[59] *THE CONCISE OXFORD DICTIONARY OF WORLD RELIGIONS* (NEW YORK: OXFORD UNIVERSITY, 2000), 176.

"mind," and "spirit."[60] *And the Spirit of God moved upon the face of the waters. And God said, 'Let there be light,' and there was light. (Genesis 1:2-3)."* With the breath of *ruwach,* the power of the word is activated, and that which is supreme and transcendent moves into mundane existence. What is known and experienced on the mountaintop comes down the trail to bring the light of greater understanding to life.

You may also notice in its definition that *ruwach* is not only "wind," "breath," and "spirit." It is mind. This implies that the activity of the mind in you is the creative activity of the Spirit in you. It translates transcendent insight into everyday language. Yet, when mind activity is of the intellect alone, the transcendent cannot be known. It behooves you, therefore, to align the intellectual activity of the mind with Spirit as it lives and breathes in and through you. This is done through *Love, Prayer,* and *Contemplation.* These are the three interpretive principles that will be addressed and experienced in the next chapter on *The Spirit of the Word.* For now, let us look at where else breath, or Spirit, takes us.

In the second chapter of Genesis, living is equated with the breath, *"...then the Lord, God, formed man from the dust of the ground, and breathed into his nostrils the breath of life; and man became a living being (Genesis 2:7)."* The term for God here is, "the Lord." This is an English translation of the Tetragrammaton. The word, *Tetragrammaton* is based on the Greek syllable *tetra,* meaning *four,* and *grammat,* meaning *letters.* It simply means *four letters.* It is a reference to the name of God, transliterated from Hebrew as *YHWH.*

---

[60] "RUWACH," *BLUE LETTER BIBLE,* ACCESSED AUGUST 20, 2017, HTTPS://WWW.BLUELETTERBIBLE.ORG/LANG/LEXICON/LEXICON.CFM?STRONGS=H7307&T=KJV.

YHWH is an idea of God from the *Jahwist*, named after the term from the tetragrammaton. The Jahwist is otherwise known as the "J" writer, using "J" for the "Y" sound from the German spelling of the name. *Jahwist* is the name for contributing writers of the Torah who were from Judah. They started writing in the 10th century BCE before the kingdom of Israel divided into the two kingdoms of Judah and Israel, and their writing continued into the time of the divided kingdom. Their stories were stories that had been passed down from generation to generation through oral tradition. They were stories that shared history as a story of God in relationship with His people.

This God of the Jahwist was not a transcendent God, but a God who was immanently, and intimately, involved with the life on Earth. He was a God of being and action who walked and talked with His people, often showing up in some phenomenal, or manifest, form. YHWH has also been known as "the Lord," "Yahweh," and the widely used name of "Jehovah," which is an amalgam of the tetragrammaton and the title Adonai (meaning "the Lord").

While Genesis 2:7 is the first appearance of "the Lord," or *YHWH*, in the Bible, the most well-known revelation of this name, however, is when Moses encounters God at the burning bush.

> *"But Moses said to God, 'If I come to the Israelites and say to them, "The God of your ancestors has sent me to you," and they ask me, "What is his name?" what shall I say to them? God said to Moses, 'I Am Who I Am.' He said further, 'Thus you shall say to the Israelites, "I Am has sent me to you."' God also said to Moses, 'Thus you shall say to the Israelites, "The Lord, the God of your ancestors, the God of Abraham, the God of Isaac, and the God of Jacob, has sent me to you." This is my name forever, and this my title for all generations.' (Exodus 3:13-15)."*

YHWH is seen here as the unpronounceable name of God. In the annotations on these verses found in *The Jewish Study Bible, Second Edition, Tanakh Translation,* we read the following:

> *"The exact pronunciation is uncertain since the vowels were forgotten in ancient times; hence scholars often refer to the name only by its consonants YHVH or, more precisely, YHWH. It was probably pronounced Yahweh. God's answer in v. 14, Ehyeh-Asher-Ehyeh, (I Am Who I Am) is actually an explanation of its meaning, probably best translated as 'I Will Be What I Will Be,' meaning 'My nature will become evident from My actions.'*
>
> *...Grammatically YHWH means, 'He who is,' or 'He who will be,' or, perhaps most likely, 'He who causes things to be.'"*[61]

YHWH is a verb in which both present and future tense exist. The present tense is about the *Being* of God. The future tense is about the *doing* of God through which the Being is known. In Exodus, the Lord God was known to be the God of the ancestors through his act of freeing his people from slavery in Egypt. As YHWH, God is both "I Am" and "I Will," - existence and motion. God both dwells on the mountaintop and moves in the fields and valleys of life. In fact, God both dwells and is the act of dwelling. Even the word, being, is an action for "to be." How, then, does God move into action? How does the "Be" become the "Be-ing?"

Remember when I said to take a breath? Well, I invite you to do it again. This time, do it a little more slowly, and listen as it moves in and out of your body. If you listen carefully

---

[61] *THE JEWISH STUDY BIBLE,* SECOND EDITION, TANAKH TRANSLATION, ED. ADELE BERLIN AND MARC ZVI BRETTLER (NEW YORK: OXFORD UNIVERSITY, 2014), 103.

enough, you can hear the name of God in the act of breathing. Without any vocalization, but with the sound of the air moving in you can hear the syllable YH, or Yah. Then, on the exhale you can hear WH, or Weh. The more audible the breath, the more you can hear the divine name. It is especially pronounced in snoring. No kidding – just listen to someone who is snoring. The point is, the name that cannot be pronounced is in fact spoken with every breath you take. YHWH is the name of God that breathes and lives in and through you.

The Spirit of God in you is also known as the I Am, or the *yachad*. *Yachad*, which in Hebrew means "together as one", is known in Jewish mysticism as that aspect of being that is one and the same as God. One form of it is found in the Hebrew prayer called the *Shema*, which means "hear." *"Hear, O Israel, the Lord is our God, the Lord is one (Deuteronomy 6:4)."* Here, the Hebrew word for "one," is *echad*, meaning "altogether." YHWH God breathes in you through every aspect of your being, bringing them "altogether" as the one being that is you. As you breathe in conscious awareness of this, your words and actions become an expression of *yachad*, of I Am, of God in you. One way God lives in you is through three aspects of your soul. It would be good to note here that these aspects of being, using Hebrew words from Scripture, are concepts that are drawn from the *Zohar* of the large body of Jewish mystical work known as Kabbalah of which a little more will be said in Chapter 7.[62]

---

[62] SEE BIBLIOGRAPHY FOR BOOKS REFERRING TO JEWISH MYSTICISM AND KABBALAH/QABALAH.

SOUL

In verse 2:7, God breathed life into Adam and Adam became a living being. The Hebrew word for "being" is *nefesh*. *Nefesh* is Hebrew for "soul," "self," "creature" and "person". It refers to the creature in each of us, the animal nature of the soul. This nature is the basic instinct that comes from the need to survive, both as an individual and as a species. The emotions that accompany this nature can be loving and nurturing, or fearful and threatening. They can be aggressive, protective, heroic, passive, or cowering. They are quick, immediate, and often experienced physiologically – like shaky knees, or a knotted stomach, or a sudden burst of energy and strength. While some basic emotions can result in generous and heroic actions, others can slide us down a slippery slope of destructive behavior. Without guidance from the higher aspects of the soul, we have no say over what happens when. The *nefesh* part of us just keeps reacting to life from a full T-shirt drawer of pre-conceived notions and outdated perceptions.

One higher aspect of the soul that has already been introduced in this chapter is *ruwach*. From Genesis 1, *ruwach* is the breath of the Elohim God in us. It is the activity of the mind expressing through the power of the creative word. In this moment as I am writing, my mind is filled with ideas moving through my consciousness. These ideas are like "a wind from God" moving over the face of the waters, forming the words that come forth on this page. As with the supreme God, *ruwach* transcends the emotions of *nefesh*. The light of new concepts and the fun of cleaning out my mental T-shirt drawer is what keeps me going in the face of my own self-doubts. *Ruwach* engages me in the creation of this book, rather than the comforting distraction of a big bowl of ice cream in front of the television. Such creative activity of the

157

mind, while using the intellect, must also reach beyond it. Even as I am writing this book, which is thoroughly researched and based on years of study and experience, the outcome is more than what I can mentally conceive. I must awaken the third aspect of the soul known as *Neshamah*.

Neshamah is the Hebrew word for "breath" in the "breath of life." It was breathed by God into the nostrils of Adam. It is more than the movement of air in and out of the body. It is the movement of heart energy that knows its connection with Spirit and anchors the mind in this awareness. *Neshamah* brings passion and vitality to the task at hand. It is experienced when the *leba*, Hebrew for "heartmind," is fully awakened. When this happens, the mind is guided by intuitive wisdom as the heart expands in its love for life. From this place, the whole soul can be engaged in the search for Truth through *History*, *Meaning* and *Logic*. *The Soul of Truth* that works with these interpretive principles will be explored in Chapter 8. In the meantime, let's look at a part of the "living being" that brings "living" to "being" by visiting the Sistine Chapel. Using the imagination, I invite you to stand with me in this very special place.

BODY

Looking up from the midst of the crowd, it takes the eyes a moment to focus on the iconic depiction of Creation. More than 4 million people each year make this effort in what could be the world's most visited room. Amid scenes from Genesis, frescos of prophets, and images of biblical events and characters, it comes into view – the hand of God giving life to Adam. The touch of the master artist reveals the touch of the master Creator.

This was Michelangelo's idea of Genesis 2:7, but is this what the birth of humanity really looked like? Was it the touch of an actual hand from an anthropomorphic God that gave life? We have seen from Genesis 2:7 that there is nothing about God's hand in the creation of man – just nostrils. Some say that the famous panel at the center of the Sistine Chapel depicts the breath of God as a great mind bestowing intelligence upon the already living being of Adam. This is indicated by the shape of the brain seen in the surrounding space of the divine figure with its cloak and accompanying cherubims. Others have noted that "the touch" is not really a touch, but the transference of creative energy, which is of a spiritual rather than physical nature, as seen in the space between the two index fingers.

I tend to lean toward the idea that Genesis 2:7 represents more than the coming together of Spirit and dense matter. It speaks to the life-energy of which we are made that reaches beyond the touch of the fingers. In the term, "breath of life," the word for "life" is the Hebrew word, *chai*. *Chai* means "alive," and "living." It refers to green vegetation and animal life as well as the vitality, or life-energy of the human being.[63] In the Hebrew Bible, the body is not so much a vehicle to be used by Spirit for a time and then set aside at death. The creation of human being is the enlivening of earth substance into an expansive expression of life that forms the ultimate masterpiece of Creation – you. The commentary on verse 2:7 in *The Jewish Study Bible* states, "...the human being is not an amalgam of perishable body and immortal soul, but a

---

[63] "CHAY" (CHAI), *BLUE LETTER BIBLE*, ACCESSED AUGUST 21, 2017, HTTPS://WWW.BLUELETTERBIBLE.ORG/LANG/LEXICON/LEXICON.CFM?STRONGS=H2416&T=KJV

psychophysical unity who depends on God for life itself."[64] This unity of body (physical), soul (psycho) and Spirit (God) is seen in the very substance of which human being was made.

According to Genesis, you, and I, and Adam, and all of humanity, are formed from "the dust of the ground." In this part of the description of human creation, the Jahwist taps into the understanding that our bodies are made of the same elements as the earth. The Hebrew word for "man," as it is used in the biblical verse, is *adam*. *Adam* also means "human being," referring to both individual man and all of humanity.[65] This is not the only play on words found in the name, Adam. The Hebrew word for "ground" in this verse is *adamah*. *Adamah* also means "land," as in "earth." and "ground."[66] Religionists and philosophers through the ages have used this to support the idea that human beings are dirt. They were right – but look at how wonderful it is to be made of dirt!

Besides meaning "human being" and "ground," *adamah* also means "earth substance."[67] What makes up the substance of the Earth? Famed cosmologist, Carl Sagan once stated the following:

> *"Matter is much older than life. Billions of years before the sun and earth even formed, atoms were being synthesized in the*

---

[64] *THE JEWISH STUDY BIBLE*, 13.

[65] *THE NEW INTERPRETER'S STUDY BIBLE, NEW REVISED STANDARD VERSION WITH THE APOCRYPHA*, ED. WALTER J. HARRELSON (NASHVILLE, TN: ABINGDON, 2003), 9.

[66] "ADAMAH," *BLUE LETTER BIBLE*, ACCESSED AUGUST 21, 2017, HTTP://WWW.BLUELETTERBIBLE.ORG/LANG/LEXICON/LEXICON.CFM?STRONGS=H12 7&T=KJV.

[67] IBID.

insides of hot stars, and then returned to space when the stars blew themselves up. Newly formed planets were made of this stellar debris. The earth, and every living thing, are made of star stuff."[68]

Again – how wonderful it is to be made of dirt, of earth substance, of star stuff, of the atoms, chemicals and biological intricacies that physically connect us with all of Creation! So the next time someone tells you that you are a piece of dirt, you can say, "Hey – thanks – and I think you're great, too!" Well, you may or may not want to say it, but you can certainly think it. As long as you are being grateful, you can also thank your body, just for being alive! After all, your body is your connection to all of life. Another well-known cosmologist, Neil deGrasse Tyson, said, "We are all connected to each other biologically, to the Earth chemically, to the rest of the universe atomically."[69]

The body does not keep you from unity with Spirit. It is in unity with Spirit, and through Spirit, in unity with life. Being made of star stuff, it does not even stop at your skin. Remember the space between the fingers of God and Adam? Famous physician and spiritual teacher, Dr. Deepak Chopra has written:

"Your body is not separate from the body of the universe, because at quantum mechanical levels there are not well-defined edges. You are like a wiggle, a wave, a fluctuation, a convolution, a whirlpool, a localized disturbance in the larger quantum field.

---

[68] CARL SAGAN, ACCESSED SEPTEMBER 17, 2014, HTTP://WWW.YOUTUBE.COM/WATCH?V=IE9DEAX5SGW.

[69] NEIL DEGRASSE TYSON, ACCESSED SEPTEMBER 17, 2014, HTTP://WWW.YOUTUBE.COM/WATCH?V=XGK84POEYNK.

The larger quantum field – the universe – is you extended body."[70]

If the universe is your extended body, then the whole world is part of who you are, just as you are part of the whole world. What, then, is your relationship with your world?

WORLD

DOMINION

In the first chapter of Genesis, the creation of humankind is one part of the whole process of Creation, and it is done in a very special way.

"Then God said, 'Let us make humankind in our image, according to our likeness; and let them have dominion over the fish of the sea, and over the birds of the air, and over the cattle, and over all the wild animals of the earth, and over every creeping thing that creeps upon the earth' (Genesis 1:26)."

When it comes to "dominion," a large portion of humanity has had the tendency to think that it is our God-given birthright to dominate, control, exploit, and manipulate our environment and relationships. Is this, however, what "dominion" really means?

From the Hebrew root, *radah,* "dominion" means to "rule;" "dominate;" "tread down;" "subjugate;" and "scrape-out."[71] To

---

[70] DEEPAK CHOPRA, *THE SEVEN SPIRITUAL LAWS OF SUCCESS*: A PRACTICAL GUIDE TO THE FULFILLMENT OF YOUR DREAMS (SAN RAFAEL AND NOVATO, CA: AMBER-ALLEN AND NEW WORLD LIBRARY, 2003), 69.

[71] "RADAH," *BLUE LETTER BIBLE*, HTTPS://WWW.BLUELETTERBIBLE.ORG/LANG/LEXICON/LEXICON.CFM?STRONGS=H7 287&T=KJV

have dominion could then mean to exercise one's birthright to subjugate people or nature for the sake of fulfilling one's own wants and needs, including the need to prove right one's perspective on how the world should be. It is not unlike the "manifest destiny" of the European descendants who settled in the Americas and felt the need to dominate whole races of people. This is not true dominion, however, for the absolute control we seek is never a given.

History, and even the world today, is full of rebellion, revolution, and the chaos of organizational and governmental systems that collapse in on themselves. One of the greatest and most well-organized empires in history, and one of the most dominating powers on earth, was the Roman Empire. Yet, while the genius of Rome, and its pertinent structures, still influence our world today, the empire itself has long since passed into history along with the preceding empires of Greece, Egypt, Persia, and many others that rose to power, only to fall at some point in time to the chaotic forces of human evolution.

One great lesson of history is that humankind cannot have absolute dominion and control over the people and things of the world – and thank God for this. For it is out of the chaos, dissolution, and even death of what has gone before, that new systems and ways of living are given birth. This is called evolution, and it is the same for individuals as it is for world governments. In fact, many people do not seek global domination, they simply want to dominate the situations and circumstances of their own lives. They think that dominion in life means controlling life so that it is for them what they think it should be. Yet, show me the person who has complete and absolute control over his or her life, who has the skill to make life go exactly as he or she wants it to go from one moment to the next, and I will show you someone who is in need of some authentic self-reflection.

Countless souls have tried to have such mastery, only to find continued emptiness and longing for something more, or frustration and disappointment at falling short of some made up standard of excellence or perfection. As human beings, we have often found ourselves dominated by our own emotional need to be in control of our own lives, or avoid the control and domination of others, with anger and resentment as the result. In fact, in the futile search for absolute dominion, violence becomes the desperate act of those who have no other means of control, resulting in war, brutalization, murder, and even suicide. Is this what the promise of dominion really brings?

Let's look this time at the first part of the verse from the Genesis passage. We read, *"Then God said, 'Let us make humankind in our image, according to our likeness; and let them have dominion...".* In my Bible classes, one of the most frequent questions I have been asked about this verse is, "Who is *us?*" Why does God say, "Let *us* make humankind in *our* image and after *our* likeness?" Scholars believe that the word *us* could be a reference to a heavenly court of beings who share the cosmic realm with God. In *The New Oxford Annotated Bible*, we find this commentary:

> *"The plural us, our probably refers to the divine beings who compose God's heavenly court. Image, likeness is often interpreted to be a spiritual likeness between God and humanity. Another view is that this text builds on ancient concepts of the king physically resembling the god and thus bearing a bodily stamp of his authority to rule. Here this idea is democratized, as*

all of humanity appears godlike. This appearance equips humans for godlike rule over the fish, birds, and animals."[72]

Just as God rules over the heavens and the heavenly court, he made his image and likeness to rule over the earth and the creatures within it. Yet, this kind of rule is not the rule of the human ego that sees the world and Creation as something to fear, conquer, and dominate. It is the "god-like" rule that sees the world the way God sees it as described a little later in the same Creation story. *God saw everything that he had made, and indeed, it was very good (Genesis 1:31)."* When we see the world as already being "good" we no longer feel the need to fix it and make it work our way, or to fight or conquer it for fear of what it might do to us.

Regarding the dominion given to humankind in the first chapter of Genesis, *The Jewish Study Bible* says, "Some have seen in that commission a license for ecological irresponsibility. Elsewhere, however, the Tanakh presents humanity not as the owner of nature but as its steward, strictly accountable to the true Owner."[73] Dominion coming from such a state of mind is not a dominion of absolute control, but one of spiritually motivated stewardship and responsibility for the world and those in it. Our practice of subjugation would then be directed at subjugating our own tendencies to let the conditions of our world be an excuse for not being a responsible steward within it. Thus, the dominion in life is found in the inner mastery that gives us the clarity of vision to see the world as good and to serve those in it.

---

[72] *THE NEW OXFORD ANNOTATED BIBLE*, THIRD EDITION, NEW REVISED STANDARD VERSION, ED. MICHAEL D. COOGAN (NEW YORK: OXFORD UNIVERSITY PRESS, 2001), 12.

[73] THE JEWISH STUDY BIBLE, 12.

CONNECTING

To be connected with all of life is to be, not just a living being, but a living doing. It is to live as a contribution to our world. How we can do this is discovered in *The Body of Life* in Chapter 9. This chapter approaches the body as being in perfect unity with Spirit, soul, and world as we complete our transformational journey through the metagetical experience. When we look at the *Message* drawn from Scripture, the *Movement* of making it real in our lives, and the *Mastery* of spiritual practice and continued contribution, the principles of Part IV, entitled *Metagetics*, come alive and we become the living language of God for humanity and all of life.

Now, here again are the questions with which we began this chapter. What is living? What does living do for me?

When Spirit (Elohim/YHWH), in its perfect unity with the individual (*yachad*), breathes in and through physical body (adamah), the soul (nefesh, ruwach, neshama) is awakened, and a connection is made with all of life (chai) through the dominion (radah) of stewardship. Living, then, is the natural outcome of God breathing, or expressing, in, through, and as us. What living does for us is offer us the opportunity to know the ecstatic and fulfilling bliss of what it means to be alive right here, and right now. What we can do, not so much *for a* living, but *for* living, is to be wise stewards of the rich gifts of life in and all around us.

SUMMARY

To look at what *living* is, we examine the elements of *being*. These elements show up in the two creation stories of Genesis as Spirit, soul, body, and world.

Spirit

- The first creation story in Genesis 1 was written four hundred years later than the second story in chapter 2 by the "P", or *Priestly* writers. It depicts God as *Elohim* and transcendent over all of Creation.
- From Genesis 1, *ruwach* is the breath of the *Elohim* God in us. It is the activity of the mind expressing through the power of the creative word.
- *Yahweh*, the God of the Jahwist writers of the second Creation story of Genesis 2 was immanently and intimately involved with His Creation and His people.
- As *Yahweh*, or YHWH, God is both "I Am" and "I Will," - existence and motion. The present tense is about the *Being* of God. The future tense is about the *doing* of God through which the Being is known.
- The Spirit of God, or I Am, in you is *yachad*. *Yachad* means "together as one". It is known in Jewish mysticism as that aspect of being that is one and the same as God.

Soul

- From Genesis 1:2, *ruwach* is the breath of the *Elohim* God in us. It is the activity of the mind expressing through the power of the creative word.
- From Genesis 2:7, *neshamah* is the Hebrew word for "breath" in the "breath of life." It is more than the movement of air in the body. It refers to both the movement of the heart energy that knows its connection with Spirit and anchors the mind in this awareness.
- The movement of *neshamah* is the awakening of the heartmind, known in Hebrew as *leba*.

167

- The Hebrew word for individual "living being" is *nefesh*. It refers to the creature in each of us, the animal nature of the soul.

Body

- The Hebrew word for "man" is *adamah*, which is also a reference to earth substance, or the physical substance of the body.
- In the term, "breath of life," the word for "life" is the Hebrew word, *chai*, which means "alive," and "living." It refers to the energy of life within all manifest forms.
- Through *chai*, the body is in unity with Spirit, and through Spirit, in unity with all of life.

World

- In Genesis 1, *radah* is the Hebrew word for "dominion". To have dominion is to be like God and to see the world, and everything in it, as good, and as your own extended body.
- Dominion coming from such a state of mind is not a dominion of absolute control, but one of spiritually motivated stewardship and responsibility for the world and those in it.
- When Spirit (*Elohim/YHWH*), in its perfect unity with the individual (*yachad*), breathes in and through the body (*adamah*), the soul (*ruwach, neshama, nefesh*) is awakened, and a connection is made with all of life (*chai*) through the dominion (*radah*) of wise stewardship in the world.
- Living, then, is the natural outcome of God breathing, or expressing, in, through, and as us.

INQUIRY

1. How do you experience the Spirit of God…
   - In you?
   - In your life?
   - In your world?

2. When is it easiest to know yourself as a living expression of God? When is most difficult?

3. What can you do in the difficult times to remind yourself who you really are?

UNIT TWO: METAGETICS AND THE BIBLE

PART V: THE SPIRIT OF THE WORD

CHAPTER 8: LOVE

"Let love be genuine; hate what is evil, hold fast to what is good; love one another with mutual affection; outdo one another in showing honor (Romans 12:9-10)."

PROLOGUE

I have had a life-long relationship with the Bible that has grown and evolved over time. Such a relationship never stays the same. As a little girl, I thought of the Bible as a book for coloring and scribbling. Later, I came to know some of its stories and related to it like a good story book. I watched old Bible movies and made Bible characters and animals out of pipe cleaner and construction paper in Sunday School. I especially liked the story of all those animals on Noah's Ark. I imagined myself on the Ark in charge of feeding and taking care of the animals.

Then, one day when I was 11 years old, I committed myself to read the entire Bible. I got one of those Bible's with the recommended reading for each day for a year and plunged into Scripture. The more I read, the more confused I became. I noticed the Bible had some parts that were not so nice. People did bad things to other people. God did bad things to people. In the Old Testament, if you did not obey God – watch out! In the New Testament, if you rejected or distorted the good news of salvation through Jesus Christ – watch out! This did not make sense to me. My God loved everybody – even the animals!

My grandmother, who was a minister, taught me that Jesus came, not to condemn those who did not believe in him, but to love unconditionally and to teach us how to do the same. My father, who was also a Unity minister, taught that we needed to look through the written word to its spirit. Thus, as a young pre-teen I began to learn how to interpret the Bible metaphysically. I did this through my teen and adult life, starting with one resource.

STUDY

SPRINGBOARD

The *Metaphysical Bible Dictionary*, also known as the *MBD*, was written by a team of researchers and writers lead by the co-founder of the Unity movement, Charles Fillmore, and was first published in 1931. It was a good guide. It had an early form of exegetical work as it defined each of the biblical names that were listed. It first gave the Hebrew or Greek meaning of the name. Then it put the person, place, or thing being addressed in its biblical context, telling the story or relating the passage in which it was found. While many of its metaphysical interpretations are still useful for people today, many others may seem outdated to the modern-day Bible student. Most people I have known who have worked with it, used it as a springboard for discovering their own metaphysical understanding. This was the book's exact intention. In its *Preface* is written the following:

"In presenting these methods of interpretation we have endeavored to give with each one sufficient explanation to enable the student to get an idea as to how and why we arrive at given metaphysical conclusions. By reasoning along the same lines the student can develop the inner interpretation of the Scriptures for

176

himself. Our real aim is to assist in leading the student into the inner or spiritual interpretation of the Bible, that he may apply it in the very best and most practical way in his own life."[74]

By the time of my early twenties, I had studied the Bible in college and was teaching its metaphysical interpretation, otherwise known in the *MBD* as "...the inner, or spiritual, interpretation of the Scriptures." The "inner interpretation" of the Bible is what my father, Dr. Paul Barrett, called "esoteric", or the search for the "hidden meaning". It is the quest for the Spirit of the Word.

The apostle, Paul, wrote, *"...our competence is from God, who has made us competent to be ministers of a new covenant, not of letter but of spirit; for the letter kills, but the Spirit gives life. (2 Corinthians 3:5b-6)."* In interpreting this scripture, my father, Dr. Paul Barrett, said the following:

Spiritual things must be spiritually discerned. ... The mind must move through the letter of the word, small "w," to the inner spirit of the word, large "W," representing the Truth of God. If we are bound in the letter of the word, we are caught up in the guilt feelings of sin that lead to punishment, and to death, and ultimately to hell. That's where the letter leads. But the spirit of the word gives us life. It gives us hope. It shows us we are loved by God. It leads us to recognize our spiritual divinity, and not lock us into an, "I am a miserable sinner" syndrome. The spirit of the word shows us how to master the throws of death, how to build our heaven right here on earth, how to live in the here and now of heaven – and not the hereafter. You have to understand,

---

[74] PREFACE, METAPHYSICAL BIBLE DICTIONARY, ED. CHARLES FILLMORE (UNITY VILLAGE: UNITY, 2011), 8.

though, that the Bible is an esoteric book. It is not meant to be taken literally. Esoteric means, "with hidden meaning".[75]

My father believed that the Logos was the invisible Word of God behind the visible word of Scripture. His way of extracting this text from the words on the biblical page involved seven principles. They are as follows: "Love of the Bible; Knowledge of Bible History; Knowledge of Truth Fundamentals; Knowledge of the Meanings of Names; Idioms, Metaphors and Symbols; Prayer and Contemplation; and Application of Spiritual Logic." [76] Through history, meaning, and the understanding of idioms, metaphors and symbols, exegesis was definitely a part of the metaphysical work. Yet, also part of this work was a belief in the eternal Word, capital "W", written on the ethers, or as we have come to know it in this book, the Logos.

I used my dad's principles in a slightly re-arranged and extended version for years in teaching metaphysical interpretation. During this time, I also continued my study of biblical history, language, and literature as my dad and my Unity teachers always encouraged me to do. I have learned of the history of Israel and its people, of many cultures that influenced Judaism, Christianity, and the writings of the Bible. I have become acquainted with some of the mystical commentaries on Biblical literature.

MYSTICSM

One great collection of such commentaries is known as *Kabbalah*. *Kabbalah* is an umbrella term for a large and

---

[75] DR. PAUL BARRETT, INTRODUCTION TO BIBLE INTERPRETATION, RECORDED 1986, FAIRFAX, VA: DIVINE LIFE MISSION, INC., 2 TAPES, TAPE 1, SIDE A.

[76] BARRETT, TAPES 1-2.

178

complex grouping of esoteric teachings from Jewish mystics that began in the Second Temple Period of Judaism from the 6th century BCE to the 1st century CE, and continued from the 1st through the 13th centuries. It would take a lifetime immersion in its teachings to begin comprehending their depth and meaning. Even so, a small portion of the teachings of a concept called *ein sof*, found in a collection of writings called *Zohar*, influenced the ideas I shared in Chapter 6 on the nature of being. Although I have worked with these ideas in a different way from how they are presented in the Zohar, I do need to acknowledge the roots from which they came.

The term *ein sof* is Hebrew for "no limitations," and is a reference to the infinite nature of God. *Zohar* is Hebrew for "splendor," and "radiance". It is a group of books whose time and authorship is in dispute among Jewish scholars. Interestingly, it proposed four approaches to biblical interpretation much like those found in John Cassian's *Fourfold Sense of Scripture* in Chapter 4. Their Hebrew terms are *peshat* (literal); *remez* (allegorical); *derash* (anagogical); and *sod* (mystical). Together they are *prds*, or Pardes, a word for that which takes us to "Paradise," and a root for that word as well.

PROCESS

The more I studied and continued to teach, the more I cleaned out my own T-shirt drawer regarding the Bible. I came to a distinct understanding that the Spirit of the Word was not so much a matter of something eternal and out there seeking to reveal itself to you through the metaphysical principles of interpretation. Rather, it is the Logos living as you and the Truth revealing itself through you that is discovered within those principles. Thus, the metaphysics of my dad's seven principles have evolved into the seven principles of metagetics of Love, Prayer, Contemplation, History, Meaning, Logic, and Mastery. The first three principles awaken the Spirit of the Word. The second three reveal the Soul of Truth, and the final principle activates the Body of Life.

"Spirit," "Soul," and "Body" are here capitalized because of the ways in which they are used. "Spirit" is a reference to your unity with the Spirit of God (*yachad*) that you experience through the heartmind (*leba*), awakening in you the ability to discern the Spirit of the Word in Scripture. "Soul" is the totality of your inner nature. It is the energy of the heart (*neshamah*) that anchors the mind (*ruwach*) and the animal nature (*nefesh*) in the deeper meaning of Truth discovered through exegesis and metaphysics. "Body" is both your personal physicality, and your extended universal body, both of which are enlivened through the metagetical experience. With our work, we will specifically look at the extended body as the world in which we live. In the process of metagetics on which we are now embarking, we begin with The Spirit of the Word, and the principles of its domain: *Love, Prayer* and *Contemplation*. This chapter is primarily focused on Love.

PERSONIFICATION

AGAPE

Love is the personification of the Word. Prayer is the proclamation of the Word. Contemplation is the doorway to the Word written on your heart. In chapter 1 we saw how the Logos evolved into its Christian form of the personification of Jesus Christ, the proclamation of the Gospel, and the written form of the Bible. In Chapter 2 we saw how the Tanakh and the Old and New Testaments became the authoritative Word of God in the Jewish and Christian traditions. Being the Word of God, these scriptures were also considered to be continuous resources for spiritual revelation. Yet, how can revelation occur from words that were written so long ago in a different language and another world context?

As referenced in the *Introduction* of this book, when my dad called the Bible "The Word of God," he said, "The Bible is Esoteric, that is to say it is filled with hidden meanings that are revealed, not so much through the literal word, as through the inspired mind and heart." The "inspired mind and heart" is the mind that is anchored in the heart, or the heartmind. No matter how hard the mind works from the intellect alone, no matter how disciplined and thoughtful it may be, it cannot know God until it feels God. When we feel God in every part of our being, we become God in living, personified expression.

There is one word for feeling God. That word is Love. Love is the foundational principle of the metagetical process and experience. In Love is found our ability to be the personification of the Word. In encouraging his readers to imitate the love God has shown through the person of Jesus Christ, the author of 1 John wrote, *"Beloved, let us love one another, because love is from God; everyone who loves is born of God and knows God. Whoever does not love does not know God, for God is love (1 John 4:7-8)."*

Looking to its deeper meaning, the word for "love" used here is the Greek word *agape*. *Agape* means "affection," "good will," "benevolence," and "brotherly love." [77] In the *Westminster Dictionary of Theological Terms*, agape is defined as, "The

---

[77] "AGAPE," BLUE LETTER BIBLE, ACCESSED AUGUST 21, 2017, HTTPS://WWW.BLUELETTERBIBLE.ORG/LANG/LEXICON/LEXICON.CFM?STRONGS=G2 6&T=KJV

self-giving love seen supremely in God's love for the world."[78] In other words, it is the experience of God loving God. For God to love God, there had to be something in existence. Hence, God loves God by loving what God created. When we experience God as love, the natural result is our love for the universe, the world, and all living things, including our fellow human beings. This is *agape*.

Agape is the love that encompasses all other kinds of love. Like the "breath of life," or *neshamah*, it comes from God and draws all things back into God. Because of this, it's meaning can encompass physical affection, brotherly and sisterly love, and benevolent good will. Agape can heal the pain of unfulfilled longing and transform the neediness of sense based desire into the generosity of compassion. This brings us to the other kinds of love found in the Bible.

EROS

In distinguishing love's different forms, we find five kinds of love in the Bible, all of which can be defined with Greek words. One kind of love is *agape*, and another is *eros*. *Eros* comes from the name of a Greek god who personified love. It means "love" in the form of "desire."[79] Since its use in the 20th century by Dr. Sigmund Freud (1856-1939) it has been known as the, "…urge to self-preservation and sexual pleasure."[80] It is the love that comes from *nefesh*, the animal nature of the

---

[78] DONALD K. McKIM, WESTMINSTER DICTIONARY OF THEOLOGICAL TERMS (LOUISVILLE, KY: WESTMINSTER JOHN KNOX PRESS, 1986), 5.

[79] DOUGLAS HARPER, "EROS," ONLINE ETYMOLGY DICTIONARY, ACCESSED AUGUST 21, 2017, HTTP://WWW.ETYMONLINE.COM/INDEX.PHP?TERM=EROS

[80] IBID.

soul which is focused on an instinct for survival and reproduction.

The word, "eros," is not in the Bible, probably because in the ancient world it was known more as a Greek god than a concept of human nature. The expression of *eros*, however, is in the Bible. The sensual nature of the poems in the Song of Solomon emulate *eros*. *"How graceful are your feet in sandals, O queenly maiden! Your rounded thighs are like jewels, the work of a master hand (Song of Solomon 7:1),"* is an example. This poetry conveys the deep and sensual passion of sexual love that was later interpreted as a metaphor of God's love for his people. Sexual love is a common metaphor in religious texts for the union between the human and the Divine. This can be seen in the *Bhagavad Purana* of Hinduism with Krishna who seduced maids who milked the cows with the music of his flute.

On a less pleasant note, with no pun intended toward the flute music, the passions of *eros* took over the mind of David.

> *"It happened, late one afternoon, when David rose from his couch and was walking about on the roof of the king's house, that he saw from the roof a woman bathing; the woman was very beautiful. David sent someone to inquire about the woman. It was reported, 'This is Bathsheba daughter of Eliam, the wife of Uriah the Hittite.' So David sent messengers to get her, and she came to him, and he lay with her. (2 Samuel 11: 2-4a)."*

This lead to a scandalous affair with Bathsheba that resulted in the murder of one of his best military officers, Uriah, and the death of the child born from that affair. *Eros* can usurp better judgment and lead to disastrous results when it is directed by the animal nature of *nefesh* alone. When it is not uplifted by a greater love, *eros* is based on self-preservation and personal gratification without thought of its impact on others or consideration of how they may respond. There is nothing wrong with *eros*. It can be a means of expressing the devotional love of the Divine, or it can be dangerously overwhelming, as with the story of David and Bathsheba. It needs to be directed by a higher form of love.

PHILEO

One such form, as has been previously indicated, is *agape*. Another is *philadelphia*. Now where have we heard that word before? I even had trouble getting my computer to stop capitalizing it. The first part of the word comes from *phileo*, which means to "approve;" "like;" "sanction;" and "treat affectionately or kindly."[81] By itself, *phileo* is another kind of love that acts only for the purposes of receiving good in return. Jesus referred to it as hypocritical, saying that those who express love in this way are inauthentic in what they do, and will receive inauthentic responses in return. *"And whenever you pray, do not be like the hypocrites; for they love (phileo) to stand and pray in the synagogues and at the street corners, so that they may be seen by others. Truly I tell you, they have received their reward (Matthew 5:6)."* *Adelphus*, meaning "brother," brings in the element of love as a sense of kinship from the authenticity of the heart. Combine *phileo* with *adelphus*, and you have a big city in Pennsylvania. I mean you have *philadelphia*.

PHILADELPHIA

As we all know, *philadelphia* means "brotherly, or sisterly, love." It refers to love that is mutually shared in a larger

---

[81] "PHILEO," BLUE LETTER BIBLE, ACCESSED AUGUST 21, 2017, HTTPS://WWW.BLUELETTERBIBLE.ORG/LANG/LEXICON/LEXICON.CFM?STRONGS=G5368&T=KJV

community. With *philadelphia* we recognize that we have a familial relationship with the larger human family. It moves *agape* into the experience of our spiritual connection with others. Through *agape*, we are awakened to our oneness with God, and with all of life, and we experience *chai*, the life-giving energy of that connection. Through *philadelphia*, we are awakened to our oneness with all of humanity, and we experience the blessings of those connections. Immersed in our connection with others, and with all of life, the fears of the animal-self subside, as we come to realize that our desires are met through the relationships we have in life.

PHILOSTORGAS

A more self-centered form of brotherly/sisterly love is *philostorgas*. The suffix of *storgas* is a reference to the natural love one has for those who are in a familial, or close, relationship.[82] *Philostorgas* calls forth the discerning ability of the mind, or *ruwach*, to meet

the needs of the animal nature, or *nefesh*. It seeks out those with whom it can bind together in a mutually beneficial relationship, like a pride of lions, a pod of orcas, or a flock of birds. These include friends, family, and community.

Philostorgas is found in combination with its more expanded form of "brotherly love" in Paul's letter to the Romans. Most letters of the apostle are named after the locations that he had visited. Romans is the only letter Paul wrote ahead of any visits to that location. It is, therefore, a self-introduction. In

---

[82] "FOUR GREEK WORDS FOR LOVE, ADAPTED FROM PRECEPT MINISTRIES INTERNATIONAL, ACCESSED AUGUST 25, 2017, HTTPS://WWW.MCLEANBIBLE.ORG/SITES/DEFAULT/FILES/MULTIPLY-RESOURCES/CHAP3/GREEKWORDSFORLOVEWS_CHAPTER3.PDF

it he shares his primary message of justification through faith in Jesus Christ. *"Therefore, since we are justified by faith, we have peace with God through our Lord Jesus Christ, through whom we have obtained access to this grace in which we stand; and we boast in our hope of sharing the glory of God (Romans 5:1-2)."*

How do we share this glory? Paul points out several ways to do so later in this letter, three of which are expressions of love. In fact, *agape, philadelphia,* and *philostorgas* all meet in two verses from Romans. *"Let love (agape) be genuine; hate what is evil, hold fast to what is good; love one another (philadelphia) with mutual affection (philostorgas); outdo one another in showing honor (Romans 12:9-10)."* The love mentioned in verse 9 is *agape.* [83] In verse 10, are both *philadelphia* and *philostorgas.*[84] Here, Paul is saying to let God's love move naturally in you to reject what is not like itself; and connect you in love and mutual affection with a larger community of people. This transforms the neediness of reciprocal love (*philostorgas*) into the generosity of communal love (*philadelphia*), leading to the experience of love that is genuine and divine. That love is *agape* love, the same love that is found in the great commandments to love God and love your neighbor as yourself.

Where does this leave eros? The passions of eros (sensual love), when directed by *agape,* (the love of God) evolve into *philostrogas* (familial love) and *philadelphia* (communal

---

[83] BLUE LETTER BIBLE,
HTTPS://WWW.BLUELETTERBIBLE.ORG/SEARCH/SEARCH.CFM?CRITERIA=LET+LOVE +BE&T=KJV&SS=1#S=S_PRIMARY_0_1

[84] BLUE LETTER BIBLE,
HTTPS://WWW.BLUELETTERBIBLE.ORG/SEARCH/SEARCH.CFM?CRITERIA=LOVE+ONE +ANOTHER&T=KJV&SS=1#S=S_PRIMARY_0_1

love). Does it feel like you are learning a new language? Well, you are. Mostly, you are learning the language of the Word, the language of God speaking to you through Scripture. When you understand this language, you live from the heartmind, the mind that is anchored in love. It is then that love, expressing as you, becomes the personification of the Word.

AWAKENED

REVEALED

When love expresses as you, nothing can stop you. When you interact with Scripture in love, nothing in the words of Scripture can be hidden from you. My dad believed that love for the Bible called forth the hidden truths within its words. He said, "When you love the Bible, you open your mind to be bonded with the Word of Truth to make it one with what you are in consciousness." He also stated that love of the Bible does four basic things. They are as follows:

1. "It attracts to mind the hidden teachings of the Scripture.

2. It unifies mind with the Truth revealed.

3. It expands the mind with spiritual understanding.

4. It dissolves from mind belief not in agreement with Truth."[85]

---

[85] BARRETT, TAPE 1, SIDE A.

Love adds to the bliss of your interaction with the Bible, but you do not have to be passionately in love with the it. In fact, you do not need to love the Bible any more than you already do. You are already willing to develop a deeper relationship with it or else you would not be reading these words right now. This willingness is love awakening in you. What kind of love? I believe when love comes genuinely from the heart, it is *agape*. *Agape* is expansive, it embraces all forms of love and can express through them. It also does what my dad said, not just with the Bible, but with all things of life. Therefore, to revise what Dr. Paul Barrett said in a way that is supported by what the Apostle Paul said in Romans 12, here is what love does:

1. Love Unifies. It unifies heart and mind as one in the soul's authentic expression of Spirit.
    "Let love be genuine... (v. 12:9a);"
2. Love Attracts. It draws you into beneficial relationships, allowing you to see the true nature of someone or something.
    "...love one another with mutual affection... (v. 12:10a);"

3. Love Dissolves. It dissolves from the heartmind belief not in alignment with Truth.
    "...hate what is evil, hold fast to what is good... (v. 9b):"

4. Love Expands. Honoring all the ways God speaks to us through the people and things of life, it expands spiritual awareness and understanding with the wisdom of the heartmind.
    "...outdo one another in showing honor (v. 10b)."

When you turn to the Bible, in love, seeking love's way, it reveals love to you. Perhaps the result of this is that you end up loving the Bible more deeply, only to have it reveal more of itself to you at a deeper, more intimate, and spiritual level. This is because the love you bring to the Bible is the same love with which you seek to experience more of God – *agape* love. *Agape* love compels you to give yourself fully to whatever you are doing. In so doing, God is revealed.

BREATH

How is *agape* love awakened? It is awakened through *neshamah*, the breath of life that anchors the mind in the heart. Neshamah can be activated through the movement of your own breath. Following are three heart opening meditative exercises using the breath. While each meditation alone is a heart opening experience, they are most effective when done together in sequence. I recommend spending 3 to 5 minutes with each, and having a 1 to 2 minute pause in between.

In "Meditation 1" as you connect with another, you are sharing the passion of love, or "com-passion." In "Meditation 2" as you learn to love in the midst of anxiety, you are experiencing the power of forgiveness, which is love given for, and in the face of, difficulty. In "Meditation 3," you begin, or revitalize, your loving relationship with the Bible. When you are ready, you can begin with Meditation 1.

MEDITATIONS

Meditation 1

- *Take a deep breath and relax into a comfortable upright position. Breathe normally for three breath cycles.*
- *Think of someone, or something, you love. Maybe it is someone close to you, or a beloved animal or friend, or a special place in nature that has opened your heart. See that person, or thing with the eye of your inner vision. Give that person, or thing, your complete focus and full attention. Take a deep breath. Envision the breath filling the mind on the inhale, and pulling the mind down into the heart on the exhale. Breathe normally for three breath cycles feeling the awakening of your heartmind at the center of your being.*
- *Take another deep breath, feeling love moving into your heartmind on the inbreath and out to your loved one on the outbreath. Breathe normally for three breath cycles.*
- *Take one more deep breath, breathing as deeply into your body and being as you can. Let love fill you all the way. Then release the breath, sending the energy of love forth to bless your world. Breathe normally and quietly say, "Amen."*

Pause and rest in your awakened compassion. When you are ready, begin with Meditation 2.

Meditation 2

- *Take a deep breath and relax into a comfortable upright position. Breathe normally for three breath cycles.*
- *Knowing you are safe in the presence of Love, think of someone or something that brings up anger, upset, worry, or grief in you. Let yourself feel that feeling, whatever that is.*
- *Imagine the energy of love wrapping around you like a blanket of light. Breathe deeply and inhale the energy of that love into the space of your heart. Let it interact with your feelings. Then exhale*

---

the feelings you wish to release and let them dissolve into the light
of love that surrounds you. Breathe normally for three breath cycles.
- Keep breathing at a normal pace, letting love move in and difficult
feelings move out, like washing the dirt out of a cotton shirt on a
gentle wash cycle. Do this until you reach a place of greater calm.
- Take a deep breath, breathing love into your being on the inbreath,
and out to the subject of your present focus on the outbreath.
- Keep breathing at a normal pace as you inwardly commit yourself to
letting the energy of love guide you in your relationship with this
person, place or thing. Quietly say, "Amen."

Pause and rest in the calm that now moves through you into
your relationships. When you are ready, begin with
Meditation 3.

Meditation 3

- Take a deep breath and relax into a comfortable upright
position. Breathe normally for three breath cycles.
- Envision the Bible or hold it in your hands. Let yourself feel all that
you have felt in your relationship with this book.
- Practice the gentle wash cycle (see Meditation 2) of the normal
breath to breathe in love and breath out any difficult feelings you
may have in working with the Bible. Do this until you reach a place
of greater calm.
- Keep breathing at a normal pace as you commit yourself to healing
what needs to be healed and awakening to what is revealed as you
advance in your relationship with Scripture. Quietly say, "Amen."

Love is the personification of the Word. The Word of God
speaks through the compassion and calm that is within you

191

as you relate to the people and things within your world. The compassion and calm come from allowing yourself to feel what you feel, and to gently release it through the breath. In this way, *agape* love comes alive, and you are ready to go to the altar of prayer in conscious communion with God.

SUMMARY

- Certain resources have been valuable in my search for the Spirit of the Word in Scripture.

- The Metaphysical Bible Dictionary has been a good guide. First compiled in 1931, it had an early form of exegetical work as it defined each of the biblical names that were listed.

- The metaphysical, or "inner interpretation" of the Bible is what Dr. Paul Barrett, called "esoteric", or the search for the "hidden meaning". It is the quest for the Spirit of the Word.

- One esotreric resource is the Kabbalah. This is an umbrella term for a large and complex grouping of esoteric teachings from the 6th century BCE through the 13th century CE. It would take a lifetime immersion in its teachings to begin comprehending their depth and meaning.

  o Found in a section of the Kabbalah called Zohar, the teachings of ein sof influenced the work in chapter six on Living and Being. Zohar is Hebrew for "splendor" and "radiance". The term ein sof is Hebrew for "no limitations," and is a reference to the infinite nature of God.

- In the process of metagetics on which we are now embarking, we begin with The Spirit of the Word, and the interpretive principles of its domain: *Love, Prayer* and *Contemplation.* Love is the personification of the Word. Prayer is the proclamation of the Word. Contemplation is the doorway to the Word written on your heart.

- The mind can only know God when it feels God. That feeling is Love. Love is the foundational principle of the metagetical process and experience. In Love is found our ability to be the personification of the Word.

193

In distinguishing love's different forms, we find five kinds of love in the Bible.

- Agape, is a term for "good will" and "benevolence". When we experience God as love, the natural result is our love for the universe, the world, and all living things, including our fellow human beings. This is agape. It encompasses all other kinds of love.

- Eros, the Greek word for sensual love is found in the Bible, although the word eros is not. Eros can be an expression of agape in the form of devotional love for the Divine, or it can be a dangerously overwhelming lust. It needs to be directed by a higher form of love.

- By itself, phileo is another kind of love that acts only for the purposes of receiving good in return.

- When combined with adelphus, meaning "brother", phileo becomes the word, philadelphia. Philadelphia brings a sense of kinship with the larger human family from the authenticity of the heart.

- The suffix of storgas is a reference to the natural love one has for family or close relations. Philostorgas is a form of love that seeks out those with whom it can bind together in a mutually beneficial relationship.

INQUIRY

1. Have you ever sought the Spirit of the Word in the Bible? If so, what has been an important resource in doing this? If not, what has been a spiritual guide that opened your heart?

2. Reflect upon and/or share an experience of agape. How does it make you feel?

3. When is *eros* an expression of *agape*? When is it not?

4. How can you give *philadelphia* manifest expression in your life and world?

5. What does it mean to anchor the mind in the heart? How does the breath help with this?

CHAPTER 9: PRAYER

"Be still and know that I am God (Psalms 46:10)."

PROCLAMATION

Prayer is the Word proclaimed. Of its relation to the process of Bible interpretation, Dr. Paul Barrett made the following two statements:

1. "Prayer attunes us to the invisible word. Prayer elevates the mind and spiritually makes it one with God -Mind, thus revealing the ideals inherent within every verse of Scripture."
2. "Prayer clears the mind and focuses it on the task at hand."[86]

In my years of working with 20th century metaphysics, I have come to understand that the word, "mind" refers to something more than the intellect. It refers to the whole of the inner consciousness of an individual. In the Hebrew terminology, it includes the *neshamah*, *ruwach*, and *nefesh*, the entire thinking and feeling natures of a human being.[87] In reference to God, the word "Mind" with a capital "M" means all that God is. Thus, according to my father's statements, prayer aligns all that we are with all that God is.

---

[86] DR. PAUL BARRETT, INTRODUCTION TO BIBLE INTERPRETATION, RECORDED 1986, FAIRFAX, VA: DIVINE LIFE MISSION, INC., 2 TAPES, TAPE 2, SIDE B.

[87] SEE CHAPTER 6 FOR THE MEANING OF THESE TERMS.

The metaphysical language that emerged in the late 19th and early 20th centuries uses the term "mind" to describe the spiritual aspects of being and existence. The implication of this language is that the dominant feature of the inner being needs to be rational thought. Emotions and feelings need to come under the direction of reason. This makes sense when emotions are sourced by the animal nature of *nefesh*. After all, the fearful mind that thinks it is fighting for its own survival can lead to dangerous and aggressive actions. So, too, can the unbridled passions of *eros* when love is directed only by a need for self-gratification.

As we have read in this book, however, there is a higher feeling nature that is awakened when the mind is anchored in the heart-center of the soul. When this happens, the wisdom of the heartmind is activated and the power of Spirit can be felt. Revelation, spiritual insight, and healing occur when we go beyond the rational mind into the realm of Spirit. Thus, I am re-phrasing, and adding to, what my father said to include the language of the heartmind and the expression of God in all things:

1. Prayer Attunes. It centers our awareness on God, healing our lives and revealing the Spirit of the Word as it speaks to us in all things.
2. Prayer Clears. Prayer clears the clutter of the mind and anchors it in the heartmind, from whence comes our ability to focus on the task at hand.
3. Prayer Unites. Prayer unites us with God by honoring God in all things, be it Bible, body, or the myriad forms of being.

Through prayer, we are attuned to the Word of God, and we can experience God speaking to us. Through prayer, we can clear the mind and anchor it in the heart. Through prayer, we can have a direct experience of God's presence in whatever is before us. Here is a story of how this works.

198

POWER

HEALING

In 1936 a young mother by the name of Mildred was living in northern Virginia. She had managed her life beautifully. Her husband found odd jobs to get through the financial stress of the Depression years, and she used her skills to work at different secretarial positions. Everything was going well – with one exception. Her nine-year-old daughter, Mary, was gravely ill with an infection of the brain. The doctors held out little hope short of a risky surgery that involved drilling a hole in the skull to relieve the fluid build-up from the infection. Mildred did not know what to do. Then a friend recommended that she call Silent Unity.

The Unity movement was built on prayer. Beginning in 1891 after the healing of its co-founder, Myrtle Fillmore, who had focused on an affirmative prayer statement for two years to heal herself of tuberculosis, the Society of Silent Help was formed to join people in affirmative prayer locally and throughout the country. This organization later evolved into what is now known as Silent Unity. Through the years of the Great Depression, Silent Unity maintained the ability to pray with people from a distance through correspondence, the *Daily Word* magazine, and a 24/7 phone-in prayer service.

Desperately worried about her only child, Mildred called Silent Unity. The voice on the other end of the line affirmed the activity of God's healing love in the body of the child, and peace for the mother. Mildred became attuned to the power of God present in the Spirit of the Word spoken through prayer. Her mind became clear and peaceful as she focused on the feeling of comfort and assurance in her heart. Staying up all night with Mary, Mildred saw the presence of God in her child, and united with that presence in love. In the morning, Mary's pillow was soaked. The infection had drained out of her ear. Within a couple of days she was as bright and energetic as any child could be.

Inspired by the power of prayer, Mildred started to study about Unity and its teachings. She attended the Unity church in Washington D.C., where she got a job working as a secretary in the Whitehouse. Over time she began a prayer and study group in Fairfax, Virginia. This evolved into a congregation with prayer and worship services and eventually became Unity of Fairfax with Mildred, my grandmother, serving as its founding minister. Mary, my mother, grew up to become an artist and teacher, giving birth to two daughters, my older sister, Harriet, and me.

AFFIRMATION

"Prayer Power" became a familiar term in the household where I was raised, and the most practiced form of prayer in my family was affirmative prayer. Affirmative prayer was, and is, a form of proclaiming the Word. It taps into the creative power of the Logos using words that proclaim the good in any situation and release the negativity of fear and doubt. The words of proclamation are known as "affirmations." The words of release are known as "denials." In the Sermon on the Mount, Jesus said, *"Let your words be 'Yes, Yes,' or 'No, No,'; anything more that this comes from the evil one (Matthew 5:37)."*

This verse completes a group of instructions Jesus is giving to not only avoid swearing false oaths, as has been taught in the Hebrew Scriptures, but to not swear any oaths at all. He refers to this practice as coming from "evil," or the "evil one." The Greek word for "evil" as it is used here is *poneros,*

200

meaning *full of labors*; *annoyances*; *hardships*; and *of a bad nature or condition*.[88] This is because the practice of swearing lead to a society full of distrust and hardship, where people would swear that something was of good value when it was not.

For example, when selling something at greater expense than what it was worth a person might say, "I swear this is the lower price for this item." Swearing was used more to get what you wanted, than to verify the authenticity of what you were saying. The clarity of simply affirming something was so, or not, of saying what you would do, or not do, would bring integrity to any conversation and strength to any community where people could be trusted to speak with truth and authenticity.

In the same way affirmations and denials bring integrity to your inner being and worldly life. They motivate you, not only to proclaim your good in every situation, but to take positive actions in the confidence of receiving the best possible results. This aligns you with the creative energy of the universe. In a pamphlet that I wrote for Unity in 1999 entitled, *Denials and Affirmations*, there is a description of the energy of this form of prayer that moves like the breath of creation:

"From the beginning, all creation has been in a great cycle of denial and affirmation. The process that began with the void and was followed by the great breath and word of creation brought all things and beings into existence, and the pattern continues in each particle of creation – including you. By touching your wrist or your neck in just the right spot, you can feel life coursing through your veins. This is just a microscopic

---

[88] "PONEROS," BLUE LETTER BIBLE, ACCESSED AUGUST 21, 2017 HTTPS://WWW.BLUELETTERBIBLE.ORG/LANG/LEXICON/LEXICON.CFM?STRONGS=G4190&T=KJV

reflection of the great pulsating life force underlying everything in our universe. The ... birth and death of stars, the ebb and flow of the tides, the shift from day to dark and from dark to day – all are expressions of the great life movement from creation to destruction and back to creation again.

When we practice the affirmative prayer processes of denial and affirmation, we immerse ourselves in the great universal cycle of life. We actually tap into the universal life energy of God. Like closing your eyes and listening to the gentle and cyclical movement of the ocean breakers, the effect of affirmative prayer is a relaxed and energized body and clear and focused mind. Through denial and affirmation, we press out the frenetic tension of old, unwanted thoughts and pull in the fresh vitality of new and inspired ideas."[89]

Like the name of God spoken with every breath, we inhale and say "Yah," or "Yea" to the influx of new life and inspiration, and we exhale and say "Weh" or "away" with the old thoughts of limitation. To work in a practical way with this movement of breath, I have taken some of the combined denials and affirmations from my pamphlet and worked them into a reversed structure of affirmations and denials. You can speak them aloud, or do a silent meditation with them. Following are the instructions and statements for this meditation.

---

[89] LAURA BARRETT BENNETT, DENIALS AND AFFIRMATIONS (UNITY VILLAGE: UNITY, 1999), 3.

Meditation 4

Silently focus on these pairs of affirmation and denials.
Breathe in on the affirmation and out on the denial. If
you do these statements in sequence, take three
normal breath cycles between each pair of statements.
At the completion of your meditation, just sit silently
for a moment or two, breathing normally to let these
prayerful statements take hold in your inner being.
Here are the statements:

- *I am filled with the life-giving Spirit of God, and I
  am made whole! No condition is greater than the
  power of God's life in me!*

- *I accept the truth that God is my unlimited source
  of abundant supply! I release and let go all ideas
  of lack of limitation!*
    - *I am safe in God's love and poised in
      God's power! Nothing can disturb the
      calm peace of my soul.*
    - *God is always with me! I am not alone!*
    - *I know love, I accept love, and I am love in
      action! Nothing can stand in the way of
      God's love bringing peace and prosperity
      to me and to my world!*

An affirmation is not a magical incantation to produce
whatever you want in the moment, nor is a denial the means
to ignore the real experiences of life. Practicing affirmations
and denials will cause a shift in your habitual thinking and
bring greater awareness of how God is present and active in
you and in your life. Practiced together, they align your
ruwach (mind) with your *leba* (heartmind), and let your
neshamah (activated heartmind) awaken you to Elohim (the
all-powerful God) showing up as YHWH (the immanent God)

203

within the specific circumstances of the present moment. Let's say that another way. The prayerful practice of affirmations and denials shifts your focus from the intellect to the heart where you experience the infinite power of God's Presence in the finite conditions of life and are motivated to act in accordance with this awareness.

In saying this, I realize that there are those who do not believe in God as a Divine Presence and who do not even like using the name. This is okay. They can call God by whatever form God shows up for them – be it Love, or Wisdom, or Life, or other forms of divine expression. They can even change the affirmations and denials to whatever wording works for them. God by any other name, is still God. There is not a finite God entity out there that will be offended by whatever name is used. It is entirely up to you how you connect with whatever God is for you. In fact, there is no name that captures all that God is. For that matter, there is no name that captures all that you are. The only pure name for God is in your own breath.

My own direct experience of God is full, permeating universal Presence, in me, all around me, as me, as all of existence, and greater than all of existence. It is to this God that I direct my prayers, whether in the moment I call it Love, Wisdom, Peace, Power, Christ, Logos, the Force – or my own higher Self. This is a God, not separate from me, but greater than I intellectually know myself to be. I know this God because I feel this God in my heartmind, I hear this God in the words of those near and dear to me, I see this God in the words of Scripture and in the people and things around me. This is the God my grandmother turned to in her human struggle. This is the God with which I have communed as my own eternal Self. This is the God of which Myrtle Fillmore spoke when she focused on the healing affirmation, "I am a child of God, and therefore, I do not inherit illness." This is the God of Myrtle's poem when she wrote, "The hours I spend with Thee, dear Lord, are pearls of priceless worth to me. My soul, my being merge in sweet accord in love for Thee, in Love for Thee!" Now, let us see what it is to spend a little time in direct communion with this God.

SILENCE

Another way to proclaim the Word of our unity with God is no proclamation at all. It is the *Silence*. What is the *Silence*? The metaphysical teacher, Ed Rabel, said, "Silence is pure power."[90] This is because the Silence is the experience of pure and absolute Being. This is why it is spelled with a capital "S". It is your immersion in the realm of Divine Spirit. It is the emptiness found beyond the third tier of knowing. In the Silence you may experience the all-pervading presence of Elohim God in which the whole universe dwells. You may hear the Logos. There are no words that can capture its definition, yet it permeates every word that is spoken or written. It is what Hindu Vedas call in the language of Sanskrit, *anahata nad*, the unstruck sound, the primordial vibration out of which all Creation comes.

To experience the Silence, the Psalmist has one simple instruction, *"Be still, and know that I Am God (Psalm 46:10)."* In our next meditation, we will use the words, along with others, to take us deep into our connection with all that is. This exercise uses the power of the word to carry the light of God from your head, through your body, to the souls of your

---

[90] ED RABEL TEACHING JESUS CHRIST HEALS BY CHARLES FILLMORE (LECTURE, UNITY VILLAGE, SEPTEMBER 1982).

feet and into the earth in four deep breaths that call you to, "Be still, and know that I Am God."

Diving this deeply, you reset in the Silence for a few minutes. Then, you return with four more deep breaths, moving the light energy back through the body to the head, and filing your whole being with light as you affirm, "God is what I know and still am." Here we will use the words as written, for they take us to the deeper place of pure understanding. Read through the instructions below first so you know what to expect and to do. Then read them again, doing what the instructions direct.

Meditation 5

- *To move into the Silence, take a deep breath and let your body move into a comfortable and upright position with your feet on the floor or ground. Breathe normally for three breath cycles.*
- *Take another deep breath and envision your breath moving into your mind focusing on the word "Be" with the inbreath, and "Still" with the outbreath. Let this quiet your thoughts. Breathe normally for three breath cycles.*
- *Take another deep breath and envision your breath pulling the mind down into the space of the heart, awakening the heartmind, with the word, "And" on the inbreath, and the word, "Know" on the outbreath. Breathe normally for three breath cycles.*
- *Take another deep breath and envision your breath moving all the way to the core of your lower abdomen, about two inches below the belly button, where your organs of digestion, elimination and pro-generation do their work to keep your body vitally alive. Focus on the word, "That," on the inbreath and on the word "I" on the outbreath. Breathe normally for three breath cycles.*
- *One final time, take a deep breath and envision it moving down your hips, legs, and through the souls of your feet into the ground. Focus on the word "Am" on the inbreath,*

and "God" on the outbreath. Affirm silently to yourself, "Be Still – And Know – That I – Am God."

- *For a minimum of 3 minutes, "Be still, and know that I Am God."*

***

- *Coming out of the Silence, pull the light up from the earth with your inward breath through your feet and into your legs and hips. Focus on the word "God" on the inward breath, and "Is" on the outward breath. Breath normally for three breath cycles.*
- *Take another deep breath and envision the light moving from your hips through your lower abdominal region, then concentrating itself just below the belly button. Focus on the word "What" on the inbreath, and "I" on the outbreath. Breathe normally for three breath cycles.*
- *Take another deep breath and envision the light moving upward into the heart-center, the space of the heartmind. Focus on the word "Know," on the inbreath and on the word, "And," on the outbreath. Breathe normally for three breath cycles.*
- *Take one more deep breath drawing upward from the heart into the head and see the mind filled with light. Focus on the word "Still" on the inbreath, and "Am," on the outbreath. Breathe normally for three breath cycles.*
- *Now, become aware of your body, and your surroundings. Take one more deep breath and stretch, breathing in with "Yah" and out with "Weh." Affirm to yourself, "God Is – What I – Know And – Still Am." "God is what I know, and still am." And so it is!*

You are now ready for contemplation.

SUMMARY

- Prayer is the Word proclaimed.
- Prayer aligns all that we are with all that God is.
- Affirmative prayer taps into the creative power of the Logos using words that proclaim the good in any situation and release the negativity of fear and doubt. The words of proclamation are known as "affirmations." The words of release are known as "denials."
- The prayerful practice of affirmations and denials shifts your focus from the intellect to the heart where you experience the infinite power of God's Presence in the finite conditions of life and are motivated to act in accordance with this awareness.
- There is no name that captures all that God is. For that matter, there is no name that captures all that you are. The only pure name for God is in your own breath.
- Another way to proclaim the Word of our unity with God is no proclamation at all. It is the *Silence.*
- The Silence is the experience of pure and absolute Being. That is why it is spelled with a capital "S". It is your immersion in the realm of Divine Spirit.
- In your practice of the Silence, you are called to *"Be still, and know that I Am God (Psalm 46:10)."* This prepares you for Contemplation.

Inquiry

1. In what ways does prayer proclaim the Word of God?

2. What is affirmative prayer? How does it work?

3. What form of prayer, if any, is most effective for you? Why?

4. What does it mean to you to "Be still, and know that I Am God?" Who, or what is God for you? What does it mean to be still?

CHAPTER 10: CONTEMPLATION

"I have more understanding than all my teachers, for your decrees are my meditation
(Psalm 119:99)."

WRITTEN

Contemplation calls forth the Spirit of the Word written on the heart. In so doing, it brings us into a state of conscious communion with God. When the author of Deuteronomy conveys God's words to his people through what became the greatest commandment of the Hebrew and Christian scriptures, he included God's instructions that what was decreed be kept in the heart. *"Hear, O Israel: The Lord is our God, the Lord is one. You shall love the Lord your God with all your heart, and with all your soul, and with all your might. Keep these words that I am commanding you today in your heart (Deuteronomy 6:4-6)."*

Connection with God through the law of love and forgiveness is also emphasized in the New Covenant of Jeremiah, and the heart is depicted as the true place where God's law is written.

"But this is the covenant that I will make with the house of Israel after those days, says the Lord: I will put my law within them, and I will write it on their hearts; and I will be their God, and they shall be my people. No longer shall they teach one another, or say to each other, 'Know the Lord,' for they shall all know me, from the least of them to the greatest, says the Lord; for I will

211

forgive their iniquity, and remember their sins no more."
(Jeremiah 31:33-34)[91]

In the annotations on these verses from *The New Interpreter's Study Bible* it says, "The new relationship will be stronger because God will inscribe the Law – that is Torah or right instruction – upon their hearts."[92] This Torah, inscribed upon the heart, is not a physical form of words. Rather it is, as the Jewish philosopher, Abraham Joshua Heschel, pointed out, "...the Torah, which is eternal in spirit,..." and which "...assumes different forms in different eons."[93]

What is written on the heart is your Torah, your divine instruction. It assumes different forms in the different stages of your life. It is the decrees, or messages, from the Lord of your being. These decrees are the treasures of love that come from direct communion with God. They are the power behind the written, or spoken, word known as the Spirit of the Word. They are unformed until they are accessed through what is formed. What is formed can include anything through which you hear the language of God speaking to you. Among the greatest forms of this language in human history are the words of Scripture found in the Bible. There are three keys to unlocking the Spirit of the Word in Scripture that we are looking at in this book. They are *Love*, *Prayer*, and *Contemplation*.

---

[91] ALSO QUOTED IN CHAPTER 3.

[92] THE NEW INTERPRETER'S STUDY BIBLE, ED. WALTER J. HARRELSON (NASHVILLE, TN: ABINGDON, 2000), 1104.

[93] HESCHEL QUOTED FROM CHAPTER 2.

LECTIO DIVINA

CULMINATION

Regarding *Contemplation,* Dr. Paul Barrett said, "Contemplation of the Scripture is the natural follow up to prayer." [94] He also said, "Through meditative inquiry, contemplation allows the intellect to be used by the greater Intelligence that is God. It leads the mind through the letter of the word to its spirit."[95] The greater Intelligence that is God is the intelligence of the heartmind. This is where God speaks directly to us, and through us. To access the intelligence, or wisdom, of the heartmind, humankind has been gifted with the ability to practice contemplation. One of the clearest expressions of this practice is found in the work of Guigo II.

As presented in Chapter 5, *Contemplation* was the top rung of the *Ladder of Monks* created by the 12th century monk, Guigo II. It was the fourth rung. *Prayer* was the third. As with the principles of metagetics, *Prayer* immediately precedes *Contemplation* on Guigo's ladder. There are more connections, but this is where the direct parallels end between these two approaches.

The first rung of Guigo's ladder was the *Reading* of Scripture. The second rung was reflection, or *Meditation.* It was *Contemplation,* however, that brought it all together. A wonderful study of Guigo was done in the book *A Taste of Silence: A Guide to the Fundamentals of Centering Prayer* by Carl Arico. In it, Guigo is quoted as writing the following:

---

[94] DR. PAUL BARRETT, INTRODUCTION TO BIBLE INTERPRETATION, RECORDED 1986, FAIRFAX, VA: DIVINE LIFE MISSION, INC., 2 TAPES, TAPE 2, SIDE B.

[95] IBID.

213

"Reading directs the mind to a careful looking at the Scriptures. Meditation is the studious activity of the mind, pondering the knowledge of some hidden truth under the guidance of our own reason. Prayer is a devout turning of the heart to God to get ills removed and to obtain good things. Contemplation is a certain elevation above itself of the mind which is suspended in God, tasting the joy of eternal sweetness."[96]

Guigo also wrote that when contemplation comes, it "rewards the labors of the preceding three."[97]

Contemplation was the culmination of the interpretive practice that Guigo called *Lectio Divina*, translated as *Sacred Reading*. *Lectio Divina* is a spiritual "how-to". It is a methodical study of Scripture that brings you into direct communion with the God. Guigo believed *Lectio Divina* connected the individual with the Spirit of the Word, and the Spirit of the Word connected the individual with God. He wrote, "The more I know you, the more I long to know you, no longer in the husks of the letter, but in the sense of the Spirit."[98]

ELEVATION

Elements of *Lectio Divina* are present in the application of the contemplation principle of metagetics. Indeed, *Lectio Divina* is a hermeneutical root of metagetics. For example, the contemplation principle of metagetics also connects you with

---

[96] GUIGO II, LADDER OF MONKS, QUOTED BY CARL ARICO, A TASTE OF SILENCE: A GUIDE TO THE FUNDAMENTALS OF CENTERING PRAYER (NEW YORK: NY, CONTINUUM PUBLISHING, 1999), 105.

[97] GUIGO II QUOTED BY ARICO, 107.

[98] GUIGO II QUOTED BY ARICO, 106.

214

the Spirit of the Word, bringing you into direct communion with God. In a slightly different order than Guigo, it begins with *Prayer*. This is done through the "Invocation" of clearing the mind and anchoring it in the heartmind where the presence of God can be felt. Guigo describes *Prayer* as, "...a devout turning of the heart to God to get ills removed and to obtain good things." Then comes "Focus" on the Scripture, what Guigo calls *Reading* that "...directs the mind to a careful looking at the Scriptures."

Meditation as Guigo sees it, is distinct from the guided and silent meditations that have been put forth in this book. It is more like the "meditative inquiry," to which my father referred that allows the "...intellect to be guided by the greater Intelligence that is God." As quoted earlier Guigo called it "...the studious activity of the mind pondering the knowledge of some hidden truth under the guidance of our own reason." He further pointed out, "Meditation earnestly inquires what we should seek and as it were, digs out and finds the treasure and shows us the treasures."[99] Earnest inquiry is the core of contemplative practice. The "treasure" we seek is communion with God. The "treasures" are insights, or the decrees that come from infinite Intelligence. With the tools of our heart-centered questions, we dig into the field of the heartmind until we go beyond all thought to find the pure Truth. This experience of *Contemplation* is described by Guigo as a "...certain elevation of the mind above itself which is suspended in God, tasting the joy of eternal sweetness."[100] Here is how Contemplation works.

---

[99] GUIGO II QUOTED BY ARICO, 107.

[100] GUIGO II QUOTED BY ARICO, 106.

GUIDELINES

In 1992, I created a contemplation method that I used in my Bible Interpretation classes for many years. It later became part of the curriculum for a class entitled, *Interpreting the Bible*, produced by what was then Unity School for Religious Studies. What follows is that method of contemplation, updated.[101]

It begins with a Bible quote, *"I have more understanding than all my teachers, for your decrees are my meditation (Psalm 119:99)."* This Psalm is an exhortation on studying the Torah. The Psalmist here proclaims that the divine teaching of the Torah, or Spirit of the Word, renders more understanding than all of the wisdom of his teachers. His blissful study culminates in a statement that was used in Chapter 1 of this book, *"Your word is a lamp to my feet and a light to my path (Psalm 119:105)."* The Psalmist had obviously invested his whole life in the study of Scripture, as did Guigo. Our work provides a little taste of their divine encounters with the sweetness of Spirit that comes from a sacred reading of Scripture through the practice of *Contemplation*. We begin with learning what *Contemplation* is.

STATEMENTS

In the section on my handout entitled, *Statements of Contemplation*, I gave four descriptions of *Contemplation*. Below is an updated version of these descriptions. Having some understanding of these things enhances the quality of your experience with this phenomenal spiritual practice.

---

[101] LAURA BARRETT BENNETT, "LESSON 5: THE CONTEMPLATIVE PROCESS," INTERPRETING THE BIBLE INSTRUCTOR'S GUIDE (UNITY VILLAGE: UNITY, 1999), 95-98.

1. Contemplation is a form of inquiry that reveals the spiritual reality of what you contemplate. This brings you into direct communion with God.

2. Contemplation gives you an experience of thought and feeling relating to what you contemplate, while at the same time allowing you to observe your experience from a state of awareness that is greater than your thoughts and feelings.

3. Contemplation is a beingness, not a thinkingness. Although you can use the intellect to trigger the process of contemplation, with true contemplation the intuition of the heartmind is your guide.

4. Contemplation gives you the experience of spiritual awakening. The more you contemplate God in specific things, the more awake you are to God in all things.

Now that we have the descriptions of what *Contemplation* is, we can experience what it does.

The act of contemplation applies to anything in life. You can contemplate a rock, and experience God in the process. When applied to Scripture, contemplation brings forth the Spirit of the Word as it is written on the heart through the following 8 steps:

1. **Invocation** – taking a prayerful pause to go into your heartmind and consciously connect with the Spirit of God as your inner guide;

2. **Focus** – concentrating your full attention on the object of your contemplation;

3. **Feelings** – becoming fully present to what you are feeling intuitively, emotionally, and physically through your focus;

217

4. **Articulation** – putting your feelings into words through single terms, brief phrases, or short sentences;

5. **Reflection** – writing down brief reflective questions based on the feelings that have taken form;

6. **Response** – asking each question of your inner being, writing down the spontaneous answers that arise;

7. **Synopsis** – synthesizing in a brief paragraph the answers and insights that stand out for you;

8. **Illumination** – creating a prayer statement or affirmation that sums up the paragraph and illuminates your spiritual understanding.

These steps anchor the thinking process of the mind firmly in the intuitive feeling of the heart. To experience this more fully, we will first select a scripture on which to focus. One of my favorite methods of selecting Scripture is what I call, "Drop the Needle."

SELECTION

Along with Religion Studies, I majored in music while in college. In the corner of the music classroom was a phonograph player for long playing vinyl record discs. In the listening room of the music department was a reel to reel tape player with a headset. This was in a time before computer apps, flash drives, and even CD's. I would spend hours with the earphones listening to different tapes of music from history's great composers. Come examination time, the professor would put the phonograph front and center in the classroom. He would hold up its arm, and drop the needle on the record. It would play for a few seconds. Then, he would lift the needle and we would have to write a short essay on what we just heard. We would have to name the piece, the composer, the period of his life in which the piece was written and what motifs or styles in the music indicated this.

There are many ways to find scripture for inspiration from the Bible. I can think of Bible stories or sayings that I learned in the past and look them up in a concordance. I can even turn to a topical concordance to help me find biblical verses that are relevant to whatever it is that has my attention, curiosity, and/or concern. When I don't have a specific topic in mind, and don't know where to turn, I like to find my Scripture by dropping the needle. I open the Bible to a random place and let the needlepoint vision of my eyes fall to a specific verse, or passage, from which I can draw my inspiration. I read it, contemplate it, and create an unwritten inspirational essay with the wisdom of the heartmind.

Sometimes I "drop the needle" on a wrath of God type of passage. If you should do this, you are welcome to try again until you find what speaks to you. As for me, I like to work with whatever shows up in front of me because I know that if I see God and hear God speak through the negative language of writers who saw it as necessary for their time, then I can hear God speak through what I perceive to be the negative circumstances of our time. Why am I telling you all of this? Because for our contemplative practice in this chapter I have – you guessed it – dropped the needle.

I have also updated my earlier "Guidelines for the Contemplative Process" with the 8 steps previously outlined in a way that fits our work here. I invite you to go through these steps with me in the next section entitled "Contemplation 1". You will need a journal, or a clean piece of paper for this, and something with which to write. The writing part of the exercise will begin with the step entitled, "Articulation". I will share my written work with you as an example of what you can do when contemplating the passage used in the following exercise, or with your choice of scripture. Now, let us experience our own encounter with the *Lectio Divina,* or the "sacred reading" of *Contemplation.*

CONTEMPLATION 1

INVOCATION

Take a deep breath and let your body move into a comfortable and upright position. Relax and breathe normally for three breath cycles. Take another deep breath. On the inhale envision the breath as light moving into the space of the mind. On the exhale, let the light that fills the mind move down into the heart-center, anchoring the mind in the heart, connecting the two as one. Breathe normally as you close your eyes for one moment and dwell in the space of the heartmind. Then, open your eyes. From the space of the heartmind, invite the Spirit of God in you to be your guide, your healer, your protector, and your identity. Let yourself be the instrument through which God can know God.

FOCUS

Take a deep breath and read the verse below.

"The wolf shall lie down with the lamb,
The leopard shall lie down with the kid,
The calf and the lion and the fatling together,
And a little child shall lead them." (Isaiah 11:6)

After you have read it once, read the verse again, focusing your full attention on its words. Then read it again, until its words fill your thoughts, and/or still your thoughts. Take a deep inward breath and envision yourself breathing the words of this verse into the space of your heartmind. Then exhale and release the breath. Breathe normally and feel the energy of the words in your heart.

FEELINGS

Allow your focus to trigger whatever response arises in you, emotional or otherwise. If emotions are intense, consciously remind yourself that the Spirit of God is in your midst and that you are greater than your thoughts and feelings.

ARTICULATION

Notice what you feel, and articulate your feelings in single words, brief phrases, or short sentences. You may want to start with the phrase, *"As I read this, I feel..."* Write your responses in a journal, or on a clean piece of paper.

> **Example**: As I read this, I feel peaceful. As I read this, I feel childlike. As I read this, I feel expansive. As I read this, I feel sad that my world is not more like this. As I read this, I feel hopeless that this will ever be a reality.

REFLECTION

Briefly write reflective questions of who, what, how, when, where and/or why that occur to you regarding what you have articulated.

> **Example**: How can I feel both peaceful and frustrated? How can I feel both childlike, and hopeless? How can I feel both expansive, and sad? What do these feelings tell me as a group? Who do I need to be to make this a reality?

RESPONSE

Ask each question of your inner being. Repeat asking each question until you intuitively feel you have reached the spontaneous answers from your heartmind. Write down these answers. In this process, other questions may arise. Feel free to write them down, treating them the same way as the others.

> **Example**: *How can I feel both peaceful and frustrated, both childlike and frustrated, both expansive and sad?* Because I have mixed feelings. *What does that mean?* It means I am human. It means that I can imagine a world of peace, but don't know how to make it happen. *Why do I have to make it happen?* I don't. I choose to make it happen. *How?* Through my willingness to be what we want to see in the world. *What is that?* A domain of peace and shared contribution.

SYNOPSIS

Synthesize in a brief paragraph the answers which stand out in meaning for you, or the insights gained from the answers received.

> **Example**: I let the wolf of my unsatisfied ego be filled with the humility of the lamb. I let the anger of the leopard, be transformed into the springing energetic joy of the kid. I let the lion of strength protect the calving of new ideas, and the fatling of the blessings they bring to others. In other words, all of the opposing forces in me are working together for my good. If that is happening, then I can transcend the adversarial conditions of my world to find peace in myself, and to share that peace with others.

ILLUMINATION

Create a prayer statement or affirmation which clearly and concisely sums up the paragraph. In this you will find a profound reminder of the spiritual reality of what you have contemplated.

> **Example**: I choose to be a center of peace in my world! Nothing can keep God from expressing through me!

ENGAGING

PRACTICE

This method is good for building your skills of contemplation, and for moving you at depth with the power of spiritual insight. Once you have a sense of how contemplation works within the metagetical process, you can abbreviate this practice. Just inwardly breathe into your mind and anchor the energy of your thoughts in the heart on the outbreath as instructed in the exercises of this book. Focus on the object of your contemplation. Let yourself experience whatever feelings arise from your focus. Ask your heartmind any who, what, where, how, when, and why questions that may arise, and inwardly listen for spontaneous and clear responses. Keep reflecting until you know you are receiving a response straight from the Spirit of God in you. Then create from that response a statement of illumination and inspiration for your life.

I practice contemplation in my relationships, in nature, in the wake of news items and events, when I am practicing or composing music, even as I write this book. All of the information gathered by my intellect to create this book has been researched from the space of my heartmind and comes through a contemplative inquiry before finding its way onto these pages. In a similar way, we will be working with the information gathered from our next two principles of *History* and *Meaning*, as they come together through the contemplative insights of spiritual *Logic*. As we engage, not just the intellectual mind, but the heartmind, we interact with the world and the people who created Scripture. In this way, we know that we know that we know, not just the concept, but "The Soul of Truth."

SUMMARY

- Contemplation calls forth the Spirit of the Word written on the heart. In so doing, it brings us into a state of conscious communion with God.
- There are three keys to unlocking the Spirit of the Word in Scripture that we are looking at in this book. They are *Love, Prayer,* and *Contemplation.*
- Contemplation was the culmination of the interpretive practice that Guigo called *Lectio Divina,* translated as *Sacred Reading. Lectio Divina* is a spiritual "how-to". It is a methodical study of Scripture that brings you into direct communion with the God.
- Earnest inquiry is the core of contemplative practice. With the tools of our heart-centered questions, we dig into the field of the heartmind until we go beyond all thought to find the pure Truth.
  - o Contemplation is...
  - o A form of inquiry that reveals the spiritual reality of what you contemplate.
  - o Both the experience of thoughts and feelings that arise in response to what you contemplate and the ability to observe the experience from an awareness that is greater than your thoughts and feelings.
  - o A beingness, not a thinkingness.
- The experience of spiritual awakening.
- When applied to Scripture, contemplation brings forth the Spirit of the Word as it is written on the heart through the 8 steps of Invocation; Focus; Feelings; Articulation; Reflection; Response; Synopsis; Illumination.
- "Dropping the Needle" is a way to spontaneously select Scripture for contemplation and interpretation. It is done by opening the Bible to a random place and letting the needlepoint vision of the eyes fall to a specific verse, or passage, from which we can draw inspiration.
- The 8 steps of Contemplation can be abbreviated and used as a continued practice that applies, not just to any chosen Scripture, but to any chosen area of life.

Inquiry

1. Share in your own words what Contemplation is.

2. How is the intellect used in Contemplation? How is it superseded?

3. How does Contemplation awaken the Spirit of the Word in Scripture?

4. Where else in life can Contemplation be applied?

PART VI: THE SOUL OF TRUTH

CHAPTER 11: HISTORY

"...you shall love your neighbor as yourself. I am the Lord (Leviticus 19:18b)."

SPECTACLE

When I was eight years old, my father took my sister and I to see the tenth anniversary re-release of Cecil B. Demille's *The Ten Commandments*. At that time my dad was a minister living in the manse of a Unity church in downtown Philadelphia, the city of "brotherly love," a term that we explored in Chapter 8. We went to the grand and glorious Fox Theater that was ornately decorated like a turn of the century opera house. The sights, sounds, and smell of the popcorn got my young senses reeling. Then came the picture.

What a spectacle for the big screen! The movie was four hours long with an Intermission. It told the story of Moses and the Exodus of the Hebrews from slavery in Egypt. The special effects were still special ten years after the movie was made. Of course, my favorite was the parting of the Red Sea. After an evening of pop-corn and pop-culture, our heads were full of images of burning bushes, golden calves, glamorous Egyptians, and Hebrews who looked like they had a Hollywood hair stylist. Oh, wait a minute – I guess they did. As we walked out of the theater, my dad paused, looked thoughtfully up to the night sky, and said, "That's not exactly the way it happened." What? How could that be? – especially when Mr. Demille had an opening scene that introduced the movie and the historical knowledge that went into making it.

I went home, picked up a Bible and started to read the book of Exodus. My dad was right! Where was Anne Baxter? Where was Yul Brynner? Of course, Charlton Heston did a pretty good visual imitation of Michelangelo's Moses, but there was nothing in there about Moses being a great Egyptian conqueror or builder of a city – let alone having an emotional breakdown over his identity. This peaked my curiosity. My interest in the Bible grew over the next couple of years. Before long I was reading it from cover to cover, and, as described in Chapter 8, my studies expanded and deepened as the years went on. I am still seeking the Truth in the Bible. Not only the ever-renewing insights of spiritual Truth gleaned from *Love*, *Prayer* and *Contemplation*, but also in the *History* of Scripture, and the *Meaning* of its words, stories, and passages.

Using breath as the vehicle of spiritual work, we have interacted with Scripture, and learned how to draw forth the "Spirit of the Word", or "Logos", as it is written on the heart. This is wonderful work, and our biblical exploration could stop right here. In fact, for many people this would be satisfactory enough when it comes to finding inspiration in Scripture. To connect with the Spirit of the Word in this way is the transformational core of our interpretive process. To give body and being to this core, we must wrap around it our own soul's experience. This brings life to its life-giving energy.

Story

Memory

The spiritual life is no good if we stay on the mountaintop. We must get back on the path. What we encounter on the path of life becomes part of who we are, bringing beauty and diversity to our existence. If we truly are the breath of God in its myriad forms, then all of what we are contributes to all of what God is, be it the animal nature of *nefesh*, the brilliant mind of *ruwach*, or the heart energy of *neshamah*. On the path of life, we are in the process of discovering, not just who and what God is, but who and what we are. We are expressions of God with different aspects of the soul that we all have in common, but what makes each of us a unique expression of God? What makes you – you?

It is your soul, the heartmind of who you are. This soul has two doorways. One is the heart. This is the great door into the temple of your innermost being wherein dwells the full power of the Divine Presence. It is through this doorway of the soul that you come to know God. There is also another doorway of the soul that carries the power of the Divine Presence into life. It is the mind of thought and reason. It is the front gate of the temple through which you step out to engage with the people and things of the world.

The world outside the gate gives you the experience and memories that are part of making you uniquely you. Yet, it is also the world of the courtyard inside the gate, but outside the great temple door, that contributes to your individual nature. This courtyard is crowded with every thought and feeling you have ever thought and felt. When in your conscious awareness you recollect, or re-collect these thoughts and feelings, this is called memory. It is like walking through the courtyard, pointing to certain thought-people who dwell there, and calling them to you. When you have a group of people, connected by the same sequence of experiences, these are the memories that give you a story. They are like the memory of seeing a movie in Philadelphia combined with the images of my dad and sister, as well as the recollection of my dad's words, that create through me the story about the experience that began my quest for biblical Truth.

HI-STORY

What started you on the quest for Truth? What has called you to deepen that quest? What do you recollect in your memory? This is part of your story, the great epic of how you got to be who you are which is much more than a movie. It could most likely be a whole series on HBO! Here is something of which you may or may not be aware. Your story is older than you. I'm not just talking about getting your story from Ancestry.com. I am talking about the high-story, or "hi-story" of all that you are. Remember from Chapter 7 how the body is made of the star-stuff that expands out into the whole universe? Well – your soul is made of the breath of the Divine – the Spirit stuff that expands out to encompass all other souls. Why else would we consider one of the Bible's greatest teachings to be, "...love your neighbor <u>as</u> yourself (Leviticus 19:18b and Matthew 22:39b)." This is because your neighbor <u>is</u> yourself, and the history of humanity is your hi-story, the elevated and expanded story of you.

When you interact with what the Bible says through the world out of which it came, as well as the experiences and intentions of its authors, you bring forth the soul of Scripture, and therefore, the soul of Truth in Scripture. The Truth emerges when the heartmind is engaged with history. This is because the soul recognizes its own high-story as depicted in

232

the Bible and learns from it. In the next chapter, we will see how this works by exploring the history and meaning of a scripture from Exodus. It is the story of the death of the firstborn of Egypt – minus the green smoke from the movie, of course.

Woaah! Wait a minute! Why so negative a subject? Couldn't we start with something sweeter and easier, like we did in the Contemplation exercise? Perhaps we can just go back to dropping the needle. Actually, this story was chosen because of its tragic circumstances. If we are to use the Bible to transform us in a way that is effective for life – we need to admit that death is part of life. For now, since we are engaging with Scripture through history, let us explore history's different aspects.

CONTEXT

FRAMEWORK

Here is what my father, Dr. Paul Barrett, said regarding what he called "knowledge of Bible history." I have put it into outline form.

1. "History puts a framework around the verse or scripture."
2. "History has 2 main aspects.
   - An accounting of past events.
     A sequential and/or factual framework.
   - An accounting of why the scriptures were written.

A literary and cultural framework."[102]

The "framework" provided by the interpretive principle of History organizes and enriches the verse or passage of Scripture. As an accounting of past events in a sequential and/or factual framework, history places the selected scripture in the context of a space-time continuum of which we are all a part and to which we each contribute. As an accounting of the literary and cultural framework that reveals why the scriptures were written, it renders insight that empowers us to put the past in the past, and wisdom that creates a new future.

For example, in 1 Timothy it says, *"Let a woman learn in silence with full submission. I permit no woman to teach or to have authority over a man; she is to keep silent (1 Timothy 2:11-12)."* Really!? I have been the senior minister and primary speaker in two churches over a total of fifteen years. I have also taught seminary courses on Bible history and interpretation for a total of 15 years. Many of my students were men. How can this be when some of the very texts about which I was teaching spoke against the fact that I was teaching? Let's look at what history tells us regarding why these scriptures were written.

By reading historical commentary we learn that it was the author's intention to align the good Christian with the social morays of the time. We also understand that, although this scripture is attributed to Paul, it was likely written after

---

[102] DR. PAUL BARRETT, INTRODUCTION TO BIBLE INTERPRETATION, RECORDED 1986, FAIRFAX, VA: DIVINE LIFE MISSION, INC., 2 TAPES, TAPE 1, SIDE B.

Paul's time by one of his followers who was trying to do what Paul did in integrating the growing Christian population into the world of the Roman Empire.[103] With this knowledge we can move away from either accepting the teaching at face value, or rejecting it entirely as having no value whatsoever. We can also understand the author's intention on instructing the leaders of a growing spiritual movement in the ways that will best grow that movement and keep it in tact. From where we are now in the space-time continuum, we can contemplatively ask ourselves how to grow what is important to us in life and how to strengthen its place in our society and world. This puts the past in the past and creates possibility for the future.

In Chapter 5, I wrote that the 20th century hermeneut, Jean Paul Gustave Ricœur, emphasized "...a relationship between the interpreter and the text which helped the interpreter better understand his, or her, self."[104] Ricœur is referenced by W. Randolph Tate in his book, *Biblical Interpretation: An Integrated Approach*, when he says, "Every text is created within some context. According to Paul Ricœur, at least three developmental stages of a text must be considered in the interpretive process. First, is the event, second the recording of the event in a text, and third the reading of the text."[105] The historical context is the framework of the Bible to which my

---

[103] SOME INFORMATION IN THIS SECTION IS DRAWN FROM THE NEW INTERPRETER'S STUDY BIBLE, ED. WALTER J. HARRELSON (NASHVILLE, TN: ABINGDON, 2000), 2129 AND 2132.

[104] SEE CHAPTER 5.

[105] JEAN PAUL GUSTAVE RICŒUR, THE CONFLICT OF INTERPRETATION (EVANSTON, IL: NORTHWESTERN UNIVERSITY PRESS, 1974) REFERENCED BY W. RANDOLPH TATE, BIBLE INTERPRETATION: AN INTEGRATED APPROACH (GRAND RAPIDS, MI: BAKER ACADEMIC, 2008), 38.

dad referred. From Ricœur's point of view, it has, not just 2, but 3 main aspects.

I see these 3 aspects as the history *in* the Bible, the history *about* the Bible, and the history *of* the Bible. The history *in* the Bible refers to the event or teaching that is in the Bible. It is the story of the Israelites and early Christianity according to the Bible. The history *about* the Bible refers to the recording of the event or teaching, the history regarding the biblical text and its author. The history *of* the Bible refers to how the reading of the text affected, and is still affecting, human history over time.

IN

The history *in* the Bible is the story of the Israelites and early Christianity according to the Bible. It is the events and teachings that have become an important part of the story of humanity - from the cleansing of the Earth by flood, to the Exodus from slavery in Egypt, to the rise and fall of a kingdom, to the sacrificial death of a great healer; to the spreading of the Gospel in the Roman world. The literal interpretation of these stories holds its own value. Those who believe that the Earth flooded, that the Red Sea parted, that Jesus raised from the dead, and that the Holy Spirit healed people through the work of the apostles just as the Bible conveys, tap into a wealth of human drama and miraculous phenomenon that give them hope for their own life struggles. They may also gain motivation to make a difference on behalf of the Lord, whether for them that is YHWH, or Jesus.

The challenge with the history *in* the Bible, is that it is finished. My friend and fellow teacher, Rev. Don Jennings, used to say, "The only problem with the Bible is its back cover." The history *in* the Bible is the full T-shirt drawer of perceptions built on pre-conceived notions, or the "first tier of knowing." [106] The perceptions of pre-conceived stories, prophecies, and ordinances are already in place. God did his big stuff and set forth his rules thousands of years ago. The best we can do is to follow God's ancient ordinances as closely as our limited humanity allows, or we can look to the grace of a vicarious human sacrifice to make up for our sinful ways. For some, this way of understanding the Bible may be what they need. This is not enough, however, for many with whom I have worked in today's world.

There is definitely a gap in the space-time continuum between the biblical event or teaching, and the life of the modern reader and interpreter. How do we bridge the gap? How does the reader understand the intention of the author in writing his, or her, memory of what happened or what was taught, and bring it into the relevance of present-day experience? Tate has written, "The preferred reading of any text is the one in which the interpreter establishes the most probable historical and cultural contexts." [107] This is the work of exegesis or understanding the text from its historical and literal context. This is the sorting out of the T-shirt drawer that conceives new insights from the "second tier of knowing." [108] This is where the history *about* the Bible is useful.

---

[106] SEE CHAPTER 4.

[107] W. RANDOLPH TATE, BIBLE INTERPRETATION: AN INTEGRATED APPROACH (GRAND RAPIDS, MI: BAKER ACADEMIC, 2008), 39.

[108] SEE CHAPTER 4.

ABOUT

The history *about* the Bible is – about the Bible. It is the history regarding the biblical text and its author. It is about the writings that make the Bible what it is. Who wrote them, when, and why? What was the world of the author in which the scriptures were written, and in which lived their initial readership? Tate writes, "...since the biblical authors stood within a particular culture proclaiming a culturally conditioned message to a culturally identified audience, does it not seem logical that the modern hermeneut must, to as great a degree as possible, return to that world?" [109] For example, acquiring an understanding of the world out of which the Gospels came, "to as great a degree as possible," can enhance our connection with the Gospels.

From Historical Criticism, which examines the political, cultural, and social conditions during the creation of Scripture, we learn about the world of Jesus and early Christianity. A good study Bible, like *The New Interpreter's Study Bible* from which I am getting some of my information, will give you a window into this world. [110] It was a world governed by the Roman Empire, in which the Emperor and an elite group ruled at the will of the gods. The Emperor, himself, was often seen as a son of God. Rome controlled political and economic conditions through a strong military structure and alliances with local kings and rulers but allowed for some flexibility in religious worship.

---

[109] TATE, 39.

[110] SOME INFORMATION IN THIS SECTION IS DRAWN FROM THE NEW INTERPRETER'S STUDY BIBLE, 1745 AND 1746.

In this world were many religious sects, some had their own stories of resurrection, while others celebrated mystical union with the Divine. Christianity grew into an amalgam of Jewish law and practices, combined with the influences of other religions, and the quest for political and personal freedom. These elements all contributed to the Gospels as we know them today. Yet, how and when were they written?

After 3 to 4 decades beyond the lifetime of Jesus, the living witnesses to his ministry were getting fewer and fewer. Who was going to tell the story? The writers of the canonical Gospels were those who dedicated themselves to preserving the stories of what Jesus said and did. Coming from insights based on what they could piece together about Jesus, as well as the influence of early Christian apostles like Paul, they did their work. It is no wonder that three Gospels have a lot of similarities in the practicalities of their stories and teachings, while a fourth Gospel brings a more mystical flavor to its depiction of Jesus. Source Criticism, the historical and textual critique that determines the authorship of Scripture, conveys these ideas, while at the same time pointing out that each Gospel has its own distinct perspective on Jesus.

We also learn from Source Criticism that to support their perspectives the Gospel authors used different writings that were available to them. Burnett Hillman Streeter (1874-1937), was a British theologian and biblical critic. He suggested a theory that four sources were used for the three similar gospels of Matthew, Mark, and Luke, or the Synoptic Gospels. Streeter's 1924 treatise, *The Four Gospels, a Study of Origins*, revealed this now widely used standard of biblical study that he called his "Four-Source Hypothesis".[111]

The four sources begin with pointing out that Mark, the earliest written Gospel, was a source of Matthew and Luke. "Q", a theorized gospel that collected sayings of Jesus, was also a source of Matthew and Luke. "Q" is the initial for the German word for source, or *quelle*. The source of writings that are only in Matthew became known as "M", and the source of writings that are only in Luke became known as – you got it – "L". Mark, Q, M, and L, then, are considered by many scholars to be documents from which the Synoptic Gospels were composed. As for John, it is believed to have its own source known as the "Gospel of Signs," a list of the miracles of Jesus.[112]

Many other authors of biblical writings have been distinguished, and many have not. As previously mentioned, a good Bible commentary will point out the most widely accepted sources of biblical scholarship, usually in the introductions to each of its books. I have often said that the two most prolific writers of the Bible go by the names of "Anonymous" and "Unknown." One of the most famous portions of the Bible where this is not the case, however, is the Torah, or Pentateuch. The work done with these sources was a breakthrough in biblical understanding. It is also relevant to our scriptural exercise in this chapter.

Since the 18th century theologians had been speculating that Moses may not have written the Torah as believed by

---

[111] INFORMATION FROM RICHARD N. AND R. KENDALL SOULEN, HANDBOOK OF BIBLICAL CRITICISM, THIRD EDITION (LOUISVILLE, KY: WESTMINSTER JOHN KNOX PRESS, 2001), 180.

[112] SOULEN AND SOULEN, 173.

tradition. For example, it would have been very difficult for Moses to write about his own death. *"Then Moses, the servant of the Lord, died there in the land of Moab, at the Lord's command (Deuteronomy 34:5)."* Jean Astruc (1864-1766) a Catholic physician in France, noticed that both YHWH and Elohim were used in the Torah as names for God. Soon scholars began to distinguish differences, not just in how God was depicted, but also in how stories were told. They discerned that there were distinct groups of writers with common intentions that were showing up throughout the first five books. The names and pronouns given these groups are used in Bible study as though they are referring to one individual. That reference to the individual, however, is a metaphor for unknowable numbers of biblical authors and editors.

One author used a lot of details and was focused on the order in which things happened, as with the seven days of creation and the genealogies in Genesis. This became known as the Priestly, or "P", writer beginning his work in the 6th century after the return of the people of Judah from the Babylonian Exile. This writer was an editor, or redactor, of earlier works from other biblical authors. One group of earlier authors wrote a lot about God's direct involvement with the activities of the people, as well as the manifest appearance of God to the people. These manifestations are known as theophany. This author became known as the Jahwist (pronounced "Yahwist"), or "J", writer of the 10th century BCE. More details can be found on both the J and P authors in chapter 7 where the names of God are explained. For example, the Priestly writer used Elohim, while the Jahwist used YHWH.

The name "Elohim" was also used by another author. Biblical hermeneuts noticed that at times elements of a primarily Jahwist story might include unusual names. Examples would be "Elohim" for God, "Horeb" for the holy mountain of Sinai, and "Ephraim", the name of a tribe to the north of Israel. These names came from old oral traditions of the northern territories of Israel and pointed to the writings of what came to be known as the Elohist, or "E", writer of the 9th century BCE. The writings of the Elohist were often seen as intertwining with the Jahwist. Exodus 3:4 is a perfect example where God is mentioned first as YHWH, or "the Lord," and then as Elohim, or God. *"When the Lord (YHWH) saw that he had turned aside to see, God (Elohim) called him out of the bush, 'Moses, Moses!' And he said, 'Here I am.'"*

Finally, the Deuteronomist, or "D" writer, emerged as the independent author of Deuteronomy from the 7th century BCE. There is also a viewpoint in post-modern scholarship that this author was a priestly redactor who wrote Deuteronomy and contributed to the books of Chronicles in the 6th century after the Babylonian Exile. Prior to this perspective, four authors of the Pentateuch were put into a sequential order of when they were presumed to have been writing. The order that became the most widely accepted theory of sources of the Pentateuch was put together by Julius Wellhausen (1844-1918). Wellhausen was a German theologian and university professor who wrote a book called *Prologue to the History of Israel.* In this book he calls the four-source theory of the Pentateuch the "Documentary Hypothesis".

In recent years, there have been those who questioned this hypothesis. One such individual was Rolf Rendtorff (1925-2014). A professor and administrator at the University of Heidelberg, who founded the German-Israeli society in 2002, Rendtorff wrote a book entitled, *The Problem of the*

Transmission of the Pentateuch.[113] In it he offers the theory that the Torah is a collection of multiple independent threads put together mostly by the Priestly and Deuteronomist redactors after the Exile. The debate and evolving understanding continues. For our purposes, we will go with the well-established idea of the Documentary Hypothesis with its chronological sequence of "JEDP," or Jahwist, Elohist, Deuteronomist, and Priestly writers and redactors. Thus, we use what we can to return to the world of the author, as Tate said, "to as great a degree as possible." This will be done in the next chapter. First, let us take a brief look at the history *of* the Bible.

OF

The history *of* the Bible reflects how the reading of the Bible affects history over time. We see it in the development of the Logos, we see it in the evolution of hermeneutics, and we see it in world changing movements and events. The vernacular translations of the Bible kindled the fires of the Protestant Reformation of the 16th and 17th centuries. Clinging to the Bible in King James English, the European settlers of Jamestown moved into the New World. The American settlers of the West moved out into the frontier to expand the territories of the United States, bringing their biblically based culture with them. In a spirit of "manifest destiny" they overwhelmed the indigenous populations to claim the riches of their "Promised Land." Today, missionaries, televangelists,

---

[113] BIBLICAL ARCHAEOLOGY STAFF, "ROLF RENDTORFF," BIBLE HISTORY DAILY, BIBLICAL ARCHAEOLOGY SOCIETY: BRINGING THE ANCIENT WORLD TO LIFE, LAST MODIFIED JUNE 11, 2014, ACCESSED AUGUST 24, 2017, HTTPS://WWW.BIBLICALARCHAEOLOGY.ORG/DAILY/ARCHAEOLOGY-TODAY/ARCHAEOLOGISTS-BIBLICAL-SCHOLARS-WORKS/ROLF-RENDTORFF-1925-2014/

and podcast preachers still spread the Word of God as they see it around the world to as many places and people as they can.

The Bible can be used for good or ill, love or hatred, expansion or isolation. It's uses have been historic in their effect on our global society. We cannot deny how much a part of our daily life it is. Our role, should we choose to accept it, is to be readers of the Bible and its history who support and uplift others, not through their acceptance of our spiritual viewpoints, but through a mutual sharing of stories that enrich us all. Mission impossible? Maybe not, if we can take what history conveys to us, and learn from it how to build a world of shared wisdom and compassionate contribution. This is possible when we let the information conveyed through history *in*, *about*, and *of* the Bible connect us with our own stories that reside in the heartmind. Let's look at an example of this in the death of the firstborn of Egypt.

PASSOVER

IN

Joshua looked up to see a thin stream of green smoke moving across the night sky. Like great fingers with the touch of death, the smoke moved down toward the Earth and Egypt. Joshua hurriedly washed the door frame with lamb's blood to protect his beloved Lilia where she was captive to Dathan, an Egyptian paid Hebrew who betrayed his own people. She would soon be freed again to marry Joshua, but for now, the final plague was collecting its toll. The payment was the firstborn of Egypt. Mournful cries filled the night as Egypt's people wept. Inside a small mud house, Moses and a few of the Hebrews, joined by his Egyptian mother, Bithia, who had been exiled, ate bitter herbs and unleavened bread in preparation for the next day's exodus out of four-hundred years of bondage in Egypt. Thus, says the book of Hollywood.

Okay, so I did put in the green smoke after all, but the Bible did not. Nor did it include Lilia or Bithia, and even though both Dathan and Joshua are in the Exodus story, neither is depicted in this part of it. To quote my dad, "That's not exactly the way it happened." Here is some of what did happen.

> "At midnight the Lord struck down all the firstborn in the land of Egypt, from the firstborn of Pharaoh who sat on his throne to the firstborn of the prisoner who was in the dungeon and all the firstborn of the livestock. Pharaoh arose in the night, he and all his officials and all the Egyptians; and there was a loud cry in Egypt, for there was not a house without someone dead. Then he summoned Moses and Aaron in the night, and said, 'Rise up, go away from my people, both you and the Israelites! Go, worship the Lord as you said. Take your flocks and your herds, as you said, and be gone. And bring a blessing on me too (Exodus 12:29-32)!'"

This part of the death of the firstborn of Egypt is actually a story within a story completing a story within a story. It is the story of death, within the story of the Passover which completes the story of the plagues of Egypt within the story of the Exodus. According to the book of Exodus, God was in a conflict with Pharaoh to free the children of Israel from slavery. *The New Interpreter's Study Bible* describes it this way:

> "The weapons of war are the forces of nature: The Lord summons reptiles, insects, and meteorological phenomena, including hail and darkness, in an initial assault on Pharaoh (chaps. 7-10). When these fail to persuade Pharaoh to release Israel from Egyptian slavery, death personified, described as the 'the destroyer,' descends upon the land of Egypt in the darkness of

245

midnight, slaying all firstborn Egyptian children and animals (chaps11-12)."[114]

Before the destroyer comes, the Lord instructs the people of Israel to select and slaughter a lamb, and to mix its blood with hyssop and spread it on the door posts and overhead block, or lintel, of the door to their homes. *"For the Lord will pass through to strike down the Egyptians; when he sees the blood on the lintel and on the two doorposts, the Lord will pass over that door and will not allow the destroyer to enter your houses to strike you down (Exodus 12:23)."*

This is the story according to what is *in* the Bible. Now let us look at the history *about* this scripture.

ABOUT

It is worth noting again that theories from recent years tell us that Exodus may be a gathering of multiple narrative threads of Israel's history, edited by Priestly and Deuteronomic editors after the Babylonian Exile. I look forward to exploring these ideas further over the next several years. Exodus has, however, traditionally been viewed as the work of three sources based on "literary style, language, and theological perspective." [115] This information from the "Documentary Hypothesis" renders the most knowledge on the history of authorship, and therefore is my choice at present for giving reference to it.

The Priestly writer wanted to ensure that the festival of unleavened bread, which was practiced during his time, had

---

[114] THE NEW INTERPRETER'S STUDY BIBLE: NEW REVISED STANDARD VERSION WITH THE APOCRYPHA, ED. WALTER J. HARRELSON (NASVILLE, TN: ABINGDON, 2003), 85.

[115] IBID, 86.

246

its roots in Mosaic history. This festival included the sacrifice of a lamb on behalf of each household. The redactor makes sure such details are included in the telling of the Passover story.

> *"If a household is too small for a whole lamb, it shall join its closest neighbor in obtaining one; the lamb shall be divided in proportion to the number of people who eat of it. Your lamb shall be without blemish, a year-old male; you may take it from the sheep or from the goats. You shall keep it until the fourteenth day of this month; then the whole assembled congregation of Israel shall slaughter it at twilight (Exodus 12:4-6)."*

It seems like the firstborn of Egypt weren't the only ones who had it rough.

Distinct from these details, the Jahwist and Elohist intertwine in vv29-32 to tell the story of a God at war with Pharaoh over the protection and freedom of His people. In these verses, the name of God is YHWH, or "The Lord." That the Lord is intimately involved with his people is a characteristic of the Jahwist. That God is also mighty enough to transcend the will of Pharaoh and the most powerful nation on Earth, is a characteristic of the Elohist. In looking at the death of the firstborn as part of the story of the Exodus, we see this about its authors.

> *"They come from a paradigm that tells them that God is literally a warrior God who doles out reward and punishment according to good or bad behavior, and that good behavior has a lot to do with spreading the power of God by destroying those who do not believe in Him, at least not in the right way. Such a paradigm views peace, not as the absence of war, but in the same meaning it had in its use in the Hebrew language, as shalom, which is the*

establishment of God's kingdom on earth and the prosperity and well-being of His people."[116]

Thus, the Yahwist/Elohist thread, or "JE", in Exodus brings forth a concept of a warrior God who protects and cares for His people like a loving parent. Without prejudicial opinions and value judgments, how do we evolve beyond our own warrior-like reactions to this kind of violent material in the Bible, let alone the war and violence that are still a part of our world? In looking at the history *in* the Bible, and the history *about* its authorship, we see that the death of the first born expands into a larger context of the Passover, the plagues, and the Exodus. In its larger context, this story is one of the most influential stories *of* human history.

OF

The Exodus from slavery in Egypt is the central story of the religion of Judaism. Passover, or *Pesach* in Hebrew, is its main yearly festival. This celebration also reaches into the holidays of Christianity. This is the festival during which Jesus shared a Passover meal, known as a Seder, with his disciples. This meal later became known as the "Last Supper". The lamb's blood of the Passover story becomes a metaphor for the death of Jesus on the cross on what is now the Christian day of atonement on God's Friday, or "Good Friday". The new life of freedom given to the Hebrews who passed through the birth canal of the Red Sea becomes the freedom of eternal life on resurrection Sunday, or Easter. All of which is in harmony with the new life of spring. In fact, Easter is

---

[116] LAURA BARRETT BENNETT, "HOLY WAR, SACRED PEACE: A LOOK AT THE PRESENT-DAY HERITAGE OF DEUTERONOMISTIC HISTORY," PRESENTED IN BIBLE HISTORY, HEBREW SCRIPTURES, SESSION 4 (UNITY WORLDWIDE SPIRITUAL INSTITUTE, OCTOBER 2016), 2.

not a biblical word, but the old English name, Eostre, the name of the goddess of spring and the rising star of the east.

What about the death of the firstborn in Egypt? Did this happen? It is possible that the first nine plagues could be explained by natural phenomenon, but the death of the firstborn was an anomaly. Even the drowning of Pharaoh's army in pursuit of the Israelites could be explained as a tidal wave or a returning of the tide. The Exodus was thought to have taken place in the time of Rameses II of Egypt. *The Jewish Study Bible* says the following:

"According to the biblical account, the Hebrew slaves worked on the construction of the city or Rameses (1:11). If there is a historical kernel to the story, the Pharaoh who enslaved them was Rameses II (1279-1213 BCE), the greatest builder in ancient Egypt, who built the city named after himself as his new capital, in the eastern delta."[117]

History *about* the world of the Bible and its authors tells us that Rameses was one of the most powerful and prosperous pharaohs of all time. How, then could this be a fact if he lost his entire slave and military force in one event? This, plus a reflection on the story from our twenty-first century ethical perspective informs us that God is not a God of mass death and destruction, whatever the stories of the Hebrew Scriptures may convey. Yet, there is no denying the biblical stories in which violent activity that shakes our current sensibilities to the core is played out. Where our present-day ethics meet the mindset of those who believed in a warrior God as a necessary part of ethnic survival is where the history of the Bible can live through us. Rather than reject outright

---

[117] THE JEWISH STUDY BIBLE, SECOND EDITION, TANAKH TRANSLATION, ED. ADELE BERLIN AND MARC ZVI BRETTLER (NEW YORK: OXFORD UNIVERSITY, 2014), 96.

anything that does not fit within our scope of what is right, or enlightened, we can look to understand its meaning for us a little better. This is where I recommended to you who are reading this now that you find time for the following Contemplation.

CONTEMPLATION 2

DIALOGUE

Take a deep breath and let your body move into a comfortable and upright position. Breathe normally for three breath cycles. Take another deep breath. On the inhale envision the breath as light moving into the space of the mind. On the exhale, let the light that fills the mind move down into the heart-center, anchoring the mind in the heart, connecting the two as one. Breathe normally as you close your eyes for one moment and dwell in the space of the heartmind. Then, open your eyes. From the space of the heartmind, invite the Spirit of God in you to be your guide, your healer, your protector, and your identity. Let yourself be the instrument through which God can know God.

Take a deep breath and read the verses below.

> "At midnight the Lord struck down all the firstborn in the land of Egypt, from the firstborn of Pharaoh who sat on his throne to the firstborn of the prisoner who was in the dungeon and all the firstborn of the livestock. Pharaoh arose in the night, he and all his officials and all the Egyptians; and there was a loud cry in Egypt, for there was not a house without someone dead. Then he summoned Moses and Aaron in the night, and said, 'Rise up, go away from my people, both you and the Israelites! Go, worship the Lord as you said. Take your flocks and your herds, as you said, and be gone. And bring a blessing on me too (Exodus 12:29-32)!'"

Since you may not want to let these words fill your thoughts, simply notice your feelings about them, without judgment. Then, take a deep inward breath and envision yourself breathing the words of this verse into the space of your heartmind. Exhale and release. Breathe normally for three breath cycles.

Take a deep breath with "Yah" on the inbreath, and "Weh" on the outbreath. See the author of these words taking form in your mind. Envision the author standing before you, ready to enter a silent and peaceful soul-to-soul dialogue about what is written. Ask the following questions of this author, knowing that he, or she, is here to answer your questions in a clear and insightful manor. Pause and listen after each question for a response. Ask the question again until the response is clear and insightful as intended by this encounter.

1. What is this story that you have written saying? (History *in* the Bible)
2. What are you saying through this story? (History *about* the Bible)
3. What is being revealed about me and my life and world in this story? (History *of* the Bible)

If nothing comes, that is okay. If something comes, write the responses in a journal. After writing, or just being present, remain in the stillness of this connection with the author through space and time. This figure before you in the space of your heartmind is part of your own self, helping you learn to grow you beyond what you know yourself to be. Be with this part of you, and feel what you feel for a brief period, knowing you are more than what you feel.

Take another deep breath with "Yah" on the inbreath and "Weh" on the outbreath. See the author with whom you have been in silent dialogue dissolving into the light of love within your heartmind. Breathe normally for three breath cycles. Take another deep breath with "Yah" on the inbreath and "Weh" on the outbreath, and thank "the Lord of your being" for this encounter. Amen.

FREEDOM

Below are the insights that I received in doing this exercise and in my own journaling of it.

1. What is this story that you have written saying? (History *in* the Bible)

   Death precedes new birth. What dies is whatever is holding me in bondage. There is nothing to fear.

2. What are you saying through this story? (History *about* the Bible)

   The Spirit of God in me is more powerful than anything I encounter in the world.

3. What is being revealed about me and my life and world in this story? (History *of* the Bible)

   My story of freedom from old limitations is a sacred reminder of who I am and who you are. We are greater than we know.

I have just one more question before moving into the chapter on *Meaning*. I want you to take it to you heartmind and let your response be a reminder of who you really are. "What is your freedom story?"

SUMMARY

- What we encounter on the path of life becomes part of who we are, bringing beauty and diversity to our existence.
- When in your awareness you recollect, or re-collect, certain thoughts and feelings you have held in consciousness, this is called memory. When you have a group of thoughts and feelings, connected by the same sequence of experiences, these are the memories that give you a story.
- The history of humanity is your high-story, or "hi-story", the elevated and expanded story of you.
- The Truth emerges when the heartmind is engaged with history. This is because the soul recognizes its own hi-story as depicted in the Bible and learns from it.
- History is an accounting of past events, as well as an accounting of the literary and cultural framework that reveals why the scriptures were written.
- Bible history has 3 aspects: the history *in* the Bible, the history *about* the Bible, and the history *of* the Bible.
  o The history *in* the Bible is history according to the Bible conveyed through events and teachings in the Bible.
  o The history *about* the Bible is history regarding the biblical text and its author.
  o The history *of* the Bible refers to how the reading of the text affected, and is still affecting, human history.
- The challenge with the history *in* the Bible, is that there is a gap in the space-time continuum between the biblical event or teaching, and the life of the modern reader and interpreter.
- History about the Bible helps close the gap by helping the modern reader connect with the biblical author.
- The "Four-Source Hypothesis" of Burnett Hillman Streeter (1874-1937) points out that Mark, Q, M, and L are considered by many scholars to be documents from which three similar, or Synoptic, Gospels were composed.
  o Mark, the earliest written Gospel, was a source of Matthew and Luke.

- o "Q", a theorized gospel that collected sayings of Jesus, was also a source of Matthew and Luke.
- o The source of writings that are only in Matthew became known as "M", and the source of writings that are only in Luke became known as "L".
- As for John, it is believed to have its own source known as the "Gospel of Signs," a list of the miracles of Jesus.
- Since the 18th century theologians had been speculating that Moses may not have written the Torah as believed by tradition.
- The "Documentary Hypothesis" was an order of theorized sources put together by Julius Wellhasen (1844-1918). It became the most widely accepted theory of sources for the Pentateuch. It is abbreviated as JEDP.
  - o J: Jahwist, pronounced Yahwist – This writer of the southern territories going back to the 10th century BCE depicts God as directly involved with the activities of the people and referred to as YHWH, or Yahweh.
  - o E: Elohist – This writer going back to the 9th century is from the northern territories of Israel depicts God as transcendent over all of Creation and referred to with the term, Elohim.

  - o D: Deuteronomist - Some post-modern scholars theorize that this author is part of the Priestly tradition of the 6th century BCE, while the most popular theory is that the "D" writer emerged as an independent author of Deuteronomy from the 7th century BCE.

  - o P: Priestly – Beginning in the 6th century BCE after the return of the people of Judah from the Babylonian Exile, this writer edited the older literature with an emphasis on detail and order according to the current religious traditions of his time.

- The Bible can be used for good or ill, love or hatred, expansion or isolation. It's uses have been historic in their effect on our global society.
- We cannot deny how much a part of our daily life the Bible is.

- Our role, should we choose to accept it, is to be readers of the Bible and its history who support and uplift others, not through their acceptance of our spiritual viewpoints, but through a mutual sharing of stories that enrich us all.
- I have just one more question before moving into the chapter on *Meaning*. I want you to take it into your heartmind and let your response be a reminder of who you really are. "What is your freedom story?"

INQUIRY

1. What is your freedom story?

2. How does Bible History contribute to the story of you?

3. Which aspect of Bible History has had the greatest influence on your life?
    a. History *in* the Bible
    b. History *about* the Bible
    c. History *of* the Bible

4. Which aspect of Bible History do you say is most important to our world today?

5. What do you say the value is in acquiring a deeper understanding of Bible History

CHAPTER 12: MEANING

"The kingdom of heaven is like treasure hidden in a field, which someone found and hid; then in his joy he goes and sells all that he has and buys that field (Matthew 13:44)."

VALUE

When you think of meaning in the Bible, what do you think? Do you think of understanding its original languages? Do you think of knowledge about its historical context, and what the author meant in writing it? Do you think of drawing meaning right off the page without even thinking about it at all? Or, do you think it is all meaningless? If the Bible doesn't mean anything to you, maybe that's a good start. If it does, you may want to go even deeper in your relationship with it.

If the Bible means something to you, no matter how good or bad it feels, or how long or short a time you have been studying it, you have a relationship with the Bible from the first tier of knowing. What the Bible means is what you have already decided it means according to your perception that comes from conclusions based on previous experience. That's good. It has brought you to where you are with the Bible. It has brought you to here. For example, if I could not recall a lot of what I already know about the Bible, I could not write this book.

If your relationship with the Bible is not working for you at this time, however, that's okay too. It just indicates a need to clean out the "been there, done that" T-shirt drawer – and what an incredible experience that can be. In fact, if you have read this book up to this point, and participated in its exercises, you have already been doing that – and more. You have been on a quest. What does that mean? It means you are seeking something meaningful, something that has value for your life.

Every quest, whether spiritually, intellectually, emotionally, politically, or materially based is a quest for meaning. You are seeking the treasure of that precious thing that will bring value to your existence. My dad once interpreted the parable of the hidden treasure from the Gospel of Matthew, seen at the beginning of this chapter. He interpreted the treasure in that parable to be the Truth with a capital "T". Yet, what is Truth but the inception of spiritual insight from the third tier of knowing that is beyond intellectual conception and formed words. When such insight is expressed in words, and those words are put into action, it brings meaning and value to life. Let's look at an example and you will see what I mean.

I had a friend when I was a minister in Flint, Michigan. Her name was Susan McCullen. Susan was a nurse who lived in Ann Arbor. Susan had a practice of walking in the woods and silently communing with God on a regular basis. In this communion, she started receiving lyrics and melodies for spiritual music. She was no musician. She did not even know how to read music or play an instrument. This did not stop her. She took the words and music that were coming to her and learned to play the guitar, so she could give them form through her own performances.

Susan made albums and began to play in churches near where she lived. I got to know her after hearing her music and inviting her to my church. Her music blessed many people and can still be heard on YouTube today. Susan went to the field of the heartmind and found the treasure she valued in the quietude of nature. It was the Truth, the language of God speaking to her from the silence of her own inner temple. She spoke this language through her music, and her music became a living treasure.

TREASURE

SEMANTICS

How do we find our treasure? Jesus said, "The kingdom of heaven is like treasure hidden in a field, which someone found and hid; then in his joy he goes and sells all that he has and buys that field (Matthew 13:44)." The tools for finding the treasure of Truth are semantic in nature. Two definitions for semantic are in the Merriam-Webster online dictionary. They are "the meaning or relationship of meanings," and "the language used." [118] In other words, when using language semantic means "meaning". How do we discover meaning in the language of the Bible? We look to its text. Randolph Tate wrote, "The meaning of the text is never that which is manifest, but exactly that which is latent. But what is stated serves as the primary context for what is unstated."[119]

As we look to the semantics of the biblical text, we find meaning through history, metaphor, etymology, and metaphysics. History, metaphor, and etymology give us our exegetical activity, while metaphysics internalizes the text to reveal what is happening in consciousness. After extracting meaning from exegesis and metaphysics, we then use what

---

[118] "DEFINITION OF SEMANTICS," MERRIAM-WEBSTER DICTIONARY, ACCESSED AUGUST 25TH, HTTPS://WWW.MERRIAM-WEBSTER.COM/DICTIONARY/SEMANTICS.

[119] W. RANDOLPH TATE, BIBLE INTERPRETATION: AN INTEGRATED APPROACH (GRAND RAPIDS, MI: BAKER ACADEMIC, 2008), 204.

259

we have discovered to go beyond meaning into the pure logic of the third tier of knowing. This we will do in the next chapter. For now, let us acquaint ourselves with the objects of treasure hunting.

HISTORY

We begin with history. History is the field in which the treasure of Truth is hidden. In Chapter 11 we explored history at depth. Here is a summary review. History in the Bible reveals the literal meaning of the text. History about the Bible reveals the text in the context of the world in which it was written and the intention of its author, and history of the Bible makes the text a living part of human history, including your own. With history in, about, and of the Bible, we have a place to begin the hunt for the treasure.

METAPHOR

Next, let's look at metaphor. Metaphor is any marker that is not the treasure, itself, but points the way to the treasure. In fact, to say that metaphor is a marker, is a metaphor. Of metaphor, Marcus Borg wrote in his book, Reading the Bible Again for the First Time, "'Metaphor' also means 'to see as': to see something as something else. Metaphor is linguistic art or verbal art. ...It emphasizes seeing, not believing. The point is not to believe in a metaphor, but to see in light of it."[120] In describing metaphor, Borg distinguishes between metaphor and simile. I paint the picture of metaphor with a broader brush that includes simile. I have, therefore, distinguished simile as one of four major kinds of intentional metaphors

---

[120] MARCUS BORG, READING THE BIBLE AGAIN FOR THE FIRST TIME (NEW YORK, NY: HARPER ONE, 1989), 41.

260

found in the biblical texts. Below are definitions and examples of each, along with how you can discern their meaning.

1. **Idiom**. My father, Dr. Paul Barrett, defined an *idiom* as, "...an expression peculiar to a language not readily understandable by the meaning of its parts." He then gave an example of a man who "lost his shirt on Wall Street."[121] This was not about someone walking around Wall Street looking for a shirt. Rather it was about someone whose Wall Street investments left him bankrupt.
   * Biblical Examples: *"...eye for an eye, tooth for a tooth..." (Deuteronomy 19:19).* Starting off as two of several literal instructions of equal retribution for a committed offense, this phrase became a blanket idiom for that same idea. If we did not have some understanding of what this phrase meant, say if we thought it referred to some form of trade in body parts, then Jesus' teaching would not have made any sense when he said, *"You have heard that it was said 'an eye for an eye, and a tooth for a tooth.' But I say to you, 'Do not resist the evildoer (Matthew 5:38-39).'"*
2. **Simile**. While others like to distinguish *simile* from *metaphor*, I believe the *simile* is a specific kind of *metaphor*. *Metaphor* is defined "...to seeing something as something else", and *simile* does that, but in a specific way. What identifies a simile from other metaphors is a little word. It can be the word, "like," or the word "as" often used in the same statement with the phrase "so is." Looking for these words in a phrase is also a good way to identify a simile in the Bible.

---

[121] DR. PAUL BARRETT, INTRODUCTION TO BIBLE INTERPRETATION, RECORDED 1986, FAIRFAX, VA: DIVINE LIFE MISSION, INC., 2 TAPES, TAPE 1, SIDE B.

- Biblical Examples: *"Like a gold ring in a pig's snout is a beautiful woman without good sense (Proverbs 11:22)."* Alright, so it's a bit misogynistic and will probably never be used in the *Daily Word Magazine* of prayer, but it's definitely a simile. Try this one. *"As an apple tree among the trees of the wood, so is my beloved among young men (Song of Solomon 2:3)."* Similes are often used in poetic form. One place where this is not the case is in the kingdom of heaven parables in Matthew, *"The kingdom of heaven is like yeast that a woman took and mixed in with three measures of flour until all of it was leavened (Matthew 13:33)."* The parable if the hidden treasure is another example.

3. **Symbol**. My dad defined a symbol as "...something chosen to represent something else." In modifying this statement I define a symbol as "some person, thing, or action chosen to represent something else."

   - Biblical Examples. Throughout the Bible we find allegorical and apocalyptic literature that is filled with symbols. We see a symbol in the flood allegory in Genesis as the "...bow in the clouds...(Genesis 9:13)," that symbolized God's covenant with Noah to never again destroy the Earth in such a way. We also see one in the book of Revelation in the "...new Jerusalem... (Revelation 21:2)," representing new life in God and a renewed world.

   - Symbols are also used outside of allegory and apocalypse. Two examples are the "...eagle's wings...(Exodus 19:4)," representing God's caring and protecting presence during the Exodus, and the "...divided tongues as of fire...(Acts 2:3)" representing the power of God's Word that descended upon the apostles and could be understood by everyone in every language.

   - And what about Jesus' famous sermons? The one in Luke was given on the plain (Luke 6:17) to represent the social equality and connection with the common person for which Jesus in Luke stood. The one in Matthew was given on the mount (Matthew 5:1) to represent the authority of the new law Jesus was revealing, just as the decalogue was given to Moses on the mountain of God. In fact, when symbols are repeated like mountains, or water, or eagles, or angels, such that they work their way into the mindset of the general population, they become archetypes.

4. **Archetype**. W. Randolph Tate wrote, "...an archetype is an image, plot, motif, character type, or concept which appears with repeated regularity."[122]

- Biblical Example. There are many good archetypes that are found throughout the Bible. One of the most prolific examples of a biblical archetype is the angel, appearing as an individual, a group, or a multitude of heavenly hosts. From the angels on the ladder of Jacob (Gen. 28.12) to those appearing to the shepherds at the birth of Jesus (Luke 2:15), angel appearances fill the Bible, and have become an archetype for the presence of God in the form of a divine message.

- Another form of biblical archetype is a number. There are several archetypal numbers throughout the Bible. One example is the number 7, seen in God's act of creation (Genesis 1:1-2:4a), in how many times we should forgive (Matthew 18:22), and in the letters to the churches (Revelation 2:1-3:22), representing the fulfillment of a goal or purpose, or how much and how long it takes to complete something. Making use of this archetypal number, this book that you are reading now has 7 parts, "7 Principles of Interpretation" and a 7-Step method of interpretation.

---

[122] TATE, 174.

Notice how I used more than one Bible reference for each of these examples. This is because many of the idioms, similes, symbols, and archetypes show up in the Bible more than once, or at least some word or phrase that identifies them does. For example, "The kingdom of heaven is like..." to identify the metaphorical similes of the parables in Matthew. The best way to identify idioms, similes, symbols and archetypes is to look for parallels in phrasing, terms, or patterns of use in more than one part of the Bible.

ETYMOLOGY

If *history* is the field in which we find the treasure of Truth, and *metaphor* refers to any of the markers that point the way, *etymology* is the shovel we use to dig-in when we have found the right spot. "*Etymology* is the study of the derivation of words."[123] This statement was made by my dad in support of his view that an important principle of Bible interpretation is the meaning of names. Part of the hermeneutical circle is the meaning of individual names of people, places and things. As mentioned in Chapter 5, the "hermeneutical circle" is the "...reciprocal interplay of text to context to reader and back to the meaning of the text...".[124] Names are particles within the larger structure of the verse and text that render meaning to that structure. The interpreter then can see the patterns within the larger structure that gives meaning back to the names.

---

[123] BARRETT, TAPE 2, SIDE A.

[124] (SEE CHAPTER 5)

For example, "Moses" is an Egyptian name that literally means, "drawing out of the water."[125] In the larger context of the Exodus story, we see even more meaning for Moses name, and we see how his name adds meaning to the story. The act of drawing out of the water is a metaphor for birth. Moses was literally floated down the river in a basket and drawn out of the water to be adopted by the daughter of Pharaoh. When the children of Israel were freed from bondage in Egypt, they crossed through the watery birth canal of the Red Sea to be given the Law of God at Mt. Sinai, and to become a nation. The Exodus, then, is the birth of freedom, of Law, and of the nation of Israel, and Moses, whose name implies "birth" is the midwife.

Pretty cool – huh? And that's just the exegetical level of working with etymology. To practice etymology, you would need to be able to look up Hebrew and Greek words for biblical names. This is because Hebrew is the root language of most of the names of people, places, and things in the Hebrew Bible, and Greek is the primary root language of these things in the New Testament. To do this, most everything we look to can be found in *Strong's Concordance with Hebrew and Greek Lexicons*, online or in print, as mentioned in Chapter 6. Just be aware that "Strong's" is presented in the King James English version of the Bible, and you may have to look up some of its words and phrases that are different than your version. Of course, if English is not your strongest language, you would have to find the best Bible Concordance in your language. I do know that "Strong's" is available in Spanish.

---

[125] JAMES STRONG, STRONG'S EXHAUSTIVE CONCORDANCE OF THE BIBLE, UPDATED EDITION (PEABODY, MA: HENDRICKSON, 2007), 1535.

There is another language. While the Greek and Roman empires, including Palestine, used Greek as the common language, Aramaic was the spoken language of both Jesus and the great prophets of the Hebrew Scriptures. This was the result of the dominant Mesopotamian Empires of Assyria and Babylon before the time of the Greeks and Romans. Because of this, there are remnants of Aramaic passages and words in both Testaments. One example is Jesus' statement on the cross, *"Eli, Eli, lema sabachthanni,"* which has been interpreted as meaning *"My God, My God, why have you forsaken me (Matthew 27:46)?"* Or – in a fifth century Aramaic manuscript of the Christian Bible called the *Peshitta* – this phrase translates as "Oh God, Oh God, to what end have you kept me?"[126] Before his death, Dr. Rocco Errico translated the Gospel of Matthew from this manuscript. If you really want to dive into any biblical Aramaic, look online for the works of Dr. George Lamsa, Dr. Rocco Errico, and/or any other good book or lexicon on biblical Aramaic.

Whatever resources you use in looking back in time to the original languages of the Bible, the derivation of words and names can sometimes be surprising, and sometimes be straight forward. Whatever meaning you find when working with etymology, it can add to the deeper meaning found when working with metaphysics.

METAPHYSICS

Once again, we visit metaphysics. Metaphysics is the key to unlocking the chest in which the treasure is found. As stated in Chapter 6, "It is the study of the Truth of Being, or the

---

[126] ROCCO A. ERRICO, THE MESSAGE OF MATTHEW: AN ANNOTATED PARALLEL ARAMAIC-ENGLISH GOSPEL OF MATTHEW (SANTA FE, NM: NOOHRA FOUNDATION, 1996), 118.

living reality and spiritual essence of all that exists."[127] As applied to metaphysical interpretation, "It includes understanding the things, characters, and stories of biblical scripture as metaphors for the qualities, states of mind, thoughts, and feelings within one's own consciousness."[128] While I believe metaphysical meanings are unintentional metaphors, that is, they were not what the author had in mind when writing the biblical text, I also believe they hold great value in our understanding of ourselves, our lives, and our world. This is because a true metaphysical meaning is reached through the exegesis of history, metaphor, and etymology in combination with self-reflection and revelation. Let's see how this works with our central text for this chapter as once again we explore *History*, *Metaphor*, *Etymology*, and *Metaphysics*.

PARABLE

HISTORY

Regarding the parable of the hidden treasure (Matthew 13:44), the history *in* the Bible tells us that Jesus was by the sea giving a discourse of seven parables. The history *about* the Bible tells us that this parable is not found in the other Gospels and is unique to Matthew. It refers to an encounter with the kingdom of God that outweighs all other value in life. To experience the kingdom of God, one must be completely committed and willing to set aside all else.

---

[127] (SEE CHAPTER 6)

[128] IBID.

To further develop this understanding, it is believed that Matthew was written after the destruction of the Temple, and the fall of Jerusalem to Rome, leaving many Jews to question where to place their religious aspirations. The author's intention with the parables of Matthew 13 is to strengthen the resolve of his Jewish-Christian audience in participating in a counter-cultural movement to follow Jesus who is believed to be the fulfillment of Jewish law and prophecy. The kingdom of heaven stands in strong contrast to imperial Rome. It's power spreads faster, *"...it is the smallest of all the seeds, but when it has grown it is the greatest of shrubs...,* (Matthew 13:32a). It is also of greater value, *"...on finding one pearl of great value, he went and sold all that had and bought it (Matthew 13:45b)."*

The history *of* the Bible shows that the influence of these parables set forth an archetypal pattern that lays the groundwork for Christian communal and monastic living. Giving all that you have to build a community that brought God's kingdom to Earth is an idea that has been practiced for centuries, right up to today. I even grew up with the Sunday School song, "Seek ye first the kingdom of God, and his righteousness, and all these things will be added unto you, Allelu, Alleluia!" Hmm! I think to some degree these parables affected my personal history. What about you? If so, great! If not, that's great too! Because now we are discovering, or re-discovering, the meaning of the hidden treasure for us.

METAPHOR

The intention of using metaphor in our selected parable is quite clear. I have even expanded on its intended metaphorical nature to write about the elements of meaning. It was not only Matthew's author who used the literary genre of parables as metaphorical similes but wrote that intention into Jesus' teachings.

> *"Jesus told the crowds all these things in parables, without a parable he told them nothing. This was to fulfill what had been spoken through the prophet; 'I will open my mouth to speak in parables; I will proclaim what has been hidden from the foundation of the world (Matthew 13:34 with a quote from Psalm 78:2).'"*

This indicates that to know spiritual Truth, we must compare it with the things of everyday life, as is done in the parables. How much more intentional can you get? After all, the word, *parable*, literally means "a comparing." [129] What are the intentional metaphors, or comparisons, of this verse. Let's take a closer look at the text. *"The kingdom of heaven is like treasure hidden in a field, which someone found and hid; then in his joy he goes and sells all that he has and buys that field (Matthew 13:44)."*

From our historical analysis, we see that the "kingdom of heaven" was a reference to the community of those who followed Jesus in the ways of God. The "treasure hidden in a field" is this community (the treasure) existing within a larger potential for growth (the field). The "someone" is a community member, or perhaps, the reader of the text who is considering being part of this community. So joyful is this "someone" at the prospect of what is to come that he makes a total commitment to its potential growth. He "...sells all that he has and buys that field." Now, let's get out the shovel of etymology and dig a little deeper.

---

[129] DONALD K. MCKIM, WESTMINSTER DICTIONARY OF THEOLOGICAL TERMS (LOUISVILLE, KY: WESTMINSTER JOHN KNOX PRESS, 1996), 200.

269

ETYMOLOGY

All of the following Greek definitions are from "Strong's."[130] Because there are so many, I have given them the reference number of where to find them in the Greek dictionary that is part of the Strong's Concordance, rather than giving each one its own footnote. They will be given with the reference numbers of where to find them in the Strong's Greek dictionary. Those numbers, of course, begin with "G", just as the references to the Hebrew dictionary begin with "H". For example, the word, "kingdom," comes from the Greek, *basileia* (G932), which means *royalty, rule,* and *realm.* Now let's look at some of the other words in the verse. The word, "heaven," comes from the Greek, *ouranos* (G3772), meaning *elevation,* and *sky.* Thus, we know that the "kingdom of heaven" is an elevated realm in which God rules.

The word "treasure," is from the Greek, *thesauros* (G2344), meaning *deposit,* and *wealth.* To find the word in "Strong's" for "hidden" I had to go to my search engine of Google, and type in "Matthew 13:44 in KJV", or King James Version. It is slightly different from the NRSV, or New Revised Standard Version, of the Bible that I use. The KJV uses the word "hid." The Greek word for "hid", or "hidden", is *krypto* (G2928), meaning *conceal,* and *keep secret.* This tells us even more. Not only is the treasure a metaphor for the kingdom, which is a metaphor for the Christ based community, it is also a *secret.* The word, "field", comes from the Greek, *agros* (G68), meaning *piece of ground, country, farm, hamlet,* and *land.* Remember the word, "agriculture"? "Someone" is from

---

[130] A REFERENCE TO JAMES STRONG, STRONG'S EXHAUSTIVE CONCORDANCE OF THE BIBLE, UPDATED EDITION (PEABODY, MA: HENDRICKSON, 2007).

antrhopos (G444), which simply means, *human being.* "Found" is *heurisko*, meaning *come upon, meet, learn, discover*, and *obtain.* Here we have a place that is rich and fertile for growth and development (field), and that contains a deposit of wealth (treasure) about which no one knows (hidden). A person (someone) comes upon and discovers (found) the wealth (treasure) and keeps it a secret (hid/hidden). In other words, *"The kingdom of heaven is like treasure hidden in a field, which someone found and hid; ... (Matthew 13:44a)."*

then in his joy he goes and sells all that he has and buys that field (Matthew 13:44)."

The verse continues, *"...then in his joy he goes and sells all that he has and buys that field (Matthew 13:44b)."* The word "joy" comes from the Greek, *chara* (G5479), meaning *gladness, calm delight*, and *greatly.* "Sells", or "selleth" in the KJV, is from *poleo* (G4453), meaning *barter.* "Has", or "hath" in the KJV, is *echo* (G2192), meaning *have, be*, and *need.* Lastly, "buys", or "buyeth" in the KJV, is *agorazo* (G59), meaning *purchase*, and *redeem.* In other words, with great delight (joy) the individual barters (sells) all that he is and thinks he needs (has) in order to redeem (buy) the wealth (treasure), that is in the fertile place (field).

METAPHYSICS

Say what?! That sure is a long way to go just to say what the verse basically says from the start. Why do it? Dr. Barrett said that there are two primary approaches to "knowledge of the meanings of names". They are "etymological", and "metaphysical". We have done some digging into the etymology, or "EM". Let's grab the keys to the treasure by taking a look at the names, or words, in the context of their phrases, then putting a metaphysical meaning, or "MP", to what we find. That is to say, let's look at what the words and phrases of this text symbolize in the consciousness of you and me, and what this means to the soul of each of us. Here is the list of phrases.

- "Kingdom of Heaven" – (EM) The elevated realm in which God rules. (MP) An expanded awareness of God's presence and power in life.
- "Treasure hidden in a field" – (EM) Secret deposit of wealth in a place of growth. (MP) The richness of Truth (treasure) buried and unacknowledged (hidden) in the depths of consciousness, or the soul (field).
- "Someone found and hid" – (EM) Someone discovered and kept secret the wealth. (MP) A positive thought takes hold of Truth (someone found) and holds it in silence (and hid).
- "In his joy" – (EM) In a calm state of great delight. (MP) Happy thoughts that bring calm to the soul.
- "Sells all that he has" – (EM) Barters his whole being, what he has, needs, and is. (MP) Total commitment and focus given to knowing the Truth and experiencing God-centered awareness.
- "Buys that field" – (EM) Redeems the deposit of wealth along with its potential for growth. (MP) Truth grows within the soul and expands consciousness into the awareness of God in all things.

As we put our metaphysical phrasing together, it will revise itself in a natural way that makes sense for what it has to teach us. I am using the first-person plural of "our", "we", and "us" to include you in the work that I have done. Here is the resulting message from doing that.

Metaphysical Meaning: An expanded awareness of God's presence and power in life is buried and unacknowledged in the depths of the soul. A positive thought calls it forth to our present awareness but holds silently to it. When in the delight of what is possible, our whole being becomes focused on growing ourselves and our world from the insight of this God-centered awareness, we give ourselves completely to that purpose. It is then that it can grow within us, and work through us to grow our world.

To summarize: *When we give ourselves wholly to knowing God, God is known through us. Or in poetry form: "It is God we know through our commitment to grow."*

WRAP-UP

This is both the "nitty gritty", and the fun of exegetical and metaphysical interpretation. It has been practiced this way, in one form or another, not just for the hundred or so years Unity has been doing it, but for the thousands of years humanity has looked for meaning in Scripture. What brings the meaning home to the heartmind, and makes it come alive in being and body, is spiritual logic. It is this *Logic* to which we will look in our next chapter to expand our experience and move toward the final stages of becoming the living language of God.

SUMMARY

- Any quest, regardless of whether it is spiritually, intellectually, emotionally, politically, or materially based is a quest for meaning.
- As we look to the semantics of the biblical text, we find meaning through history, metaphor, etymology, and metaphysics.
- History, metaphor, and etymology give us our exegetical activity, while metaphysics internalizes the text to reveal what is happening in consciousness.
- History *in, about,* and *of* the Bible forms the field in which the treasure of Truth is hidden.
- Metaphor is any marker that is not the treasure, itself, but points the way to the treasure. According to Dr. Marcus Borg, metaphor means "to see something as something else."
- There are four kinds of metaphor.
    - **Idiom**: Dr. Paul Barrett defined an *idiom* as, "...an expression peculiar to a language not readily understandable by the meaning of its parts."
    - **Simile**: What identifies a simile from other metaphors is a little word. It can be the word, "like," or the word "as" often used with the words "so is," or to compare one thing to another.
    - **Symbol**: A symbol is some person, thing, or action chosen to represent something else.
    - **Archetype**: When symbols are repeated like mountains, or water, or eagles, or angels, such that they work their way into the mindset of the general population, they become archetypes.
- The best way to identify idioms, similes, symbols and archetypes is to look for parallels in phrasing, terms, or patterns of use in more than one part of the Bible.

- Etymology is the shovel used to dig for the treasure. It is defined by Dr. Barrett as "...the study of the derivation of words."
- Part of the hermeneutical circle is the meaning of individual names of people, places and things. Names are particles within the larger structure of the verse and text that render meaning to that structure. The interpreter then can see the patterns within the larger structure that gives meaning back to the names.
- Metaphysics is the key to unlocking the chest in which the treasure is found. It is defined in Chapter 6 as "...the study of the Truth of Being, or the living reality and spiritual essence of all that exists."
- Metaphysical interpretation includes understanding the things of Scripture as metaphors for the qualities, states of mind, thoughts, and feelings within one's own consciousness."
- Metaphysical meanings are unintentional metaphors, that is, they were not what the author had in mind when writing the biblical text. Yet, they are important in our quest for Truth.
- Because a true metaphysical meaning is reached through the exegesis of history, metaphor, and etymology in combination with self-reflection and revelation, its holds great value in understanding ourselves, our lives and our world.
- Exegesis and Metaphysical Interpretation have been practiced in one form or another for thousands of years as humanity has looked for meaning in Scripture.

INQUIRY

1. Share something that brings meaning to your life. What does it mean to you?

2. Why is finding Truth like digging for hidden treasure?

3. Why is it important to understand metaphor when finding meaning in the Bible?

4. Did the authors of the Bible intend for their writings to be metaphysically interpreted? Why or why not?

5. What is the value of metaphysical interpretation as it applies to the Bible?

CHAPTER 13: LOGIC

"For the trumpet will sound, and the dead will be raised imperishable, and we will be changed (1 Corinthians 15:52b)."

INTUITION

Logic from the mind of reason brought me to the metaphysical meanings found in the interpreted scripture of Chapter 12, but logic goes even deeper than that. My father, Dr. Paul Barrett, said that spiritual logic assimilates knowledge into knowingness. He explained further with the following:

"Logic deals with spiritual reason. It is the kind of reason that uses the intellect, but is not governed by it. We are all capable of reasoning from a spiritual base. The base is called intuition. Ideas conveyed through Scripture are spiritually based. They are alive and the spiritually discerning mind can assimilate them through logic."[131]

Logic is our connection with the Logos, or the Word of God. It goes beyond the intellect to the heartmind where we awaken our inner knowing, or intuition.

In this chapter, we engage the breath of life, or *neshamah*, to move into the space of the heartmind, or *leba*, as we work with a challenging passage in the Bible when it comes to how it applies to our lives today. We begin with a method that brings

---

[131] DR. PAUL BARRETT, INTRODUCTION TO BIBLE INTERPRETATION, RECORDED 1986, FAIRFAX, VA: DIVINE LIFE MISSION, INC., 2 TAPES, TAPE 2, SIDE B.

together the principles of metagetical interpretation to establish a relationship with Scripture. In so doing, we discern the meaning of Scripture through exegesis and metaphysics. Then, we let the language of God reveal itself through the intuition of pure spiritual *Logic*, and we see what message emerges for us.

METHOD

RECIPE

Logic is the sixth of the "7 Principles of Interpretation" known as *Love, Prayer, Contemplation, History, Meaning, Logic,* and *Mastery.* These principles are the ingredients of the interpretive stew. If they are the ingredients of the stew, the "7-Step Method of Metagetics" provides the recipe on how to put them together, blend their flavors, and create a delicious experience. These 7 steps are *Choose, Commune, Contextualize, Combine, Conclude, Constitute,* and *Contribute.* In this chapter, we are engaging 6 of the 7 principles along with 5 of the 7 steps. In the next chapter we complete the process with the last principle and the final 2 steps.

This may sound complex, but it follows a simple pattern. First come the principles, then the steps. First, we gather the ingredients of our stew, then we apply the recipe. Just as when you are working with the ingredients and instructions of a recipe, you put your principles together and then do your steps in portions according to the recipe. There are 5 portions in the metagetical recipe. Within these portions, each principle will be shared as an exercise that gives you the experience of that principle. For greater clarity, each of these exercises will be laid out before you in a table, just as you lay out each ingredient on the table where you work with your recipe.

With *Portion 1* the ingredient, or principle, is *Love* and the recipe instruction, or step, is to *Choose*. *Portion 2* puts together the principles of *Prayer* and *Contemplation* with the step to *Connect*. In *Portion 3*, the principles of *History* and *Meaning* share the two-part step to *Contextualize*, while *Meaning* also includes the step to *Combine*. *Portion 4* assimilates the previous work with the ingredient of *Logic* applied through the step to *Conclude*. Finally, in the last chapter, *Mastery* is the great ingredient whose full flavor is epitomized through the steps to *Constitute* and to *Contribute* in *Portion 5*. We begin with *Portion 1*.

PORTION 1

For this portion of the recipe, we have laid out a contemplative exercise that invites *Love* to guide the way as you *Choose* a Scripture. Your chosen scripture can be a verse, a passage, or a story. Your choice may be from coming across a writing that leapt out at you and cried for further understanding. Or – it may be one that you went to the concordance to find to locate something that speaks to a theme or project on which you are working. Or – it may be one you already know, either a little or a lot, and are seeking a new relationship with it. Or – maybe you are looking for inspiration and you just "dropped the needle," as explained in chapter 10. However your choice is made, it is just right for you at the time you choose it when you choose it from a place of love.

For now, I have chosen a scripture for you. This is to guide you in the learning process of Chapters 13 and 14. I recommend following along with what is chosen, and then going back through these steps with a scripture of your choice. When I chose this scripture, I did it from love. When you choose your scripture, you can come from love as well. Here is a contemplative exercise designed to awaken love in you.

Principle 1: *Love*
• Focus on the name of God within you as you deeply breathe in - and breathe out. Let your body relax into a comfortable and upright posture, then breathe normally for three breath cycles.
• Take another deep breath and let the spirit of the Logos move into the mind as a vision of light on the inbreath. On the outbreath, bring the focus of the mind down into the heart and anchor yourself in the space of the heartmind.
• Breathe normally for a moment, feeling love in the space of your heartmind. If you have trouble centering on love, think of someone or something you love and let that awaken love in you.
• Take a deep breath and ask your heartmind, "Through what Scripture can I expand my capacity to love?" Breathe normally for three or more breath cycles and listen for an answer.
• Repeat this until you have a response.

STEP 1: *CHOOSE*

In choosing your own scripture, when you receive a response from your contemplation on love, pursue it. You may get a few words in your mind, or an idea of what the Scripture is supposed to be, and may have to do some searching for it. Sometimes this can be an obvious scripture, such as *"Love your enemies, ... (Matthew 5:44)."* Sometimes it can be a challenging scripture through which you can learn to love more greatly. If it is right for you, your heartmind will know it. Once you have found your scripture, choose it. Let yourself be in a relationship of open anticipation that will attract the right message from it for you.

Since I have chosen our scripture for the time being, I invite you to be open to its gifts as well. This means you must also choose it, if only to learn more about this process. To do so, read through the passage below:

> *"Listen, I will tell you a mystery! We will not all die, but we will all be changed, in a moment, in the twinkling of an eye, at the last trumpet. For the trumpet will sound, and the dead will be raised imperishable, and we will be changed. For this perishable body must put on imperishability, and this mortal body must put on immortality. When this perishable body puts on imperishability, and this mortal body puts on immortality, then the saying that is written will be fulfilled: 'Death has been swallowed up in victory. Where, O death, is your victory? Where, O death, is your sting?' The sign of death is sin, and the power of sin is the law. But thanks be to God, who gives us the victory through our Lord Jesus Christ (1 Corinthians 15:51-57)."*

Now, take a brief pause, and consciously choose to engage with this passage. This does not mean you have to agree with it or judge it in any way. You can simply choose to have a relationship with it that reveals Truth to you, whether you are attracted to what it says, or not. When you are ready, you may continue the process with *Portion 2*.

PORTION 2

In this portion, we bring forth the ingredients of *Prayer* and *Contemplation*.

Principle 2: *Prayer*

- Take a deep breath and focus on the name of God within you as you breathe in – and out. You can use *Yah* on the inbreath and *Weh* on the outbreath, or if you prefer, you can use *I* on the inbreath and *Am* on the outbreath. Do this again. And one more time.
- Remain silent and still. Breathe normally until you feel a direct connection, or communion, with the Spirit of God in the space of your heartmind, whatever that Spirit is for you. Silence...
- When you are ready, you can stretch and open your eyes.

Following your prayer time, you can return to the chosen scripture in the preceding text or look it up in your Bible. While the chosen scripture is from the New Testament, and speaks to Christian ideals, bear in mind that it belongs to no religion in this moment. What these words hold for you is a spiritual insight that speaks specifically to you, just as you are.

Principle 3: *Contemplation*

- Focus your eyes on the chosen scripture. Read its words. Remember, these are words on a page that are there to reveal the Spirit of the Word in you.
- After you have read it once, read the verse again, focusing your full attention on its words. Simply notice your feelings about them, without judgment. Take a deep inward breath and envision yourself breathing the words

---

of this verse into the space of your heartmind. Exhale and
release. Breathe normally for three breath cycles.
- Take another deep breath and ask this question of the
scripture before you. "What do you have to reveal to me?"
Repeat this inquiry two more times. Then relax and
breathe normally.

STEP 2 – COMMUNE

Like milk and flour blending in a bowl, *Prayer* and
Contemplation come together to create an experience that is
more than the sum of these two ingredients. It is the
experience of spiritual communion. To *Commune* is to come
into conscious union with both the Spirit within you, and the
words before you. It is to completely connect with what you
seek - the Spirit of the Word in Scripture.

PORTION 3

This is the exegetical piece where the bulk of the intellectual
work is done. Let your mind be anchored in the heartmind as
you move through this. When you do it with your own chosen
scripture, enjoy the research! Have fun digging for the
treasures of Truth in each word. You may choose to work with
short passages of 2 to 3 verses, or longer passages between 3
to 10 verses. I do not recommend working in detail with
passages of more than 10 verses. It simply takes too long. Of
course, if you want to put in the time and effort, it can be a
very enlightening process.

Following the historical research, you can select words or
terms that stand out for you and discern their meanings
through etymological and metaphysical interpretation. If in
your research you discover the presence of any metaphorical

terms, you can also make note of those. Here are some instructions on how to do this with the answers drawn from the work I did on *History* and *Meaning* with our currently chosen scripture of *1 Corinthians 15:51-57*.

Principle 4: *History*
Acquaint yourself with the history *in*, *about*, and *of* the scripture. In a good Study Bible, read the scriptural annotations, and/or look through the introduction to the book in which the chosen passage is found.

STEP 3A: *CONTEXTUALIZE HISTORY*

To *Contextualize History* is to move into the world of the author, familiarizing yourself with the story and intention of the Scripture through an exploration of the known facts. For our scripture, I turned to *The New Interpreter's Study Bible*.[132] Here is a paraphrased summary of what I discovered based on the history in, about, and of the Bible.

1. *History In*: This is Paul's treatise to the Corinthians on Jesus' resurrection and the resurrection of the dead bringing forth his theme of justification, or salvation, through faith in Jesus Christ.
2. *History About*: Paul had been corresponding with the Corinthians for more than three years. In this correspondence, they asked him to elaborate on some of the things he taught. In this passage he is addressing their

---

[132] THE NEW INTERPRETER'S STUDY BIBLE, ED. WALTER J. HARRELSON (NASHVILLE, TN: ABINGDON, 2000), 2037 AND.

questions about the resurrection of the dead and their concerns regarding those in their community who had already died before the return of Christ.

3. ***History of***: Resurrection and eternal life following death is a theme that has worked its way into the common belief system of countless people around the world. You can discern how the ideas put forth in this scripture have affected your life by contemplating the following: What is your story of comforting those who have lost loved ones, or things, that are precious to them. What is your belief about these things? How has that shown up in your life?

This understanding of History helps to shape our ideas for what this scripture can mean for us and who we are as eternal and unlimited beings. With the context, let us now look at *Meaning*.

Principle 5: *Meaning*

Discern the meaning of the passage in one of two ways: "Verse by Verse", or "As a Whole". Here is how to apply meaning:

Verse by Verse:
  a. Break down the passage into its individual phrases or verses.
  b. List specific words that stand out in these phrases.
  c. Research the metaphorical and/or etymological meanings of these words.
  d. Take a deep breath, move into the heartmind, and discern the metaphysical meaning of each word.
  e. Follow it up with a "Key Phrase" of metaphysical insight from the quoted statement.
  f. Put these phrases together in a paragraph of "Metaphysical Meaning."

As a Whole:

---

a. List 6 or 7 words that stand out for you within the whole passage.
b. Research the metaphorical and/or etymological meanings of these words.
c. Take a deep breath, move into the heartmind, and discern the metaphysical meaning of each word.
d. Bring the meanings together in a summarized phrase.

STEP 3B *CONTEXTUALIZE MEANING*

To *Contextualize Meaning* is not only to put the words on the page in the context of their ancient languages, but also to find the deeper meaning that emerges through these words from the context of our own spiritual understanding. On the following pages is an example of how meaning is applied with our chosen passage "verse by verse". Again, I am using the Greek words from *Strong's* accompanied by their reference numbers.[133] The etymology of each word is presented first, then the metaphysical meaning is below the word. Also added is the symbolic meaning where metaphor is present. For clarity with its categories, each verse is presented in its own table outline. There are 8 tables, one for each verse. The categories are the "*Verse #*", followed by the definitions of the "Key Words," followed by a metaphysical translation of the verse called "Key Phrase". Here are the verses of the chosen passage with etymology and metaphysics.

Verse 51:

---

[133] JAMES STRONG, STRONG'S EXHAUSTIVE CONCORDANCE OF THE BIBLE, UPDATED EDITION (PEABODY, MA: HENDRICKSON, 2007).

"Listen, I will tell you a mystery! We will not all die, but we will all be changed,…"

Key Words:
- Listen: (G2400) *idou*, meaning *behold*, and *see*.
  - The state of being alert.
- Tell: (G3004) *lego*, meaning *speak, affirm, teach.*
  - The receiving of a teaching in consciousness
- Mystery: (G3466) *mysterion*, meaning *hidden thing, hidden purpose, secret.*
  - Truth buried within consciousness.
- Die/Death: (G2837) *koimao*, meaning *sleep.* Even though Paul was writing about the actuality of dying and death, it is clear from the linguistics that dying is a metaphor for going to sleep.
  - Falling asleep in consciousness. The unconscious state.
- Changed: (G236) *alasso*, meaning *exchanged, transformed.*
  - Transformation in Consciousness.

Key Phrase:
"Be alert to the teaching of the Truth that has been buried in your consciousness. You are no longer unconscious. You are transformed."

Verse 52:
"…in a moment, in the twinkling of and eye, at the last trumpet. For the trumpet will sound, and the dead will be raised imperishable, and we will be changed."

Key Words:
- Moment: (G823) *atomos*, meaning *indivisible.*
  - Undivided attention

- Twinkling: (G4493) *rhipe*, meaning *a stroke, a beat.*
  - o Instantaneous awakening.
- Trumpet: (G2536) *salpigx*, meaning *quavering*, and *reverberation.* As a metaphor, a trumpet symbolizes the call of a great event or happening. The last trumpet indicates the end of one thing and the beginning of another.
  - o Resounding spiritual awareness. A paradigm shift in consciousness.
- Imperishable: (G852) *aphthartos*, meaning *uncorrupted, undecaying, immortal.*
- New Life. That in us which is eternal.

Key Phrase: "With undivided attention, instantaneous awakening creates a paradigm shift in your consciousness. Resounding spiritual awareness awakens that which has gone unconscious to its eternal nature, and transformation is the result."

Verse 53:
"For this perishable body must put on imperishability and this mortal body must put on immortality."

Key Words:
- Perishable: (G5349) *phthartos*, meaning *decayed.*
  - o Forgotten ideas.
- Mortal: Greek *thnetos* (G 2349), meaning, *liable to death.*
  - o Thoughts of limitation
- Immortality: Greek *athanasia* (G 110), meaning *undying, everlasting.*
  - o Ideas of possibility.

Key Phrase:

"Forgotten ideas will find new life and thoughts of limitation will become ideas of possibility."

288

Verse 54:
"When this perishable body puts on imperishability, and this mortal body puts on immortality, then the saying that is written will be fulfilled: 'Death has been swallowed up in victory.'"

Key Words:
- Swallowed: (G2666) *katapino*, meaning *drink down, devour, destroy.*
  - The activity in consciousness of dissolution.
- Victory: (G3534) *nikos*, meaning *to utterly vanquish.*
  - To eliminate, or release

Key Phrase:
"When forgotten ideas find new life and thoughts of limitation become ideas of possibility the unconscious state of mind will be eliminated."

Verse 55:
"'Where, O death, is your victory? Where, O death, is your sting?'"

Key Words:
- Sting: Greek *kentron* (G2759), meaning *wounding from a stinging animal.*
  - Emotional Pain.

Key Phrase:
"The power of the unconscious state of mind is released. The pain of the unconscious state of mind is no more."

Verse 56:
"The sting of death is sin, and the power of sin is the law."

Key Words:
- Sin (G266) *hamartia*, meaning *miss the mark.*
  - Misunderstanding.
  - Error thinking.
- Power (G1411) *dynamis*, meaning *strength*, and *ability.*
  - Fortitude
- Law (G3551) *nomos*, meaning *established, custom, command.*
  - Pre-determined and established ways of being.
  - Limitation

Key Phrase:
"The pain of being unconscious is error thinking. The fortitude of error thinking is limitation."

Verse 57:
"But thanks be to God, who gives us the victory through our Lord Jesus Christ."

Key Words:
- Thanks: (G5485) *charis*, meaning *grace, loving-kindness, goodwill.*
  - State of grace.
- God: (G2316) *theos*, meaning *a god*, as well as *the only true God.*
  - The Spirit of God within.
- Lord: (G2962) *kyrios*, meaning *he who has power to decide over a thing, he to whom a person or thing belongs, master, owner.*
  - Consciousness of mastery.
  - The Lord of your being.
- Jesus: (G2424) *Iesous*, meaning *Jehovah is salvation.*
  - Integral being. Being whole in spirit, soul, and body.
- Christ: (G5547) *kristos*, meaning "anointed".
  - The anointed one in all people. The sacred self.
  - That in us which makes us whole.

Key Phrase:
"In a state of grace, awaken to the Spirit of God within, and release limitation through the mastery of your own whole and sacred being."

STEP 4: *COMBINE*

From the preceding 8 verses, new meaning has emerged through the greater understanding rendered by history, etymology, metaphor, and metaphysics. Now, we combine the Key Phrases to come up with a Metaphysical Meaning for the entire passage. To *Combine* is to bring what is known together in a way that makes sense. Following is the new passage.

> **Metaphysical Meaning.** "Be alert to the teaching of the Truth that has been buried in your consciousness. You are no longer unconscious. You are transformed. With undivided attention, instantaneous awakening creates a paradigm shift in your consciousness. Resounding spiritual awareness awakens that which has gone unconscious to its eternal nature, and transformation is the result. Forgotten ideas will find new life and thoughts of limitation will become ideas of possibility. When lost ideas find new life, and thoughts of limitation become ideas of possibility, the unconscious state of mind will be eliminated. The power of the unconscious state of mind is released. The pain of the unconscious state of mind is no more. The pain of being unconscious is error thinking. The fortitude of error thinking is limitation. In a state of grace, awaken to the Spirit of God within, and release limitation through the mastery of your own whole and sacred being."

If you prefer a simplified approach to finding meaning, you can do the historical research, then take the passage "As a Whole". To do this, you choose 6 or 7 words to research the etymology and interpret metaphysically. Then, you combine their meanings through a statement that sums up what you have learned. Below is the example of a single table in which the outline is like those of the individual verses, using the categories of "Biblical Reference", "Key Words", and "Summarized Meaning".

Biblical Reference: *1 Corinthians 15:51-1*

Key Words:

- Mystery: (G3466) *mysterion*, meaning *hidden thing, hidden purpose, secret*.
  - o Truth buried within consciousness.
- Die/Death: (G2837) *koimao*, meaning *sleep*. Even though Paul was writing about the actuality of dying and death, it is clear from the linguistics that dying is a metaphor for going to sleep.
  - o Falling asleep in consciousness. The unconscious state.
- Changed: (G236) *alasso*, meaning *exchanged, transformed*.
  - o Transformation in Consciousness
- Imperishable: (G852) *aphthartos*, meaning *uncorrupted, undecaying, immortal*.
  - o New Life. That in us which is eternal.
- Victory: (G3534) *nikos*, meaning *to utterly vanquish*.
  - o To Release
- Law (G3551) *nomos*, meaning *established, custom, command*.
  - o Pre-determined and established ways of being.
  - o Limitation
- Christ: (G5547) *kristos*, meaning "anointed".
  - o The anointed one in all people. The sacred and unlimited self.
  - o That in us which makes us whole.

Summarized Meaning:

To know the Truth, be alert and conscious to your eternal self. You will be transformed as all limitation of unconscious awareness falls away. Your true nature is unlimited!

This approach not only simplifies your efforts, it gives you a clear and abbreviated form of the "Metaphysical Meaning". You can attain similar results by contemplating the metaphysical meaning in the paragraph from the entire verse by verse passage and creating an abbreviated form of it.

PORTION 4

Underlying the metagetical process that has been done with history, metaphor, etymology, and metaphysics there has been an interpretive principle at work that renders the ability to bring it all together in a way that makes sense. That principle is Logic. Not just any logic, but spiritual logic that comes from the center of the intuitive heartmind, the inner sanctum of the Temple of consciousness, the third tier of knowing, beyond intellectual thought. We have been applying this logic without being consciously aware of doing that. Now, we become consciously aware of our innate spiritual logic as we transform the work we have done into a "Message" for life. Since I cannot go to your third tier of knowing, the message that emerges for you must come from you and be yours. As I apply *Logic* for myself, and *Conclude* with my message, I invite you to do this for yourself.

To aid us in doing this we re-visit the paragraph of "Metaphysical Meaning", as well as the statement of "Summarized Meaning". Here they are:

Metaphysical Meaning. Be alert to the teaching this Truth that has been buried in your consciousness. You are no longer unconscious. You are transformed. With undivided attention, instantaneous awakening creates a paradigm shift in your consciousness. Resounding spiritual awareness awakens that which has gone unconscious to its eternal nature, and transformation is the result. For lost ideas will find new life and thoughts of limitation will become ideas of possibility. When lost ideas find new life, and thoughts of limitation become ideas of possibility, unconscious thinking will be dissolved through the activity of release. Unconscious state you are released. Unconscious state, your wounds are healed. The ill effect of being unconscious is misunderstanding. The accomplishment of misunderstanding is old dependencies. The Spirit of God is grace in us, giving us the ability to let go all limitation through its mastery in our consciousness, and its ability to make us whole.

Summarized Meaning: Be alert and conscious to your eternal self, and all limitation of unconscious awareness will fall away. Your true nature is unlimited!

Now, we bring Logic to the table in the form of a contemplative exercise. Here is the exercise.

Principle 4: *Logic*
• Take a deep breath and focus on the name of God within you as you breathe in – and out. Do this again. And one more time.
• Remain silent and still and breathe normally until you feel a direct connection, or conscious communion, with the Spirit of God in the space of your heartmind.
• When you experience this communion, take another deep breath and meditatively read the passage of Metaphysical Meaning and the statement of Summarized Meaning.
• Once again remain silent and still and reconnect in conscious communion with the Spirit of God in the space of your heartmind.
• When you experience this reconnection, ask this question regarding the above passage of you inner being: "What do you have to reveal to me?" Then relax and breathe normally, listening for your message.
• Repeat asking this question and listening to your inner being until a message comes from the place beyond intellectual thought. You will know it when it comes. It will be simple, direct, and clear, and there will not be any thinking to it. When it comes, write it down.

STEP 5: *CONCLUDE*

To create a message from the place beyond intellectual thought is to bring your previous effort to a clear and concise conclusion. To *Conclude* is to arrive at a new and expanded state of spiritual awareness through the guidance of your own inner logic. Only you can do this for yourself. As an example, here is the message I received for me.

> **Message:** This is the moment of transformation. Now is the time to know your eternal self and claim your unlimited potential.

What is your message? As it comes to you, write it down, read it, and become fully present to it. In teaching about spiritual logic, my father said, "In Bible interpretation when logic has been correctly applied, and a Truth conclusion reached, the soul will invariably emit a sort of 'Aha!' It henceforth has no doubt as to the value of that conclusion."

AHA!

READY

It has been implied that a deeper scholastic understanding interferes with a direct spiritual experience. That can be true, but only if you don't get out of the boat. There is an ancient metaphor of crossing a river to get to the other shore, then getting stuck by remaining in the boat. We have crossed the flowing energy of thought and feeling between earthly life and our pure spiritual awareness. Yet, once we have reached the other shore, it is time to get out of the boat, because that is where our "Aha!" awaits.

You have stepped onto the other shore by taking the "Metaphysical Meaning" and "Summarized Meaning" into the Silence and asking, "What do you have to reveal to me?" If a message came for you – wonderful! If not, just stay in the inquiry and it will reveal itself to you in the right way at the right time. When this happens, it is time to explore the new land on the other side of the river, to walk back down from the mountain heights of quiet spiritual connection into the activity of life. In other words, you are ready for Mastery.

SUMMARY

- *Logic* is our connection with the Logos, or the Word of God. It goes beyond the intellect to the heartmind where we awaken our inner knowing, or intuition.
- *Logic* is the sixth of 7 principles of biblical interpretation known as *Love, Prayer, Contemplation, History, Meaning, Logic, and Mastery*. These principles are the ingredients of the interpretive stew.
- If the principles are the ingredients of the stew, the "7-Step Method of Metagetics" provides the recipe on how to put them together, blend their flavors, and create a delicious experience. These 7 steps are *Choose, Commune, Contextualize, Combine, Conclude, Constitute,* and *Contribute*.

  - To *Choose* is to have the will and intention for a relationship of open anticipation with Scripture that will attract the right message from it for you.
  - To *Commune* is to come into conscious union with both the Spirit within you, and the words before you. It is to completely connect with what you seek - the Spirit of the Word in Scripture.
  - To *Contextualize History* is to move into the world of the author, familiarizing yourself with the story and intention of the Scripture through an exploration of the known facts. To *Contextualize Meaning* is not only to put the words on the page in the context of their ancient languages, but also to find the deeper meaning that emerges through these words from the context of our own spiritual understanding.
  - To *Combine* is to bring what is known together in a way that makes sense.
  - To *Conclude* is to arrive at a new and expanded state of spiritual awareness through the guidance of your inner logic.

Just as when you are working with the ingredients and instructions of a recipe, you put your principles together and then do your steps in portions, according to the recipe. There are 5 portions in the metagetical recipe.

Here is the outline of the recipe:

Portion 1
- Principle 1: *Love* (an exercise)
- Step 1: *Choose*

Portion 2
- Principle 2: *Prayer*
- Principle 3: *Contemplation*
- Step 2: *Commune*

Portion 3
- Principle 4: *History*
- Step 3a: *Contextualize History*
- Principle 5: *Meaning*
- Step 3b: *Contextualize Meaning*
- Step 4: *Combine*

Portion 4
- Principle 6: *Logic*
- Step 5: *Conclude*

- Dr. Paul Barrett said, "In Bible interpretation when logic has been correctly applied, and a Truth conclusion reached, the soul will invariably emit a sort of 'Aha!' It henceforth has no doubt as to the value of that conclusion."

- When this happens, you are ready for Mastery.

INQUIRY

1. What is the difference between spiritual logic and intellectual reason?

2. Share an experience you have had of communing with the Word, or creative power, of God.

3. How are metaphor and metaphysics alike? How are they different?

4. Share an experience of an "Aha!' moment in life.

5. What is your message for life?

PART VII: THE BODY OF LIFE

CHAPTER 14: MASTERY

"Therefore, my beloved, be steadfast, immovable, always excelling in the work of the Lord, because you know that in the Lord your labor is not in vain (1 Corinthians 15:58)."

HERO

There is no known precedent of Bible Interpretation that does what we are about to do. Oh sure, there have been practical applications of what a Bible message revealed, but there has been no conscious engagement with embodying the living message on an ongoing basis – at least not that I know. There are, however, precedents in the Bible.

After the burning bush...

"So Moses took his wife and his sons, put them on a donkey, and went back to the land of Egypt; and Moses carried the staff of God in his hand." (Exodus 4:20)

In response to the vision of God...

"Then I heard the voice of the Lord saying, 'Whom shall I send, and who will go for us?' And I said, 'Here am I; send me.'" (Isaiah 6:8)

After the baptism and time in the wilderness...

"Now when John was arrested, Jesus came to Galilee proclaiming the good news of God." (Mark 1:14)

After three days of blindness following the vision of Jesus on the road to Damascus...

303

"For several days he was with the disciples in Damascus, and immediately he began to proclaim Jesus in the synagogues saying, 'He is the Son of God.'" (Acts 9:19b-20)

These are examples of archetypal metaphor. The archetype is the hero who has had an encounter with the Divine, or God, and becomes the vehicle through which the message of that encounter comes into the world. In so doing, the hero attains mastery. Moses was a master leader, Isaiah was a master prophet, Jesus was a master teacher and healer, and Paul was a master apostle. Why were they masters? Was it because of the exquisite skill they applied to what they did? Perhaps. Was it the perfection with which they expressed themselves? Hardly – even Jesus tossed some tables in the Temple. They were masters, not because they thought of themselves that way, but because they got their own fears and concerns out of the way. They took the energy of their commission into the very cells of their body and being, and moved into action, letting the pure purpose of what they were doing shine as them. *Mastery* is a state of clear and present awareness that renders the ability to take hold of what is spiritual and give it tangible form in life and manifest expression in the world. It is to be the embodiment of God's message in the world.

ENCOUNTER

JOURNEY

The biblical hero who has an encounter with God and becomes a master of God's message in the world is a metaphor for you on your spiritual journey. If you have been to the third tier of knowing, you have had an encounter with the Divine. If you have been in the stillness of silence, you have had an encounter with the Divine. If you have heard God's name in your breath, you have had an encounter with the Divine. If you have had any form of spiritual insight from the work of this book, or any other book for that matter, you have had an encounter with the Divine.

Your encounter with God is not a matter of you coming together with something outside of yourself. Rather, it is you going deep enough within yourself to know your unity with all that is, was, and will be. Whatever activities or circumstances have taken you there, they have been part of your sacred journey. It has been my intention that the exercises and interpretations of this book have been part of that journey for you as well, right up through the experiences of *Logic* that have revealed a message from the center of your soul. While spiritual logic can take you deep within your own being to understand how God is speaking to you, there is no mastery of the message until you become a living embodiment of it. Before we work with the message and its expression through us, let us take a better look at *Mastery* – what it is, and what it is not.

MAESTRO

The audience waited as the maestro approached the piano. The internationally renowned and award-winning master of Mozart and Beethoven on the keyboard, Lily Kraus, had come to do a benefit concert for our small college in Pennsylvania. Once we had barely survived the threat that almost closed our school, as addressed in Chapter 3, we needed to raise funds to keep the school going and to renew its organizational infrastructure. One of the music professors had a connection with Mrs. Kraus, who was living in the United States at that time, and the request of her visit was made. Lili Kraus knew what it was to survive and thrive after a two-year internment in a Japanese concentration camp while touring Asia during the second world war. She gladly offered her services and gifts. The generosity of who she was came pouring through her music and teaching skills. She even gave me some pointers for a Beethoven Sonata I was working on at the time.

I slipped in on the balcony of the music hall to watch her rehearse. Without even looking at her music, she would decide which piece to play, and then play it. The music was deeply embedded in her soul and seemed to be coming out of every fiber of her being as she moved, not just her fingers, but her whole body to connect with the Steinway grand through which the music came. After weeks of advertisement and preparation, the music hall was packed-in in silent anticipation of the upcoming experience.

It all came down to this: a moment in time in which the music, the pianist, the piano, the audience, and the composer came together as one. There was no distinction between the varied elements, for all were actively engaged in creating the musical experience. The focused awareness and energy of the maestro poured into the keyboard through her performance, and the audience was drawn into the lyrical ecstasy that inspired the composer. All separation of person, thing, time and space disappeared. There was only music.

Whether it is found in a musical performance, or a painting, or a good play; whether it is on the race track, the balance beam, or the football field; whether it is in a seminar, or a class, or a sermon – the touch of the master at work is unmistakable in its ability to crack the shell of daily concerns and take us into the full ecstasy of the present moment. No individual personality can accomplish such mastery. It happens only when the artist is not the artist, but the art, and the athlete is not the athlete, but grace in motion.

The experience of mastery takes place in the moment when the individual is so at one with the source of the experience that time and space disappear, leaving only the experience. I have had such moments as a musician, as a speaker, as a teacher, and as a writer. I have also had them in meditation, conversation, doing business, chopping vegetables, folding laundry, and even balancing the checkbook. All the activities of life have the potential of being such moments in which all sense of self and others, all concerns of past or future, melt into the purity of the present. All of us have had these moments. They are part of the human experience. While some have been able to sustain this state of awareness, for many of us it comes and goes. That is okay. Mastery has room for our humanity as well.

In the mastery state, we are not preoccupied with passing judgment on the impurities in ourselves, in others, or in the conditions of life. Nor do we see or think of ourselves as being masters of anything, except maybe our own inner being. Mastery is not about domination or control of anyone or anything, as many might think. It is not even about being dominated or controlled by anyone or anything. In mastery, there is no one to dominate, or be dominated. There is nothing to control, or by which to be controlled. There is only what is. What is so is simply what is so.

This doesn't mean things stay the same, for by nature, as Heraclitus pointed out back in Chapter 2, things are in a constant state of change, flux, and transformation. When we recognize, however, that life is whole and complete just the way it is and just the way it is not, then transformation comes from the vision of what is possible, not what is wrong. To focus on what is wrong creates resistance, dispute, division, and more of what is wrong. To focus on what is possible nurtures and builds our dreams and visions.

Mastery inspires transformation, for to be transformed is not about fixing anything or anyone, not even ourselves. It is about going beyond the clutter of thoughts, opinions, concepts, and emotions to the core of who we already are. It does not mean we do not think our thoughts, have our opinions, or feel our emotions. It means we anchor ourselves in the heartmind where we are greater than all of these things put together. In the state of mastery, we can still be feeling the difficult feelings, while at the same time loving ourselves through them, maybe even learning something from our vulnerabilities and failures.

When the needs of the ego are laid aside for the rich experience of being fully human, it is then that we can hear God speaking a message of encouragement, healing, and possibility, even when we have fallen flat on our faces. Just as we can discern God's message for us in the difficult passages of the Bible, we can do the same in the difficult times of life. We can breathe in the breath of life, connect with the name of God within us, go to the space of our heartminds, ask our contemplative questions, and listen for the response. In that listening, we know our message will come, whether it is immediate and clear, or whether it unfolds over time with the events and encounters in our lives.

MESSAGE

FORWARD

Like the piano in the practice room for the aspiring musician, the Bible is our training ground for hearing the message of God speak to us in all things in life, and for becoming that message in the world. God speaks to us in many ways. I have heard God speaking in beautiful music, or the purr of my cat.

One effective way that God speaks to me for becoming a living message in my world is through clear statements that connect me with the "Aha!" of spiritual Truth. Even the sound of "Aha!" is like the breath of life bringing new inspiration and fresh motivation.

These inspiring and motivational statements can be messages that bring us an awareness of the gifts that are available in the present moment. They can be messages of "situational guidance" that move us through specific projects or challenges of life. They can be daily messages, like those found in the *Daily Word Magazine*. They can be universal messages that we carry with us through life for ourselves, and for our world. These messages can be drawn from the words of Scripture, whether it is by way of "dropping the needle" or searching out a meaningful passage.

The message with which we ended the last chapter is a message for you. You can apply it to something momentary or situational. You can let it inspire your day. You can also develop it into a universal message, not only for you, but for your world. In doing any of these things, you become the embodiment of that message, and the maestro of its music for the souls who experience it through you.

PORTION 5

To develop a message that speaks to others, and to become the embodiment of that message in the world, we work with *Portion 5* from the metagetical recipe of the "7 Principles of Interpretation" and the "7-Step Method of Metagetics". We addressed Steps 1 through 5 in the last chapter with a pre-selected passage. They were *Choose, Commune, Conceptualize, Combine,* and *Conclude.* We continue forward into Steps 6 and 7 with the message that came from that same biblical passage. In other words, we begin with the interpretive principle of *Mastery*, and complete with the steps to *Constitute* and to *Contribute*. Let's move forward with our recipe.

Principle 7: *Mastery*

- *Mastery* takes place at all levels of being: *Spirit, Soul, Body,* and *World*. Mastery has many forms of expression. Your message is one of those forms.
- To commune with *Spirit*, to embrace your message in the *Soul*, to put it into a language that connects you soul to soul with others, and to let the energy of that message move throughout your *Body* is to *Constitute* yourself as that message.
- To embody the message through positive action is to *Contribute* to your *World*. Let us now put into practice the principle of *Mastery*.

STEP 6: *CONSTITUTE*

The word, "constitute", comes from the Latin root constituere. With the prefix of con, meaning together, constituere means coming together to establish, set up, make firm, cause to stand, and form something new.[134] To Constitute means to form a union with something that causes it to be established in your life and world. When you constitute yourself as your message you establish yourself as that message through who you are being.

---

[134] "Constitue," *Online Etymology Dictionary*, accessed June 1, 2018, https://www.etymonline.com/word/constitute.

310

To do this, you connect with the Source of your message by simply noticing your thoughts and letting yourself relax in the Silence where you commune with the Spirit of God in you and in all of Creation. Then, you embrace the message with your soul through Lectio Divina, or Sacred Reading. You follow with the Revision of the message into a language that speaks simply and clearly to the souls of others. Finally, you move the energy of the message into every part of your body, becoming the Embodiment of it in your world.

In Chapters 8 and 9 we experienced Meditations 1 through 4 to awaken Love and put Prayer into practice. In the following text you will find Meditations 5 through 8 based on the Silence, Sacred Reading, Revision, and Embodiment experiences of what it is to Constitute yourself as your message.

SILENCE

To practice the Silence is simple, but not always easy. To feel as though one has spent time in this state, many people think the thoughts of the mind need to be completely quiet and still. To think about what an experience with the Silence should be can interfere with the experience itself. You might be thinking that you are thinking too much and judging yourself for it, instead of just relaxing into the moment. Having a focus helps to quiet the busy mind and allow the experience to be whatever it is. In our previous Meditation and Contemplation exercises, our focus has been the breath. The meditations of this chapter are not much different. If you notice your mind is busy, just notice it.

Meditation 5

- Take a deep breath and relax into a comfortable and upright posture, listening for the name of God in your breath. Breathe normally.

- Notice the thoughts going through your mind. Do not judge them. Just watch them like you would watch squirrels running through your yard.

- Now, notice the one who is watching your thoughts – and be that. Then, notice the one who notices - and be that. Then, just be.

- Breathe normally, remaining silent and still until you feel at one with all that is, within and without. *Silence...*

- If you do not have the experience of absolute *Silence*, do not be concerned. Know that you are having the exact experience you need – and relax.

- When you are ready, you can stretch and open your eyes.

SACRED READING

Having spent time in silent communion with all that is, you have touched the Source out of which your message has come. The message you received in Chapter 13 is God speaking directly to you from the space of your heartmind. It is a message for you, from the Spirit of God within you. Let the thoughts and feelings of your soul embrace the message as you become present to it. If you have not yet written it down, write it down. Of course, if my message speaks to you, you may use that for now, but I recommend doing this work later to see what words emerge through you. You may even want to work with another Scripture that has a stronger calling for you. For the time being, we will go through these steps with the pre-selected scriptural passage. We will begin by breathing, moving into the space of the heartmind, and reading the Scripture and its resulting message.

Meditation 6

- Take a deep breath and relax into a comfortable and upright posture, listening for the name of God in your breath. Breathe normally for three breath cycles.
- Take another deep breath, breathing the light of God into the space of your mind on the inbreath, then drawing that light down into the heart and anchoring the mind there on the outbreath. Breathe normally for three breath cycles.
- From this sacred space, read the scriptural passage once again.

Scripture:

"Listen, I will tell you a mystery! We will not all die, but we will all be changed, in a moment, in the twinkling of an eye, at the last trumpet. For the trumpet will sound, and the dead will be raised imperishable, and we will be changed. For this perishable body must put on imperishability, and this mortal body must put on immortality. When this perishable body puts on imperishability, and this mortal body puts on immortality, then the saying that is written will be fulfilled: 'Death has been swallowed up in victory. Where, O death, is your victory? Where, O death, is your sting?' The sign of death is sin, and the power of sin is the law. But thanks be to God, who gives us the victory through our Lord Jesus Christ (1 Corinthians 15:50)."

- Take a deep breath and read the "Message" you have written as though the Spirit of God is speaking to you from the space of your heartmind. The message is what you developed from your inner *Logic* following the "Summarized Meaning" in the last chapter.
- Here again, as an example, is my message: "Through the Spirit of God in me, I become conscious to the unlimited potential of my eternal self."

What is your message?

- Close your eyes and let your soul embrace the Truth of your message...

When you are ready, you can stretch and open your eyes.

REVISION

A revision is literally a re-envisioning, or new way of seeing. To see your message anew, is to see it in a form that speaks, not just to your soul from the Spirit of God in you, but to the souls of others as well. This is your key to Mastery. It is becoming the hero who is the living message of the Divine in the world. As you re-envision this message, keep two things in mind:

This new message is about the people who are receiving it. The natural result of their greater awakening to this message will be your greater awakening as this message, just as the master musician becomes the music while preparing to share it with others.

Keep your message short and simple. If you share its words, let those who hear it remember it after one hearing. Let that hearing be an "Aha!" for their lives.

314

Now it is time for your new message.

Meditation 7
<ul><li>Take a deep breath and once again move into the space of your heartmind. Being present to your message, ask yourself the following question: "What does the Spirit of God in me have to say to the Spirit of God in others?" "What is there for me to reveal?"</li><li>Take another deep breath and write the message that comes. Then revise it, and revise it again, until you feel it is a short, sweet, "Aha!" that speaks clearly to all.</li></ul>
<ul><li>As an example, here is my message for you, for others, and for the world.</li><li>You are eternal and unlimited!</li><li>What is your message for others and for the world?</li></ul>
<ul><li>Close your eyes and let your soul embrace the Truth of your message...</li><li>When you are ready, you can stretch and open your eyes.</li><li>When you can, share your message with another.</li></ul>

a. Embodiment

My cat is the embodiment of love. She stays close to me when I am not feeling well and watches me while I work. She meditates with me and loves to purr and snuggle. I look at her and I hear the message, "You are loved." It is that simple. Being the embodiment of a message has to do with who you are being on a day-to-day basis. Are you being the embodiment of your message? If not – you don't need to feel bad or start judging yourself. You don't even need to start judging the message as not the right one, or ineffective. Life is a dance of remembering and forgetting.

When you forget who you are, just remember your message and make it present in you once again. In her rehearsal, Lily Kraus paused, remembered a Mozart Sonata that she knew, took a deep breath and stretched her body and fingers, and started to play. When you forget that you are your message, you can pause and remember the message, take a deep breath, stretch, and infuse it into your body and being. Then – play! Go out and express yourself from the basis of this message. You don't even have to say the words. My cat cannot speak English, yet in her way of being, I know I am loved.

Let's do the following meditative exercise to remember the message that we are.

Meditation 8
• Take a deep breath and move your awareness into the heartmind. Breathe normally and relax into a comfortable and upright position. • Take another deep breath and go to the central core of the heartmind. There, see the letters of your message appearing in radiant gold. Breathe normally and relax. • Take another deep breath in – and on the outbreath let the energy of *neshamah*, the breath of life, radiate the golden light of the letters out into the *ruwach* of the rational mind wherein dwells your intellectual and creative thought. In other words, breathe the golden light of the message into your mind. Then, breathe normally and relax.

- Take another deep breath in – and on the outbreath let the *neshamah*, the breath of life, radiate the golden light of the letters out into the emotions of the animal self, the living *nefesh* of you. Let the radiant light of the message soothe your soul. Breathe normally and relax.
- Take another deep breath in - and on the outbreath, envision the golden light of your message radiating through the pathways of every nerve and blood vessel of your body. Then stretch, moving its life energy right out to your fingers and toes, through the souls of your feet, and out the crown of your head. Do this once again.
- Breathe normally and relax as you experience every cell, organ, and fiber of your body filled with the energy of your message.
- What does your message reveal to you as you become its living expression in your world? Contemplate these things in the space of your heartmind for a silent moment...

When you are ready, you can stretch and open your eyes. And so it is!

STEP 7 – *CONTRIBUTE*

The way to *Contribute* to your world is to act within it from your message. This is where the fingers connect with the keys, where the rubber meets the road, where the message meets the movement. As the embodiment of your message, you become the living language of God by committing yourself to the following:

Contribute to God. Whatever God is for you, give That some of your time and attention every day. As part of your daily meditative or prayerful activities, spend at least 1 full minute listening to the name of God in the movement of your breath. Through this conscious connection you contribute to God, for

317

you are the way that God knows God, or the universe knows itself.

Contribute to You. Forgive yourself for any perceived shortcomings in what you should do or be, and remember who you are by remembering your message. Read the Scripture that inspired your message, and give yourself a daily "message stretch" as we did in this chapter. If you want to add another message, or shift the message you have, find a Bible verse or passage and discern what it means for you in any of the ways suggested in this book.

Contribute to Others. After a Scripture reading and message stretch, ask yourself, "How can I be my message for others today?" "What words can I speak?" "What actions can I take?" "How can I leave others better for having encountered my presence in their world?" Then, from the space of your heartmind, seek out the opportunities and commit yourself to acting on them.

Contribute to Your World. Choose one person, cause, or thing that brings love into the local, or global, community of which you are a part – and offer your time and service. You can choose something each day, or become engaged with a long, or short-term project. If you volunteer for an organization in a way that consumes a lot of your spare time already, choose something fresh for a change that won't require much of you, or take away from what you contribute. You can always turn to the Bible for a message of "situational guidance" in what you are doing.

Remember, bring the breath of life to each action by going to the space of the heartmind and breathing the name of God in and out of your being. Then, bring to your awareness a Scripture and message that speaks to you and what you are

318

doing. Take a "message stretch" and move into action. In this way, you become the living language of God in your world.

BUILDING

FOUNDATION

In this book, we have built the foundation for you to be the living language of God in the world, using God as your Source, and the Bible as a primary resource. We have looked at depth into Word, Truth, and Life, and have transformed them into "The Spirit of the Word", "The Soul of Truth", and "The Body of Life". We have immersed ourselves in the experience of the "7 Principles of Interpretation" and the "7-Step Method of Metagetics." Here are the "Building Blocks of Metagetics" as a reminder.

Building Blocks of Metagetics		
Domains	**Principles**	**Method**
The Spirit of the WORD	Love	Choose
	Prayer	Commune
	Contemplation	
The Soul of TRUTH	History	Contextualize
	Meaning	
		Combine
	Logic	Conclude
The Body of LIFE	Mastery	Constitute
		Contribute

STAGE

To know what you are building with this foundation, ask yourself this, "Who am I as a message of the Divine in my world?" This can be revealed through your engagement with the verses, passages, stories, and/or teachings of the Bible. When you engage with the Bible to know God in yourself, people will know God in themselves when they engage with you. It is then that the words of Paul that follow up on the biblical passage with which we have been working, seem written just for you, just the way they are. *"Therefore, my beloved, be steadfast, immovable, always excelling in the work of the Lord, because you know that in the Lord your labor is not in vain (1 Corinthians 15:51-57)."* Welcome maestro to your world stage!

SUMMARY

- *Mastery* is a state of clear and present awareness that renders the ability to take hold of what is spiritual and give it tangible form in life and manifest expression in the world.
- The experience of mastery takes place in the moment when the individual is so at one with the source of the experience so that time and space disappear, leaving only the experience.
- In mastery, there is no one to dominate, or be dominated. There is nothing to control, or by which to be controlled. There is only what is. What is so is simply what is so.
- When we recognize that life is whole and complete just the way it is and just the way it is not, then transformation comes from the vision of what is possible, not what is wrong.
- In the state of mastery, we can still be feeling the difficult feelings, while at the same time loving ourselves through them, maybe even learning something from our vulnerabilities and failures.
- *Mastery* takes place at all levels of being: *Spirit*, *Soul*, *Body*, and *World*. Mastery has many forms of expression. Your message is one of those forms.
- The Bible is our training ground for hearing the message of God speak to us in all things in life, and for becoming that message in the world.
- You can apply your message to something momentary or situational. You can let it inspire your day. You can also develop it into a universal message, not only for you, but for your world.
- We move forward with *Portion 5*.
  - Principle 7: *Mastery*
  - Step 6: *Constitute*
  - Step 7: *Contribute*

- To *Constitute* yourself as your message you establish yourself as that message through who you are being.
  - To do this, you relax in the *Silence* where you commune with the Spirit of God in you and in all of Creation.
  - Then, you embrace the message with your soul through *Lectio Divina*, or *Sacred Reading*.
  - You follow with the *Revision* of the message into a language that speaks simply and clearly to the souls of others.
  - Finally, you breathe and stretch the message into every part of your body, becoming the *Embodiment* of it in your world.
- The way to *Contribute* to your world is to act within it from your message.
  1. Contribute to God. Whatever God is for you, give That some of your time and attention every day.
  2. Contribute to You. Forgive yourself for any perceived shortcomings in what you should do or be and remember who you are by remembering your message.
  3. Contribute to Others. After a Scripture reading and message stretch, ask yourself, "How can I be my message for others today?" Then seek out the opportunities and commit yourself to acting on them.
  4. Contribute to Your World. Choose one person, cause, or thing that brings love into the local, or global, community of which you are a part – and offer your time and service.
- When you engage with the Bible to know God in yourself, people will know God in themselves when they engage with you.

INQUIRY

1. What is Mastery? What isn't Mastery?

2. Describe in your own words how drawing a Message from Scripture can support you in experiencing Mastery.

3. What is your message ...for yourself? ...for your world?

4. Who are you as message for the Divine in your world?

5. How can you leave others better for having encountered your presence in their world?

Made in the USA
Coppell, TX
27 July 2021